Free Speech and Democracy in Ancient Athens

This book illuminates the distinctive character of our modern understanding of the basis and value of free speech by contrasting it with
the very different form of free speech that was practiced by the ancient
Athenians in their democratic regime. Free speech in the ancient democracy was not a protected right but an expression of the freedom from
hierarchy, awe, reverence, and shame. It was thus an essential ingredient
of the egalitarianism of that regime. That freedom was challenged by
the consequences of the rejection of shame (*aidôs*), which had served
as a cohesive force within the polity. Socrates' "shameless" free speech
at his trial captures the paradoxical consequences of democracy's theoretical grounding on the unbridled speech in which the Athenians
expressed great pride and the polity's dependence on traditions that
evoke shame. Through readings of Socrates' trial, Greek tragedy and
comedy, Thucydides' *History*, and Plato's *Protagoras*, this volume
explores the paradoxical connections between free speech, democracy,
shame, and Socratic philosophy and Thucydidean history as practices
of uncovering.

Arlene W. Saxonhouse is the Caroline Robbins Collegiate Professor of
Political Science and Women's Studies at the University of Michigan.
She is the author of *Athenian Democracy: Modern Mythmakers and
Ancient Theorists* (1996), *Fear of Diversity: The Birth of Political Sci-
ence in Ancient Greek Thought* (1992), and *Women in the History of
Political Thought: Ancient Greece to Machiavelli* (1985) and is editor
with Noel B. Reynolds of *Hobbes's Three Discourses: A Modern, Crit-
ical Edition of Newly Identified Works by the Young Thomas Hobbes*
(1995). She has been a Fellow at the Center for Advanced Study in the
Behavioral Sciences at Stanford and the University Center for Human
Values at Princeton University. She has received fellowships from the
National Endowment for the Humanities. She served as a Phi Beta
Kappa Visiting Scholar during the 2001–2 academic year and is a Fellow
of the American Academy of Arts and Sciences. In 1998 she received
the Distinguished Faculty Achievement Award from the University of
Michigan. She was Chair of the Political Science Department at the
University of Michigan from 1990 to 1993.

Free Speech and Democracy in Ancient Athens

ARLENE W. SAXONHOUSE

University of Michigan

CAMBRIDGE
UNIVERSITY PRESS

CAMBRIDGE
UNIVERSITY PRESS

32 Avenue of the Americas, New York NY 10013-2473, USA

Cambridge University Press is part of the University of Cambridge.

It furthers the University's mission by disseminating knowledge in the pursuit of education, learning and research at the highest international levels of excellence.

www.cambridge.org
Information on this title: www.cambridge.org/9780521721585

First published 2006
First paperback edition 2008

A catalogue record for this publication is available from the British Library

Library of Congress Cataloguing in Publication data

Saxonhouse, Arlene W.
Free speech and democracy in ancient Athens / Arlene W. Saxonhouse.
p. cm.
Includes bibliographical references and index.
ISBN 0-521-81985-7 (hardback)
1. Freedom of speech – Greece – Athens – History – To 1500. 2. Shame – Greece – Athens – History – To 1500. 3. Athens (Greece) – Politics and government. I. Title.
JC75.F74S29   2005
323.44'3'09385–dc22   2005008711

ISBN 978-0-521-81985-5 Hardback
ISBN 978-0-521-72158-5 Paperback

For my children – Lilly, Noam, and Elena – with love.

Now fear no more shall bridle speech;
Uncurbed, the common tongue shall prate
Of freedom; for the yoke of State
Lies broken on the bloody beach.
> Aeschylus, *The Persians* 584–94
> (Vellacott translation)

For as I detest the doorways of Death, I detest that man, who hides one thing in the depths of his heart, and speaks of another.
> Homer, *Iliad* 9.312–13 (Lattimore translation)

Contents

Acknowledgments

Many institutions and individuals have supported and encouraged me during the several years that I have been at work on this project. My debts are many; my gratitude great. The University of Michigan was willing to break out of traditional disciplinary boundaries and give this member of a social science department a Humanities Fellowship for the winter of 2000. At the same time the Center for Advanced Study in the Behavioral Sciences at Stanford provided the idyllic surroundings, institutional support, and intellectual environment for the early stages of this project. That setting in the Stanford hills gave me the freedom (and confidence) to move into intellectual arenas I had never before explored.

A fellowship from the National Endowment for the Humanities for the 2002–3 academic year, plus support from the University Center for Human Values at Princeton University and from the University of Michigan's "topping-off" program, enabled me to devote a full year to working on this book. The University Center for Human Values provided the perfect office in Marx Hall overlooking the Princeton campus where intellectual engagement with fellow Fellows was a constant and important resource during that year. Finally, a sabbatical from the University of Michigan in the winter of 2005 freed me from the usual teaching and service commitments, giving me the necessary time to complete the manuscript. I hope that the project justifies all the support that I have received.

I have been especially fortunate over the past several years in having a variety of venues in which I was able to present parts of this project before particularly lively and helpful audiences. In each case the comments I received have worked their way into the text. I thank the following institutions for their invitations to present my work: University of Notre Dame, University of Oklahoma, University of California at Davis, University of Toronto, the Toronto Political Theory Workshop, Rutgers University, University of Houston, American University, the Yale University Political Theory Colloquium, Princeton University Political Philosophy Colloquium, and the

University Center for Human Values at Princeton. For the thoughtful care and critical engagement with which these audiences read and heard my work, I am most thankful. The volume has improved significantly as the result of their interventions.

Colleagues have also been generous with their time. Several have read specific chapters, offered extraordinarily helpful written comments, and alerted me to resources of which I had not been previously aware. For such readings I would like to thank Ryan Balot, Peter Euben, Thomas Foster, Don Herzog, Duncan Ivison, Lorraine Pangle, Josiah Ober, Tracy Strong, and Roslyn Weiss. Others provided guidance along the way concerning specific aspects of the work: Christopher Eisgruber, Andreas Kalyvas, Sara Monoson, Bill Scheuermann, and Jerry Schneewind. Fred Rosen was an early reviewer for Cambridge University Press and I especially appreciate his encouragement to go beyond my initial American focus. I also benefited greatly from the comments of the anonymous reviewers for the Press, and I feel fortunate to have had the encouragement and confidence of Lewis Bateman.

And then there are the fellow travelers who sustain one in the effort to engage with the texts of political theory that enable us to confront the political world in which we live – those with whom conversations over the years keep one focused on what a life in political theory can mean: Jennifer Ring, Stephen Salkever, Molly Shanley, Cathy Zuckert, and Michael Zuckert. Monicka Tutschka was much more than a research assistant and more of an intellectual companion as the project progressed. I am thankful for her help and presence.

I dedicate this book to my children. Their varied lives, their constantly challenging thoughts (and speech), their diverse commitments all continue to teach me and enrich me. I am grateful for their willingness to continue sharing them with me. And, as always – wonderfully, marvelously – Gary is there.

Washington, DC
February 2005

Prologue

Four Stories

THE FIRST: THERSITES

In the second book of Homer's *Iliad* a character named Thersites appears. According to Homer, Thersites was "the ugliest soldier at the siege of Troy/ Bowlegged, walked with a limp, his shoulders/ Slumped over his caved in chest, and up top/ Scraggly fuzz sprouted on his pointy head."[1] Homer continues the insults: Thersites was "a blathering fool/ And a rabble rouser, [who] had a repertory/ Of choice insults he used at random to revile the nobles," and yet this blathering fool with a pointy head steps into the circle of kings who are deliberating about whether to end their siege of Troy. There Thersites states his views and the words Homer gives to this rabble rouser are not at all those of a blathering fool. Instead, in many instances, he repeats the speech Achilles gave in Book 1: Agamemnon is greedy, he does not appreciate the energy and ability of Achilles or of the men who fight for him. Yet, this Thersites who has spoken truth to power is an intruder into the Assembly of the deliberating kings. For this, Odysseus "was on him in a flash. . . .: 'Mind your tongue, Thersites. Better think twice/ About being the only man here to quarrel with his betters. I don't care how bell-toned an orator you are,/ You're nothing but trash.'" Odysseus strikes Thersites, leaving bloody welts on his back and tears in his eyes (2.212–77). Obviously, Thersites was not allowed to speak freely. The aristocratically structured society of the Achaean camp excluded him from participation in political deliberation. In particular, Thersites did not show what the Greeks called *aidôs*, shame, respect, for those in positions of authority or for the norms that governed the community of the Achaeans laying siege to the city of Troy.

Insofar as we impose continuities on history, we can say that the birth of democracy in ancient Athens is marked by the entrance of Thersites into

---

[1] Here I use Lombardo's translation; elsewhere throughout this book, I use Lattimore's translation of Homer.

the deliberative circle, by opportunities granted to the everyman to speak in the Assembly, even if his head is pointy with scraggly fuzz growing on it.[2] Accompanying this expansion of the deliberative circle is the freedom of speech, the freedom to say what one thinks without the restraints that shame or respect for the prestige of the "kingliest" of men might place on what is said. Thersites as Athenian citizen need not fear the staff of Odysseus when he speaks the same words as an Achilles – or when he speaks his own.

THE SECOND: DIOMEDES SON OF TYDEUS

In the fourth book of the *Iliad* the king Agamemnon comes upon the son of Tydeus, "high-spirited Diomedes."[3] But Diomedes is not fighting well and Agamemnon urges him on with the vision of his father's courage, "Tydeus, that daring breaker of horses . . . [whose way was never] to lurk in the background/ but to fight the enemy far ahead of his own companions" (4.365–73). So spoke Agamemnon scolding Diomedes. The strong Diomedes did not answer, so "in awe and shame (*aidestheis*) before the rebuke of the awe-inspiring (*aidoioio*) king" (402)[4] was he. After much battle and several books in which Diomedes proves his courage on the battlefield, he no longer displays the same awe before the mighty king of the Achaeans. He has proven himself as a warrior and now sees himself as one who no longer needs to hold back his speech in respectful awe and shame before the king.

   In the ninth book of the *Iliad* Agamemnon has called yet another meeting of the Achaeans, again to propose a return to their "beloved homeland" (9.27). This time it is not the misshapen Thersites who opposes the proposal, but now the proven warrior Diomedes son of Tydeus breaks the silence, transferring the language of battle to the discourse of the agora. "I will be the first to fight with your folly," he says to Agamemnon. He claims this as his "right" (*themis*)[5] in the agora of princes and so he speaks and insults Agamemnon. "With scepter he [Zeus] gave you honor beyond all/ but he did not give you a heart (*alkên*), and of all power this is the greatest" (9.33–9). Diomedes then urges Agamemnon to retreat with the numerous ships that lie on the shore while those who are brave and strong will stay to finish the war they came to fight. "So he spoke, and all the sons of the Achaians shouted/ acclaim for the word of Diomedes, breaker of horses" (9.50–1). The

---

[2] As Ober (2003b: 6–7) nicely describes the democratic scene: "Now the vote of 'nobody, son of nobody' had precisely the same weight in deciding the outcome of a debate as that of the noblest scion of the noblest house. Moreover 'nobody, son of nobody' might actually choose to raise his voice in public – if not as a formal speaker in the citizen Assembly, then in concert with his fellow nobodies attending that Assembly as voting members, hooting and jeering at the distinguished men who dared to speak."

[3] I am grateful to Dean Hammer for alerting me to the significance of the Diomedes passages.

[4] My own, not Lattimore's, translation.

[5] See Hammer (2002: 132–3) for a fuller discussion of the use of *themis* here.

staff of Odysseus does not come down upon his back as it did on the back of Thersites. Nevertheless, while he has earned his stature as a warrior, he is still a youth, speaking with audacity before powerful Agamemnon, ruler of the troops at Troy. This time the aged Nestor rises and speaks to Diomedes. Even though he accepts the validity of Diomedes' words, he still warns: "Yet you have not made complete your argument,/since you are a young man still and could even be my own son" (9.56–7). Thus, the aged Nestor speaks his own views, "since I can call myself older than you are... and since there is none who can dishonour/the thing I say, not even powerful Agamemnon" (9.60– 2). This time it is age, not nobility nor beauty, to which the speaker turns to assert his authority over another in speech. Underlying the portrayals of the Achaean kings in deliberation in Book 2 and in Book 9 is a hierarchy controlling both who speaks and what is spoken. Diomedes is not excluded from the deliberative circle as was Thersites, but the impetuous youth who has gained the stature to speak through his deeds on the battlefield must nevertheless yield to the deliberate wisdom of the aged Nestor. And it is the latter's speech that ultimately persuades Agamemnon to send his embassy to Achilles.

The transition to democracy in the fifth and fourth centuries in Athens is marked by the purging of the hierarchies so evident in these scenes of deliberation in the *Iliad*. There, in democratic Athens, there will be no limits on who can speak, on what they can say, on the insults they can hurl at their supposed superiors. There we will find the healing of Thersites' welts; there we will find the shedding of Diomedes' awe, his *aidôs*; there we will find the dismantling of a hierarchy of age.

THE THIRD: THRASYMACHUS

We are settled comfortably in the home of Cephalus awaiting dinner. Socrates has posed to Cephalus the uncomfortable question of what is justice and watched him bequeath to his son Polemarchus the question. Polemarchus has fared no better than his father under the probing questioning of Socrates, and the Sophist Thrasymachus, eager for the young men gathered at Cephalus' house to pay him to learn the art of rhetoric, has intervened challenging Socrates to provide himself the meaning of justice. Socrates demurs, opening the way for Thrasymachus to present his own famous (or perhaps infamous) definition: justice, Thrasymachus tells Socrates and his potential students, is nothing other than what is the interest of the stronger. He then waits for the expected applause. "But why do you not offer any praise?" (338c) he asks. None is forthcoming. Instead, Socrates demolishes the defenses that Thrasymachus offers for his definition, asking questions about what the words "stronger" and "interest" – so crucial for Thrasymachus' definition – may mean. At last, he brings Thrasymachus through assorted twists and turns in the argument to the point where Thrasymachus must agree that the just man is good and wise and the unjust man unlearned and bad. This is not where Thrasymachus wanted to be when he started out challenging Socrates a few moments earlier. Socrates has twisted his words so that he appears weak before those he had sought to impress. And, as Socrates famously reports the event: "Thrasymachus produced a wondrous amount of sweat, since it was summer – and then I saw what I had never seen before, Thrasymachus blushing" (350d).

Thrasymachus, so cocksure and daring, so eager to recruit the young men gathered in the Piraeus as students in the art that will give them the tools by which they can become the "stronger," persuading the many to serve their own interests, reveals his weaknesses under the piercing questioning of a persistent Socrates. He has challenged Socrates to a duel and he has lost. He is vulnerable and those vulnerabilities have been uncovered by Socrates' skills. He stands, in a sense, naked before others now with the inadequacies of his speech revealed. Thrasymachus is aware that others are gazing at him, those from whom he wants praise and applause – and employment. His blush reveals his concern with what others think; the blush reveals his shame. It is this quality of shame that allows Thrasymachus to reenter the *Republic* in Book 5 and become a founding member of the city of Callipolis.

THE FOURTH: SOCRATES IN JAIL

At dawn Crito arrives in Socrates' jail cell, eager to convince his old friend to take advantage of the opportunity he and others have arranged for him to escape from jail. Socrates is not so willing to run and rather engages Crito in discourse about whether he should run away. Crito pleads with Socrates to accept Crito's willingness to spend whatever it takes to arrange for the escape and asks: "What reputation would be more shameful than to appear to make more of money than of friends?" (44c). But, responds Socrates, why should Crito care about his reputation, about how he appears. Or to phrase it another way, why should he feel shame before others? So eager is Crito to persuade Socrates that he ignores the admonition not to care about the opinion of the many that he continues to appeal to Socrates with similar language: "How I am ashamed (*aischunomai*) on your behalf and on behalf of us your companions lest it seem the entire affair concerning yourself has been done with a certain lack of courage on our part ... O Socrates, see to it that these things are not shameful along with bad for both yourself and us" (45d–46a). Socrates is not persuaded by these appeals. Instead, he offers in response a revised view of what is shameful. "Is not being unjust (harming, *to adikein*) both bad and shameful (*aischron*) in every way for those who are unjust?" he asks (49b).

In an act of friendship, Socrates offers Crito a speech that the laws and what is shared in the city (*hoi nomoi kai to koinon tês poleôs*, 50a) might make and in their voice he asks himself whether he as a man of seventy with but a little time left to live would not be "ashamed" to think his life so valuable that he would run away. Ashamed before whom, we should ask. If he is speaking about the many who will judge him now a coward, he would be reversing the earlier conversation with Crito that concluded that he should not care about what the many may think. Unlike Crito, Socrates is not governed by the opinion of the many. The Laws, which we can call the speech of the many over time, in Socrates' recitation evoke a shame before the many. Their speech, though, appeals to Crito, not Socrates. They explain to Crito, living within a world in which one cares about how one appears before others, why Socrates must stay. They explain nothing to Socrates.[6]

From Crito's concern with the self as viewed by others, Socrates turns the conversation to an independence, to a shame that comes into being in relation to a justice that exists independently of the "laws and the community" of which he is a part. The universals to which he turns release him from shame before his fellow citizens and his friends, and thereby release his speech and his actions. Socrates freed from the expectations that others may have, that others try to impose on him, defines for himself the source of shame.

These four stories capture the themes that will dominate this book: democracy as the expansion of the deliberative circle not only in the admission of Thersites to the circle, but in the freedom to speak both the truth and insults without the young Diomedes' initial awe before "those who hold the scepter" and those who are more advanced in years. It is democracy as the egalitarian world that has shed the hierarchies of tradition. In the expanded deliberative circle gathered for the sake of self-rule, criticism and counsel, affronts and demands find expression by those who are uninhibited by shame. And as awe before others disappears from the councils of kings and democracy replaces the hierarchical world that characterized the Achaeans before Troy, so does awe before others disappear from the life of the Socratic philosopher. We have seen Thrasymachus blush when Socrates uncovered his vulnerabilities, but can we imagine Socrates ever blushing? I think not. And I argue that Socrates' failure to blush – to care what others think of him, to be ashamed were he to stand openly with his vulnerabilities revealed – lies behind the decision of the Athenians to execute him. Those who condemned him let the community's need for the sort of shame that Socrates resisted override its commitment to the freedom of speech on which their self-rule was based. The democratic regime cannot in the end practice complete shamelessness, cannot ignore its history or its traditions. The democratic regime cannot be pure in its commitment to unbridled speech.

We tend to delight in Thrasymachus' blush; we delight because the failings of the self-assured, pompous Sophist are suddenly revealed. His private motives become apparent, his inadequacies uncovered, and his vulnerabilities

---

[6] See especially Weiss (1998: chap. 8), but also Congleton (1974).

exposed before those he expected to impress with his wit and strength. We also tend to glory in Socrates' resistance to shame, in his (ironic) pride in his claimed weakness (his ignorance). We delight in the notion that indeed we cannot imagine Socrates blushing, that he speaks freely without reverence for the traditional hierarchies of the world in which he lives, without concern for what others may think of him. His independence delights us. We savor this Socrates in part, I suspect, because it also appeals to our democratic spirit, a devotion to openness and to an egalitarianism that does not force us to appear to be other than we are before supposed superiors. We also feel a sympathy that I doubt Homer intended for Thersites with his welts, for again the democratic egalitarianism in us wants to be inclusive, to ask all to join in deliberation about our common future (be that the fate of the Achaeans or the communities in which we currently live) without regard to status, wealth, age, or physical appearance.

The philosophic and the Socratic and the democratic all seem to connect here in their common opposition to hierarchy and to shame. And yet, as the myth told by the character Protagoras in a Platonic dialogue of the same name (and to be discussed in detail in Chapters 3 and 8) suggests, the polis or the political community can only come into being after humans receive (courtesy of Zeus in Protagoras' myth) the gift of shame, *aidôs* in the Greek, a word that includes reverence and the perception of the self as others see one. The tension in our democratic lives as independent, autonomous creatures is the resistance to the limits that this *aidôs* may cast over us and yet the need that any community has for it. The balance is delicate and while Thersites' welts have no place in the modern democratic world, Thrasymachus' blush might.

This volume explores the significance and implications of understanding democracy as the venue for the freedom of speech, the opening of public speech to all, and specifically the rejection of shame or *aidôs* as a limit on what one says. Little excuse is necessary to pursue issues of free speech today. It has become a focal point for many contemporary controversies – whether they be debates about political correctness and Stanley Fish's claim that there's no such thing as free speech; or discussions of deliberative democracy where ideal speech situations require that all participants speak openly; or arguments from feminist theorists about the need to limit speech demeaning to women; or concerns about the misuse of the internet as inhibiting – or, on the contrary, opening up – the opportunities for meaningful debate. Mostly, when the topic of free speech arises today in America, attention turns to the First Amendment and, given the protections affirmed there, the grounds on which one can or cannot limit speech in the contemporary world. Or, more recently, the Fourteenth Amendment and questions of equal protection come into play when free speech debates surface. I aim to take the concept of free speech away from the intellectual and political framework in which the debates about free speech are currently nestled, though in

Chapters 1 and 2 I try to connect those debates to our understanding of democratic principles. I discuss free speech instead as it appears in the practice and writings of the ancient Athenians freed from the liberal language of rights and protections that dominates (and, I believe, inhibits) contemporary discussions. I present free speech as grounded in the democratic environment of self-rule that developed in the Athens especially of the fifth and fourth centuries BCE and explore its place in the theoretical foundations of democracy.

The issue of freedom of speech in ancient Athens has often, indeed mostly, been raised in the context of the trial of Socrates who was accused of corrupting the young and introducing new gods into the city.[7] I. F. Stone's popular book *The Trial of Socrates* emerged from the great bewilderment Stone – that notable defender of the freedom of speech – felt at Athens' supposed betrayal of its principles with the execution of Socrates. For Stone, who correctly equated free speech with democratic practice in Athens, it was Socrates' unremitting attacks on the recently reinstituted and insecure democracy that accounted for his execution. Nevertheless, Stone still could not forgive the Athenians for their violation of his beloved principle of free speech, which was so integral to his own understanding of democracy.

In what follows I go beyond Stone's focus on the trial of Socrates to propose that the issue at hand in Socrates' trial in 399 BCE was not Socrates' hostility to Athenian democracy, but rather the incapacity of any regime – even, or especially, one devoted to openness of speech in the practice of self-rule and equality for those allowed to participate in that self-rule – to ignore the needs of "shame," that which restrains behavior not simply through laws or the threat of punishment, but by the sensitivity to the judgmental gaze of others and to the historical and social setting in which one lives. We can perhaps describe (as I try to do in Chapter 2) the emergence of the earliest democratic society as an act of historical amnesia. Cleisthenes, the so-called founder of Athenian democracy, liberated Athens from the patriarchal tribes that had dominated Athenian political history previously and replaced them with new units apparently created simply by administrative fiat.[8] Democracy as an open regime depends on such historical amnesia, a breaking away from the chains of the past in order to allow those living in the present to make choices for themselves, to rule themselves. Shame, as respect for modes of behavior derived from and dependent on the past, on decisions that others

---

[7] Since I began this project there has been a flurry of activity by historians of ancient Greece on this topic. See most especially, Rosen and Sluiter (2004).

[8] Different moments in Athenian history surface in different interpretations of that history as the founding moment of Athenian democracy. See Chapter 2, pages 40–2 for a discussion of why I focus on Cleisthenes.

have made and traditions established well before one was born, sets limits on both the exercise of democratic self-rule and the freedom of speech that goes along with it.

The Athenian practice of free speech – *parrhêsia*, the saying of all by the unbridled tongue – becomes a hallmark of the democratic regime, to such an extent that *Parrhêsia* becomes the name of one of the ships built with public funds. As I point out in Chapter 4, the term *parrhêsia* flows through the defenses of democracy in the fifth and fourth centuries and appears often in the Platonic dialogues as Socrates eggs his interlocutors on to practice *parrhêsia*, to speak freely – without shame – since they are conversing in the democratic city of Athens. Free speech in both politics and philosophical inquiry is bound up with the rejection of shame, with an independence from a limiting past. The execution of Socrates was not an expression of the excesses of democracy, but a violation of Athens' basic democratic principles. Athens, when it executed Socrates, acknowledged the city's dependence on *aidôs* and was eager to preserve its traditions, to resist the exposure of their inadequacies that Socratic *parrhêsia* was ready to uncover. Socrates, in contrast, uninhibited by respect for the past and free from limits imposed by the judgmental gaze of others, was the truly democratic man. The rejection of shame, though, as Protagoras makes clear in his myth, also creates a certain groundlessness and loss of foundations that exposes a society to a profound instability. Shame and free speech represent opposing points in the political order that play off one another in the construction of a stable democratic polity. The authors and experiences of ancient Athens enable us to explore the nature and implications of this opposition for democratic regimes.

Contained within the analysis below of free speech and shame in a democracy is the place of philosophy in a democratic society. Through a study of selected Platonic dialogues (primarily the *Apology of Socrates* and the *Protagoras*), I contend that Plato illustrates the compatibility between philosophy and democracy in the common rejection of shame. Thus, contrary to the familiar readings of a Platonic hostility to democracy, I find a Plato sympathetic to a democratic Socrates struggling against the socially controlling power of a hierarchically based shame.[9] The challenge that Plato faces is whether the forms (*eidê*) are an adequate alternative to the historically grounded feelings of shame in providing new foundations for a political

---

[9] Certainly there are numerous places in the Platonic dialogues that suggest hostility to the rule of the people. Book 6 of the *Republic* with its parables of the boat, of the wild beast and the corruption of the philosophic soul is just one notorious example. Yet, Socrates does adopt the principle of *parrhêsia* as the guide for his philosophic engagement. For other ways in which I believe the antidemocratic Plato is too harshly embedded in our consciousness, see Saxonhouse (1996: chap. 4).

order that previously depended so much on the power of *aidôs* – whether *eidos* can replace *aidôs*.[10]

While the Athenians, in their praise of their democracy and in the rhetoric of the fourth-century orators, exalted *parrhêsia* as emblematic of their status as free men in a free city, it is in the texts that I analyze in the second half of this volume that we find the hesitations about the practice. Free speech may lead to the egalitarianism denied poor Thersites, it may be at the foundation of the deliberations on which self-rule is based, and it may be the condition for the investigations by a Socratic philosopher, but it also has its limits. Aristophanes, Euripides, Thucydides, and Plato's *Protagoras* all offer poignant reservations about the "unbridled tongue" as they uncover the dangers of free speech and the challenges it poses to the very ideal of self-rule.

I recognize that by using the language of freedom of speech as a translation of *parrhêsia* I am wading into a deep pond – or really an ocean – of controversy about speech within the political community, whether any assertion of such freedom is merely a figment of the imagination, whether speech may really serve to oppress rather than liberate, and even what constitutes "speech," whether it is words spoken or any form of communicative behavior.[11] I do not propose that we turn to the ancient authors in order to arbitrate between those caught up in the midst of these numerous controversies, but rather to suggest how the experience of the ancient Athenians offers insights into the connections between democracy and the practice of speaking without regard to hierarchy and shame.

By removing the discussion of freedom of speech from the controversies of political correctness, pornography, the internet, and the like that inhabit the contemporary world and by setting it within the realm of the Athenian political experience, we do not discover answers to the troubling question of where precisely we ought to set limits on freedom of speech, but we come to understand better its place in the foundational principles of democratic regimes and the practice of philosophic inquiry. Perhaps we generate greater problems by pointing to the instability of regimes founded on freedom of speech and democratic principles unmoderated by the inhibitions of shame, but my goal here is not to provide certain answers. It is rather to open alternative ways of thinking about the issues raised by free speech when we set ourselves loose from the language of individual rights. The story of free speech and shame, as I see it, is the story of the possibilities and limits of democracy. Athens as the first democratic regime and the writings of its self-reflective authors let us explore this story. The first half of what follows illustrates the potential that the Greeks saw in the liberation of speech; the

[10] I return to this point in Chapter 8, pages 198–204.
[11] The essays in Bollinger and Stone (2002: 22) provide a series of discussions of such issues.

second half, though, uncovers through the analyses of specific ancient texts the limits – indeed the dangers – of free speech.

Bernard Williams, for one, at the beginning of *Shame and Necessity* argues against progressivism with regard to the ancients (1993: 5–6), a practice that has had a long and illustrious career bound up in the question of whether we have improved/degenerated/remained unchanged since the time and thought of the ancient Greeks. Williams is also well aware of the dangers of romanticizing the past. I intend to do neither, but rather assert the claim that the ancients can help us think through our contemporary issues and dilemmas. This book is an effort to justify such an assertion.

PART I

INTRODUCTION

THE INVOCATION OF ATHENS

In the early decades of the nineteenth century, George Grote wrote his memorable multivolume history of Greece. In striking contrast to the popular view of the historians of his time and earlier centuries, democratic Athens shines forth in his work as a wondrous regime of freedom and creativity rather than as a warning about the chaos and tyranny of mob rule. After recording several paragraphs of Pericles' Funeral Oration as presented in Thucydides' history, Grote reflects wistfully: "nor can we dissemble the fact that none of the governments of modern times . . . presents any thing like the picture of generous tolerance towards social dissent, and spontaneity of individual taste, which we read in the speech of the Athenian statesman" ([1851–56] 1900:6.150). If only "the governments of modern times" could recapture those practices of freedom of which Pericles spoke, Grote seems to muse here, then the modern world might again be able to produce the monuments of culture that emerged from the freedoms of ancient Athens.[1] Benjamin Constant in his justly famous speech of 1819 warns Europe about romanticizing the liberty of the ancients so praised in authors like Rousseau and imagined in the events of the French Revolution.[2] But among the ancients he excepted the Athenians whose dedication to commerce gave, he writes, "its citizens an infinitely greater liberty than Sparta or Rome" (1988: 315). If one sought to define the benefits of liberty in the nineteenth century, Athens could serve as a potent model.

On the other side of the Atlantic in the early decades of the twentieth century, Justice Louis Brandeis writes his concurrence in the landmark Supreme Court case of *Whitney v. California* (1927), a case that is considered by

---

[1] On the tradition of using Pericles' Funeral Oration in modern times as the inspiration for the defense of liberty see Turner (1981: 187).

[2] Translated and reprinted in Constant ([1819] 1988: 307–28).

many (whether rightly or wrongly) to be pivotal in the development of free speech jurisprudence in the United States. Brandeis here urges his readers to recall "[t]hose who won our independence." These were men who "believed that the final end of the state was to make men free to develop their faculties...They believed that freedom to think as you will and to speak as you think are means indispensable to the discovery and spread of political truth; that without free speech and assembly discussion would be futile...that public discussion is a political duty; and that this should be a fundamental principle of American government."[3] Brandeis footnotes these remarks with a quotation from Thomas Jefferson,[4] but those commenting on Brandeis's opinion often go further back than the founding fathers to whom Brandeis himself refers. They find echoes in his language to the world of ancient Athens, most particularly to the same Funeral Oration by Pericles that had so inspired Grote a century earlier. Specifically, Brandeis uses a phrase from that oration to describe "those who won our independence": "They believed liberty to be the secret of happiness and courage to be the secret of liberty" (1927: 375).

Though Jefferson may receive the footnote in Brandeis's opinion, the legacy of ancient Athenian democracy resonates in this powerful paean to benefits of freedom of speech. Brandeis may indeed have had, to use Robert Cover's language, a "somewhat romantic view" of Athens (1993: 149), but he brought that romantic view to his judicial writings on freedom of speech. Brandeis's perspective on Athens most likely came to him courtesy of Alfred Zimmern's *The Greek Commonwealth* ([1911] 1924), a work he "quoted throughout his life and made certain that all members of his extended family read" (Strum 1984: 237). In that volume, Zimmern writes: " 'To say everything' (*parrhêsia*) was one of his [an Athenian's] rights, and he exercised it in a large and liberal spirit, which our public men and even our Press cannot hope to rival" ([1911] 1924: 64).[5] Zimmern with his voluble Athenians

---

3 *Whitney v. California* 274 U.S. 357 (375). The case concerned Charlotte Whitney who had been convicted of assisting in organizing the Communist Labor Party of California, which was formed to teach criminals syndicalism.

4 Brandeis quotes a passage, cited by Charles A. Beard in *The Nation* of 1926, in which Jefferson had written: "We have nothing to fear from the demoralizing reasons of some, if others are left free to demonstrate their errors," and then adds his own quote from Jefferson's first Inaugural Address: "If there be any among us who would wish to dissolve this union or change its republican form, let them stand undisturbed as monuments of the safety with which error of opinion may be tolerated where reason is left free to combat it" (1927: 375n33).

5 One of the epigraphs for Chapter 8 in Zimmern's book, the chapter titled "The Ideal of Citizenship," and subtitled "Happiness, or the Rule of Love," is *to eudaimon to eleutheron, to de eleutheron to eupsuchon krinantes* and is attributed to Pericles. (It comes from Thucydides 2.43, though Zimmern does not cite the location of the passage.) The translation of the Greek here is sufficiently close to the phrase in Brandeis's opinion in *Whitney v. California*, which suggests that Brandeis may well have gotten it from here. Strum cites Brandeis's law clerk and friend, Paul Freund, as identifying the Periclean origins of this passage from *Whitney* (1984:

and Brandeis with his recourse to the language of Pericles both exemplify a familiar effort to draw from the experience of ancient Athens lessons for a modern world, one which often sees itself as the heir to Athens' democratic principles of freedom and self-rule.

The allure of tying Athenian democracy to favored contemporary practices and ideologies has a distinguished history that goes back at least two centuries.[6] But does this practice of recalling and revering an ancient political system actually legitimize current practice or goals?[7] Or does it simply supply us with rhetorical analogies that obscure the foundational and theoretical principles underlying commitments to democracy and to freedom of speech? After all, even though Brandeis might refer us to Thomas Jefferson in his footnote and echo Pericles' Funeral Oration in his opinion in *Whitney v. California*, Jefferson himself seemed more interested in the pronunciation and structure of the Greek language and the style of their poetry than in the political and moral lessons one might gain from reading the texts of the ancient Athenians or learn from their history.[8] Indeed, Jefferson himself wrote of the ancients in 1816: "But so different was the style of society then and with those people, from what is now and with us, that I think little edification can be obtained from their writings on the subject of government... The introduction of this principle of representative democracy has rendered useless almost everything written before on the structure of government; and in great measure, relieves our regret, if the political writings of Aristotle, or of any other ancient, have been lost, or are unfaithfully rendered or explained to us."[9] Heeding Jefferson's admonitions about recourse to ancient models, I do not try in this book to draw from Athens prescriptions or justifications for contemporary practices of free speech, nor do I make Athens a general guide for our own pursuit of freedom. Rather,

---

237). Blasi (2002: 78–83), working off of Strum's biography, offers an extensive discussion of the Funeral Oration and its possible meaning for Brandeis. Brandeis also writes in *Whitney v. California* "[T]he greatest menace to freedom is an inert people... [and]... public discussion is a political duty" (1927: 375), sentiments that could certainly be gleaned from reading Zimmern and Thucydides, though, for sure, others have articulated similar views.

[6] For the checkered history of Athenian democracy in the eyes of assorted interpreters and in the language of political oratory through the ages see especially the following: Turner (1981: chap. 5); Roberts (1994); Saxonhouse (1996: chap. 1); Demetriou (1996; 1999: esp. chap. 2); Urbinati (2002).

[7] A practice that Josiah Ober would call relying on "the moral authority of the past" (2003a).

[8] See for example the letters to John Waldo ([Aug. 16, 1813] 1984: 1296–8); Nathaniel F. Moore ([Sept. 22, 1819] 1984: 1428–30); and John Brazier ([Aug. 24, 1819] 1984: 1423–4) where Jefferson writes that with regard to ethical writings in his opinion the "moderns are far advanced beyond [the Greeks] in this line of science." With regard to lessons in political organization, he recommends Montesquieu or summaries of his work frequently (e.g., 1984: 1024, 1378) and if one is to look at history at all, it is the history of England, not Greece, that surfaces.

[9] Letter to Isaac Tiffany, 1816, cited by Reinhold (1984: 65–6).

I want to use Athens' experiences with the practice of free speech to reflect
on the interconnections between that practice and both democracy and philosophy. These are interconnections I believe to be obscured by a "romantic"
return to the ancient world. The Athenians eulogized free speech as a practice that allowed them to express an egalitarianism that rejected hierarchy
and the restraints of a reverence for superiors or for the past. "To say all,"
to speak freely was to uncover and thus to question what has been and
to ignore the restraints of status. Socrates is the great advocate of free
speech – irreverent in his questioning of others and their ingrained beliefs.
Thus, Athenian democracy becomes a regime that fosters – but also ends up
executing – the man who fully expresses the principles of *parrhêsia*.

It is in pursuit of the obscured interconnections between free speech and
democracy in Athens that I approach first in the next chapter, most briefly
and with a profound sense of awe, more recent efforts at uniting democracy
and free speech by surveying the history of the wide range of justificatory
efforts in the vast literature on the freedom of speech. The effort here is to
exhibit the range of ways of thinking about the practice of free speech that
have surfaced over time. By presenting this brief overview, I hope to illuminate how the discourse from Machiavelli forward concerning freedom
of speech differs from what we shall encounter in the return to the world of
ancient Athens. I certainly do not offer an adequate overview of the topic
in today's world. Others are far more able than I to do this,[10] but I hope
that the array of contexts for discussions of free speech will serve as warning
about the too easy transfer of language from one historical period to another
and help to clarify the different setting and goals of the *parrhêsia* that the
Athenians so treasured and considered their own.

In the second chapter of this Introduction, I explain the distinctive understanding of democracy and democratic theory that runs through this book.
There are many definitions of democracy and the institutionalization of
democracy encompasses a wide variety of particular (and often peculiar)
institutions. In my treatment of democracy here I simply try to distill one
aspect that I believe is critical to the understanding of democratic practices,
which the experience of ancient Athens helps us appreciate. This is the freedom that allows us to break away from the restraints of deference – to
history, to hierarchy, to shame. This allows one to uncover oneself, to speak

[10] First Amendment jurisprudence is a major industry in law journals and books and the challenges of working through the labyrinth of issues raised by the judicial applications of principles inherent in notions of freedom of speech appear almost daily in the nation's newspapers.
The literature on this topic is so extensive that no summary can even begin to do justice to
the range of issues the practice has raised. In this discussion, I refer only to some of the works
that have been especially helpful in my efforts to learn about this topic. Schauer (1982) provides a valuable summary of the topic unto the time of publication, but there had been much
written in the last twenty-five years. I thank especially Christopher Eisgruber for guidance
here.

shamelessly. To refer back to one of the stories offered previously, this is an understanding of democracy that focuses on what allows Thersites to toss aside reverence and shame and to tell Agamemnon all that he thinks about Agamemnon's leadership without the fear of Odysseus' rod. It is only when this reverence is dismissed, when a people can say freely what they think that they are able to practice a politics of self-rule. It is not so much that Thersites says what is true, but that he can disregard the status differences between himself and an Agamemnon or Odysseus.

The definition of democracy emphasizing this release from the chains of the past emerges from the discussion in Chapter 2. It highlights just this one aspect of democracy in order to distinguish democracy from a liberalism and libertarianism that focus on the protection of rights from governmental interference and then from a constitutionalism that relies on the past to limit the present. In this distilling of democratic principles much is omitted from the institutions that characterize our contemporary democracies – most especially the language of constitutionalism and liberal rights. And, indeed, ancient Athens was hardly a pure expression of the democratic principles that I see captured by their language of free speech, however much the Athenians may have identified with their regime with *parrhêsia*. Yet, I believe that by going back to these underlying principles highlighted by the Athenian experience, we sense the challenges we face when we try to incorporate them into any working democratic regime that encompass multiple and often contradictory principles.

I

The Legacy of Free Speech

Today the challenges of practicing and protecting freedom of speech seldom fade from the headlines of our newspapers or the controversies in our courts. This was not always the case.[1] Though in the series of amendments that constitute the Bill of Rights in the U.S. Constitution freedom of speech takes pride of place as part of the First Amendment, its inclusion at that point is the result more of chance than of its perceived importance when the amendments were adopted. Over time the interest in free speech has varied greatly as have the justificatory arguments about its place in political regimes. On occasion, Athens and its democratic regime surface as part of a justificatory argument as writers connect free speech with the Athenian experience of self-rule. The more contemporary recourse to the language of freedom of speech underscores for the most part, however, the differences in the ways in which this practice becomes part of the life of a regime. The brief story of the inclusion of freedom of speech among the "first" protections in the Bill of Rights will serve as preface to a synopsis of some of the many ways that

---

[1] In the contemporary world of free speech debates, the argument is frequently made that free speech jurisprudence in America dates only to the early decades of the twentieth century with Holmes' opinion in *Schenck v. United States* (1919) and *Abrams v. United States* (1919) and with the influential writings of the Harvard law professor Zechariah Chafee (1920; also 1941). Though the adequacy of this claim has been subject to much debate it arises, it seems, because it is only after *Schenck v. United States* and Holmes' dissent in *Abrams v. United States* that the jurisprudential literature about free speech engages seriously in identifying justifications that go beyond the libertarian worry about governmental oppression and the so-called fortress model of freedom of speech, to be discussed below. See especially Rabban (1997) for an exhaustive discussion of nineteenth-century cases dealing with freedom of speech and Rabban (1985) for a careful and persuasive critique of the argument by Levy (1960) that the Americans had not moved much beyond English common law in the eighteenth century. The controversy swirls around the question of whether the protection of seditious libel is an issue that separates the government from the people and how the people's role of checking the government fits in with the judicial decisions of the nineteenth century.

freedom of speech enters our discourse as we reflect on the goals of political life.

1. GOVERNMENT AS OGRE

Sitting in the first session of the U.S. Congress in 1789, Representative James Madison, one of the architects of the Constitution, acknowledged that document's inadequacies. Sensitive to the challenges that had been raised by the anti-Federalists during the debates over ratification as well as to the letters appended to a number of the documents of ratification asking for greater assurances of protection against the newly formed government, Madison urged the House to address the question of the amendments at once: "[T]he great mass of the people who opposed it [ratification of the Constitution], disliked it because it did not contain effectual provisions against encroachments on particular rights, and those safeguards which they have been long accustomed to have interposed between them and the magistrate who exercises the sovereign power" (June 8, 1789 *Annals of Congress* 1834–56: 1.450). When Madison offered his own list of amendments and changes to the now ratified Constitution in order to address this problem, among the protections he recommended in his "fourth article" was the following: "The people shall not be deprived or abridged of their right to speak, to write, or to publish their sentiments; and the freedom of the press, as one of the great bulwarks of liberty, shall be inviolable" (1.451–2). He explained this proposal by noting that "the great object in view is to limit and qualify the powers of Government, by excepting out of the grant of power those cases in which the Government ought not to act" (1.454). This is about as much as we hear concerning the "whys" of freedom of speech during the debates about the adoption of the Bill of Rights. Since most state constitutions had provided such protections for the individual already, the debate in Congress at first was over whether such liberties needed to be affirmed at the federal level by so quickly amending the new Constitution or whether Congress had more important things on its agenda than tending to what may have been redundant concerns.

In the debates surrounding the adoption of what has come to be known as the Bill of Rights, freedom of speech does not emerge as a central issue.[2] Indeed, what we know as the First Amendment appeared as either the Third or Fourth Article in the several versions put forth by the congressional committee specifically assigned to draft the amendments. Congress finally approved twelve amendments that were to be submitted to the states for their approval before becoming part of the Constitution; only ten of those twelve received the requisite support for adoption. The first one of those sent to the states went into greater detail about adjusting the number of

---

[2] On the history of the adoption of the Bill of Rights see Berns (1976), Amar (1998), and Levy (1999).

representatives in Congress as the size of the population changes than the existing Constitution did; the second prevented congressional self-dealing by requiring elections to intervene before pay raises for members of Congress and the Senate could go into effect. Both of these proposals met with defeat.[3] Only with the rejection of those original first two amendments, then, did the protection of freedom of speech acquire the value-laden appellation of being part of the "First" Amendment.

Though discussions of why a nation should so care about freedom of speech as to include protections for it in its constitution do not surface in the congressional debates,[4] we can note, if we consider the early versions of the proposals to protect freedom of speech, that they all are framed largely in terms of the protections such a provision would offer a free people from excessive governmental intervention into the lives of its citizens. Thus, Madison's proposed amendments of June 8, 1789 had included the freedom of speech in his lengthy "Fourthly." There he writes of "equal rights of conscience," and the "right to speak, to write, or publish sentiments," and proposes that "the freedom of the press, as one of the great bulwarks of liberty, shall be inviolable" (*Annals of Congress* 1.451). He adds to this list in the same "Fourthly" the right to bear arms, the right to resist military service, protection from the quartering of soldiers, protection against double jeopardy, protection against self-incrimination, and so forth. For Madison, the freedom of speech is just one of many bulwarks against oppression – some of which are natural rights, others of which (e.g., trial by jury) result from "compact" (*Annals* 1.451).

After considerable debate over whether the House itself should consider the issue of these amendments to the Constitution or delegate the task of writing them to a select committee, the House voted on July 21, 1789 to appoint a committee to draft the amendments (*Annals* 1.685–91). Subsequently, the House constituting itself as a Committee of the Whole began consideration of the Select Committee's report on August 13, 1789 and continued its discussions through August 24, 1789 when seventeen proposed amendments went from the House to the Senate (*Annals* 1.730–809). We find from the record of the discussion that the Select Committee had used language in its Article 1, Section 9 that was similar to Madison's original proposal: "The freedom of speech, and of the press, and the right of the people peaceably to assemble and to consult for their common good, and to apply to the government for redress of grievances, shall not be infringed" (*Annals* 1.759). Again, though, this passage appears amidst a potpourri of other protections. Freedom of speech is just one among many.

---

[3] See further Amar (1998: chap. 1) and Levy (1999: chap. 1).
[4] There is no record of the discussion in the Senate, which met in closed session during this period.

The considerably slimmed down version of the amendments passed by the House on August 24, 1789 has as Article the Third freedom of religion and Article the Fourth ensuring freedom of speech, the press, and assembly for "the common good." The separation of the Third and Fourth Articles here may underscore somewhat different concerns. The Fourth Article addresses the citizens' role as protectors of the public welfare. The Third Article ensures protection of the individual liberty of conscience. By September and in the even slimmer version proposed by the Senate, the House's Third and Fourth Articles are made one, freedom of religion joins freedom of speech, and the language of consultation for "the common good" disappears (*Annals* 1.948).[5] The progress of what will become the First Amendment through its assorted permutations takes it specifically in the direction of protection from government as oppressor (as in the freedom of conscience associated with freedom of religion) and away from a focus on the freedom to deliberate for the common good that appeared in some of the earlier versions. The protective rather than the participatory concerns survived the pruning process.

This model for understanding freedom of speech as protection against governmental oppression has its roots in a much earlier English tradition, a tradition that ultimately develops into the language of government by consent. Sir Edward Coke's *Institutes of the Laws of England* (1628–1644) offers the English phrase "freedom of speech" for the first time. It seems to mean here the "privilege of free debate belonging to members in parliament"[6] and it retains this meaning in the English Bill of Rights of 1689 as well, but extends that freedom beyond Parliament: "[T]he freedom of speech and debates or proceedings in Parliament ought not to be impeached or questioned in any court or place out of Parliament." Yet, the tradition in England established early on that this "freedom" did not mean "license" and precautions needed to be taken – that is, publications needed to be licensed – lest speech have what was referred to later in Blackstone's *Commentaries* of the late-eighteenth century as a "pernicious tendency," and thus be harmful to the common welfare – even if the speech itself were true.[7]

---

[5] Cogan (1997: 86–7) records the various documents that chronicle the changing form of the amendment; according to his documentary records, "for the common good" disappears from the amendment during the Senate discussions on September 9, 1789 when the Senate combines freedom of religion with freedom of speech, the press, assembly, and petition into "Article the Third."

[6] According to Stoner (2003: 48) at the beginning of each session of Parliament, the Commons would petition the king for the privilege of free speech during the session and he would grant it. We find a recollection of this British practice in Article 1, Section 6 of the U.S. Constitution where the members of Congress are assured: "for any speech or debate in either House, they shall not be questioned in any other place."

[7] The discussion in this paragraph draws on Kersch (2003: 47–50).

It was this practice of governmental licensing or "prior restraint" that was the immediate impetus for one of the great documents associated with the practice of freedom of expression, Milton's *Areopagitica: A Speech for the Liberty of Unlicenc'd Printing* written in the middle of the seventeenth century (1644). In this work protesting the licensing of books and the restraints thereby placed on free expression in published works, we find the worry about the impact of governmental restraint. Milton embeds this argument in a series of allusions to the world of ancient Athens. The very title of the piece derives from the *Areopagitica* delivered by the fourth-century orator Isocrates to the Athenians and ties Milton to the values expressed by the ancient Athenian. Though Milton's explicit concern is the censorship of works in print, the allusion to Isocrates draws on images of Athens in order to connect freedom of speech to human virtue and political freedom. Free Athens, as Milton develops it in the rest of the piece, becomes the model for free speech. Isocrates' *Areopagitica* had invoked the virtues of the older generation of Athenians, virtues that were supposedly embodied in the judges who sat on the Areopagus in the early-fifth century, virtues that Isocrates found so sorely lacking among the Athenians of his own time. Both Milton's essay and Isocrates' oration ask for a return to these ancient virtues. In making this appeal, however, Isocrates focuses on an equality of merit that he claims characterized the Athenian democracy of Solon's and Cleisthenes' time, not on a freedom to speak. In fact, *parrhêsia* appears only once in the speech (20) and then pejoratively as the opposite of *isonomia*, equality in the law. Milton, in contrast, makes his plea for freedom of expression by affirming that the sought-after virtues only flourish when there is the opportunity to express contradictory (even if incorrect) views and with the intellectual stimulation allowed by the freedom to offer in print one's own speculations.[8] In other words, Milton's return to the *Areopagitica* of Isocrates speaks in language that is quite different from Isocrates'. Milton sees the connection between free speech and virtue, Isocrates between virtue and equality of merit without any expression of Milton's worry about government oppression.

To the title that recalls Isocrates' appeal to an ancient virtue, Milton adds as an epigraph a passage from Euripides' *Suppliant Women* (437–42) that may in fact be more appropriate to the theme of freedom of expression to which Milton appeals. In Euripides' play Theseus as the nominal ruler in Athens explains to a Theban messenger, who expects a single man to rule in Athens, that Athens is a city where (in Milton's translation) "freeborn men/ Having to advise the public, may speak free" ([1644] 1999: 3). Britain,

---

[8] Both Pangle (1992: 124–5) and Canavan (1978) emphasize this aspect of Milton's speech as a way of affirming Milton's interest not so much in the freedom of "expression" but in the freedom to search for the truth as the exercise of reason. See also Pangle and Pangle (1993: 48–9).

Milton suggests, should not appear inferior to Athens in its devotion to liberty and he includes in his speech numerous allusions to Athens and to the authors from Athens who enjoyed freedom of speech. Milton even defends the ancient devotion to freedom of speech to such a degree that he explains away the censorship Plato seems to advocate in his political writings; Plato only included provisions for censorship, Milton tells us, because Plato knew that the regime he was proposing would be impossible to found ([1644] 1999: 21–2). Milton seeks no Platonic utopia for Britain, nor does he imagine a commonwealth free of complaints, but remarks that "when complaints are freely heard, deeply consider'd, and speedily reform'd, then is the utmost bound of civil liberty attain'd, that wise men looke for" ([1644] 1999: 4). Milton's arguments against the practice of licensing go in many directions – from the *ad absurdum* argument that such restraints could carry over to restraints on "all recreations and pastimes, all that is delightfull to man" (22) to the general inefficacy of such a policy to the view that such licensing will keep men perpetual children, unable to reason, unable to make their own choices. Yet the bundle of arguments he offers his readers all conform to a consistent theme in the modern world, that of freedom of speech as a tool to restrain governmental oppression of Parliament or the people. Two centuries later when William Blackstone compiles his *Commentaries on the Laws of England*, he appeals to the same vision: "The liberty of the press is indeed essential to the nature of a free state." He, like Milton, sees this liberty as consisting "in laying no *previous* restraints upon publications" and insists that "[e]very freeman has an undoubted right to say what sentiments he pleases before the public." And again, like Milton, he nevertheless does not see this freedom as a right to avoid punishment for publishing "what is improper, mischievous or illegal" or "any dangerous or offensive writings," which many judged to be "of a pernicious tendency" ([1769: Book 4, Chapter 11.13] 2002: 151–2).

The argument of Milton, of Blackstone, and of others who turned to the freedom of speech as a tool of liberty is cogently and succinctly captured in the February 4, 1720 Letter 15 included in the vastly popular writings of John Trenchard and Thomas Gordon and compiled as *Cato's Letters*:

That Men ought to speak well of their Governors, is true, while their Governors deserve to be well spoken of; but to do publick Mischief, without hearing of it, is only the prerogative and felicity of tyranny: A free people will be shewing that they are so, by their freedom of speech...it is the Interest, and ought to be the ambition, of all honest magistrates, to have their Deeds openly examined, and publickly scanned...Freedom of speech is the great bulwark of liberty; they prosper and die together. ([1720] 1995: 111, 114)

Though scholars may debate whether Trenchard and Gordon writing under the pseudonym of Cato, a hero of the Roman Republic, expressed a "republican synthesis," there is little debate about the popularity of these letters. These letters were not only widely circulated in England; the ideas and even the language resonated in the literature of eighteenth-century colonial America.[9] The "bulwark of liberty" is the language we find in the eighteenth-century Trenchard and Gordon, but similar military metaphors surface as well in writings about free speech among today's scholars: for Bollinger, freedom of speech is a "fortress" (1986: chap. 3; 2002: 25)[10] and so great is the fear of a government power that might limit speech that even extremist speech must be protected lest the fortress be weakened.[11]

Speech as primarily a protection against an oppressive government surfaces in the assortment of libertarian justifications that one finds scattered in the opinions of justices and other works reflecting on the place of free speech in a free society.[12] All these views, whether they use the language of bulwark or fortress, however, derive from the model of government introduced by the social contract theories of John Locke. Locke had argued that government is simply the agent of the people, created by the people to protect their individual rights and entrusted by them with the power to ensure their safety and welfare through impartial adjudication. The eternal threat of resistance ensures for Locke that the government will not assume a role independent of the welfare of the people who have contracted together to create it. In this model, freedom of speech belongs to the people as a necessary tool for them to "check" the actions of those in power. The libertarian view, the "fortress," the "bulwark," the "checking" models that we find in the formulation and many analyses of the First Amendment, in the English tradition of Coke and Blackstone, in *Cato's Letters*, and in some sections of Milton's *Areopagitica* emphasize this Lockean orientation with its separation and distinction

---

9 On Cato's influence on freedom of speech in America see, for example, Curtis (2000: 37–42); for the scholarly debates concerning the nature of Cato's influence at the time of the American founding see especially Zuckert (1994: 297–319).

10 Blasi in his review of Bollinger and elsewhere (1987; 2002) uses similar language. Owen Fiss's slender book on free speech recognizes the view that the state is often seen as the "natural enemy of freedom" and that freedom may need protections from government, but he wants to focus on how the state can be a source and indeed a friend of freedom rather than the object of restraint (1996a: 2).

11 Continuing with such metaphors of almost quasi-military resonance, Bollinger and Stone (2002) entitle their volume of collected essays on the First Amendment "Eternally Vigilant," picking up from Justice Holmes in *Abrams v. United States* (1919) a phrase that captures the necessity of protecting our freedom of speech, even "the expression of opinions that we loathe," from the reach of governmental control unless "an immediate check is required to save the country" (1919: 630).

12 See Graber (1991) who offers an almost overwhelming typology of differing versions of the "libertarian" model, but primarily identifies the "natural rights" libertarianism of the nineteenth and early-twentieth centuries that focuses on the individual and a free speech theory that focuses on groups within the American polity rather than individuals. Schauer (1982) distinguishes libertarian arguments that favor the absence of government control over self-regarding actions from those that limit government control over other-regarding actions like speech.

between the "people" and the government as their agent.[13] Because of its strength, the government, though created by the people themselves, nevertheless always stands as an ogre-in-waiting, ready to tyrannize and enslave the free people by whom it was created. A constitutional system, a legal system sets limits on the government's capacity to oppress and the freedom of speech is but one of the many freedoms assured by the constitution to protect the individual and the people threatened by a potentially aggressive government.[14] This libertarian model and its concomitant "checking" or "fortress" model offer the framework within which we largely debate and discuss the practice of freedom of speech today.

This model where the practice and defense of freedom of speech works against a political power, however, must be set in contrast to what we will find when we turn to the *parrhêsia* and democratic institutions of ancient Athens in Chapter 4. Then there will be no reference to an "oppressive government" against which the people, the *dêmos*, need to protect themselves; there will be no "checking" of a government that serves as their agent; there will be no ogre-in-waiting to oppress. And there will be no government limited by constitutional restraints. There was in ancient Athens no distinction between the government and the people such as exists in contemporary conceptual frameworks deriving from the liberal Lockean model. The *dêmos is* the government. The *dêmos* meet to pass the laws by which they themselves will be governed. The *dêmos* meet to make the policy choices for the city – whether to go to war, whether to kill the women and children of a colony that resisted Athenian rule, or whether to recall troops or send reinforcements.[15]

The members of the *dêmos* fill the assorted administrative offices of the city, chosen for their positions by lot, not election. And the *dêmos* – or rather

---

[13] Freedom of the press is obviously closely connected with freedom of speech and has created a huge interpretive industry of its own, at times indistinguishable from the freedom of speech debates. Freedom of the press concerns, though, have centered around questions of "seditious libel," which, as Rabban (1985) nicely points out, addresses the key issue of popular sovereignty that lies at the heart of this debate. The point Rabban clarifies is that seditious libel raises the question of whether the government is a partner in a contract or the agent of the people. The point here is that the government is seen as an alien force, whether it is understood as a partner or as the people's agent, and that in both situations the government needs to be controlled by freedom of speech and freedom of the press and constitutionally restrained from interfering with those freedoms.

[14] John Stuart Mill's great innovation on this theme (drawing its own inspiration from Tocqueville's *Democracy in America*) is, of course, to see the threat of oppression stemming not from government, but from the people themselves now constituted as "society" and the "majority." "[T]he tyranny of the majority was at first, and is still vulgarly, held in dread, chiefly as operating through the acts of the public authorities. But reflecting persons perceived that when society is itself the tyrant ... its means of tyrannizing are not restricted to the acts which it may do by the hands of its political functionaries" ([1859] 1978: 4).

[15] The references here are to Thucydides 1.140–4 (Pericles on facing the war with Sparta); 3.36–49 (Mytilenian Debate); 7.15 (Nicias' letter from Sicily).

a selection of citizens again chosen by lot – hold those who have been chosen by lot to be officers in the city accountable for their actions. Before citizens left the office in which they served annually and for which they had been selected by lot, they were subjected to an official "scrutiny" assessing whether they abused their offices. The question during the scrutiny, though, was not whether they had deprived the *dêmos* of their freedom but whether they had enriched themselves by embezzling monies from the public treasuries. "Participation in decisions and rule," to use Aristotle's definition of the citizen (*Politics* 3.1: 1275a23), characterized the life of the ancient polity. It was not a world where one consented to be ruled by a distant power nor was it an issue of establishing a "bulwark" to protect oneself from an overaggressive government.[16] The Athenians certainly understood and feared tyranny. They celebrated as great heroes their tyrannicides, but they, as citizens ruling over themselves, were not the tyrants they feared. The separation of the people and its government, so much a part of our language today and so ingrained in our understanding of the freedoms affirmed in the Bill of Rights, has no place in the political culture of the ancient Athenians. The regime was the self-rule of a democracy; it was not the liberal playing field of the individual protected by constitutional fences ensuring assorted rights claims against a potentially oppressive government, nor was it a world where citizens were to be "eternally vigilant" in their commitment to prevent the potential abuses of a political power. The modern individual possesses freedom of speech so that the government as his or her agent acts in the interest of the governed, so that those in authority do not misuse their power. This modern individual has little in common with the Athenian citizens sitting on the hillside of the Pnyx and participating in the Assembly in order to take upon themselves the responsibility of making decisions for the city as a whole. The Athenian freedom of speech is the affirmation of the equality of participation and self-rule.

Despite these fundamental differences, Athens surfaces regularly for many as the paradigmatic democracy to which one turns to defend freedom of speech in the modern world. Given that the emphasis for these thinkers is on democracy as a community of citizens, the concern is less with the fortress or bulwark and more with political life as a school of virtue. In the next section I look at the most prominent of such efforts.

2. GOVERNMENT AS "THE PEOPLE"

In his slim, but exceedingly influential, volume *Free Speech and Its Relation to Self-Government* (1948), originally presented as the Walgreen lectures

---

[16] See Manin (1997) for an excellent study of the differences between a regime based on lot and participation and one based on consent and evaluation. Of course, the portrait of the participatory Athenian democracy is overdrawn. Not all citizens participated, and certainly not all who lived in Athens were citizens.

at the University of Chicago, Alexander Meiklejohn eloquently presents the dependence of a self-governing people on their practice of free speech. Meiklejohn, one-time president of Amherst College, life-long activist on behalf of free speech, and deeply devoted to the study of the classics, was the founder in 1928 of the Experimental College at the University of Wisconsin with its intensive study of Greek civilization for the first year.[17] An appreciation for the ancient world guided his multiple pedagogical efforts. The health of modern democracy derived, for him, from the understanding of Athenian democracy. In the 1940s and 1950s, Meiklejohn was widely acknowledged as a national spokesman for the protections of free speech and his writings, especially the published version of the Walgreen lectures, set the agenda for those exploring the theory of free speech and democracy after him. Volume after volume on the topic of freedom of speech for the next half century has felt the need to devote at least some pages, if not whole chapters, to addressing Meiklejohn's thesis about the relation of free speech to self-government.[18]

Much of Meiklejohn's book is an attack on Justice Oliver Wendell Holmes's justification for limiting speech with the language of a "clear and imminent danger" that appeared in his dissent in *Abrams v. United States*. Such language of restraint contradicts what Meiklejohn reads into the constitutional principles of "We the People...." Meiklejohn begins his famous lectures by presenting the familiar view that the government is the agent of the "People." Writing in 1948, he prefaces his book with reference to the Attorney General who has "restricted the speech of temporary visitors to our shores." The Attorney General "is afraid that we, whose agent he is, will be led astray by opinions which are alien and subversive," writes Meiklejohn. Meiklejohn then asks rhetorically, "Do We, the People of the United States, wish to be thus mentally 'protected'? To say that would seem to be an admission that we are intellectually and morally unfit to play our part in what Justice Holmes has called the 'experiment' of self-government" (1948: xiii–iv). Yet, as Meiklejohn proceeds with his lectures, he loses interest in the Attorney General and focuses instead on the "people": "There is only one group – the self-governing people. Rulers and ruled are the same individuals" (1948: 6). Further, "Self-government is nonsense unless the 'self' which governs is able and determined to make its will effective" (1948: 9). It is this self-government that depends on the free flow of ideas and so Meiklejohn brings forth as his political ideal self-rule through the town meeting where "[t]he basic principle

---

[17] Though it lasted only from 1928–32, this experimental college inspired programs, such as that of St. Johns College, Annapolis, which emphasize the study of the ancient, and especially the Greek, classical texts. The commitment to regaining the Athenian political model extended to his role as educator as well.

[18] See, for example, Shiffrin (1990: 47–56); Bollinger (1986: chap. 5); Schauer (1982: chap. 3); Baker (1989: 25–37). See also Post's article entitled "Meiklejohn's Mistake" (1993) and Fiss's response to that article (1996b: chap. 6).

is that the freedom of speech shall be unabridged" (1948: 22). Leaving the "fortress/bulwark" model far behind, Meiklejohn turns free speech not into a tool intended to protect a people from its government, but into the very condition of self-rule.[19]

Though Meiklejohn's lectures ignored a host of thorny theoretical (and historical) issues, the lectures and his subsequent writings were rhetorically powerful pleas for a democracy dependent on the assurances of free speech for its proper functioning. Meiklejohn's work defended the notion that free speech and democracy were to be understood as mutually constitutive. Yet, despite (or perhaps because) of the huge impact that Meiklejohn had on First Amendment jurisprudence in America, his work called forth its share of critical commentary. Frederick Schauer, for one, describes Meiklejohn's argument as a "sterile formulation" and urges his own readers to resist a "conception of the electorate as a national debating society" (1982: 42). For Schauer, the justifications for the protections of free speech offered by Meiklejohn evoke a false image of democratic assemblies, perhaps reminiscent of the Athens to which Meiklejohn was so partial, but not especially relevant to an understanding of democracy in the twentieth century.

Nevertheless, others still attracted to the democratic potential of Meiklejohn's argument develop his arguments with assorted and often idiosyncratic modifications.[20] Robert Post, for example, distinguishes between

---

[19] Those currently writing under the influence of Jurgens Habermas (see e.g., 1996) and articulating the benefits and expectations of deliberative democracy are in many ways the unacknowledged heirs to Meiklejohn in their invocations of freedom of speech as a fundamental condition for the success of that form of democracy. Joshua Cohen, as just one of many such participants in this discussion, writes: "A framework of free expression is required for the reasoned consideration of alternatives that comprises deliberation. The deliberative conception holds that free expression is required for *determining* what advances the common good, because what is good is fixed by public deliberation, and not prior to it. It is fixed by informed and autonomous judgments, involving the exercise of the deliberative capacities. So the ideal of deliberative democracy is not hostile to free expression; it rather presupposes such freedom . . . the deliberative conception supports protection for the full range of expression, regardless of the content of that expression. It would violate the core of the ideal of free deliberation among equals to fix preferences and convictions in advance by restricting the content of expression, or by barring access to expression" (1997: 83–4). See also Benhabib (1996).

[20] I discuss Robert Post's work briefly in the text, but see also Fiss (1996a: 2) who explicitly attributes the theory he is going to adopt – that free speech protection is a protection of popular sovereignty – to Meiklejohn. Fiss builds his case on the view that speech "is valued in the Constitution . . . not because it is a form of self-actualization but rather because it is essential for collective self-determination" (1996a: 3). Sunstein makes an appeal to Meiklejohn's work as a resource that "would help solve many of our current controversies . . . while maintaining our focus on deliberative democracy . . . without sacrificing the basic features of free speech law as it now stands" (1995: 122). The great complexity of the effort to associate free speech with deliberative democracy becomes apparent in Post's discussion of *Hustler Magazine v. Falwell* (1990) where he points to the ways in which a freedom of speech that allows for "outrageous speech" can, by enabling the violation of community values, discourage the practice of public discourse.

the "Meiklejohnian" (as he calls it) democratic free speech that is identified with the mechanisms of decision making and his own theory, a participatory theory focusing on a democracy that "requires that citizens experience their state as an example of authentic self-determination" (2000: 2367–8). Post defends an interest in freedom of speech as foundational for the ideal of deliberative self-determination that sits at the core of democratic practice. Doing so, Post suggests, allows for the protection of free speech to extend the concern simply with the processes of collective deliberation in the town meeting that Meiklejohn had defended to protections that facilitate the development of the individual autonomy of the citizen. Thus, freedom of speech becomes a vehicle to enhance (not simply allow, as for Meiklejohn) participation in the deliberative processes of democracy (1991: 279–85). Post in this way moves the discussion of freedom of speech from its place in the political life of the Meiklejohnian regime to its role as promoting individual growth through the encouragement of autonomy.[21]

Post thus expands Meiklejohn's theories in the direction of private benefits that go beyond the public advantages of full deliberation among citizens as they rule themselves. In doing so, though, we see the perhaps inevitable move to a *liberal* theory that distinguishes contemporary discussions of democracy and that exists in uneasy tension with the Meiklejohnian or Athenian perspective. While on one level Post echoes the longing for the Athenian participatory regime, he does so with a widely different agenda when he refocuses on the individual and introduces such phrases as "authentic self-determination." By doing this, he affirms a central distinction between the public and private individual and opens up an important (for him) chasm between public and private discourse. Public speech in Post's model concerns the world of self-ruling citizens; private speech rests in the private realm and is subject to different forms of analysis and especially different forms of control and limit. This distinction allows Post to raise questions about the blanket application of the principles and freedoms of public discourse to private discourse, and enables him to ask whether private speech should enjoy the same protected status as speech engaged in the life of self-rule (Post 1990). His worry is about speech that harms individuals. Post senses the need (that Meiklejohn did not) to bring this familiar liberal dichotomy between public and private into play in order to address the controversies surrounding expressions of hate speech and to explore the conditions under which one could argue for protection against that form of harm and yet still insist on the freedom of speech as a vital political practice in a democratic regime of self-government. Meiklejohn, so enamored of the Athenian model he was teaching in his experimental colleges, scorned any reading of the First Amendment's freedom of speech that looked to it as a doctrine intended to

---

[21] Post here is moving in the direction of the arguments based on self-development so prominent in Mill's *On Liberty*. I discuss those arguments in more detail in the next section of this chapter.

nurture individual autonomy. Athens, not Mill, dominated the writings and endeavors of Meiklejohn. Post searches in his writings for a unity between Athens and Mill that Meiklejohn forthrightly rejected.[22]

The distinctions between public and private speech that underlie Post's analysis, so dependent on the liberal distinctions between those two worlds that emerged with the rise of Lockean liberalism, do indeed sit uneasily in discussions of the world of ancient Athens.[23] When Socrates explored the meaning of virtue, he spoke in the agora, in the gymnasium, in the homes of Cephalus and Callias, on paths outside the city walls; wherever he engaged in conversation, though, his was public speech that the Athenians (under the prodding of his accusers Meletus, Lycos, and Anytus) saw as affecting the stability and foundation of the political regime. That his speeches occurred outside the Assembly or law courts was irrelevant to whether his speech was part of the public life of the city. Athenian democracy was a regime that depended on its citizens, in Pericles' words, becoming "lovers (*erastes*)" of the city (Thucydides 2.43). Though Socrates may have made much in his *Apology* of speaking in private to his interlocutors (31b) in order to distinguish what he did as a philosopher from those who were active politically, Socrates' speech about the nature of virtue, the soul, and what was worthy and unworthy, nevertheless was a public threat to the life of a political regime that had not encountered early liberalism's efforts to distinguish between public and private worlds.

Parrhêsia is not toleration of diversity. No wall of separation divided a protected public speech in the Assembly from a potentially unprotected private speech – or the reverse. The speech of Socrates in a literal marketplace of ideas was a speech that challenged the life of the community, whether it was spoken from a seat among the assembled *dêmos* sitting on the Pnyx or from a bench in a wrestling school (*Lysis*) or the home of the metic Cephalus (*Republic*). The speech of Socrates played this public role precisely because there was not the liberal distinction between public speech and private speech, precisely because the practice of free speech was exercised publicly as an attribute of a free people who governed themselves; it was not the speech intended to

---

[22] This seems to form the crux of the various critiques of Meiklejohn's position – namely, that he focused primarily on political speech and did not pay enough attention to the need to protect the private speech of citizens. This topic did not interest Meiklejohn and he is dismissive about the "needs of many men to express their opinions" (1948: 63) and warns about an "excessive individualism" (1948: 71) of such concern to Chafee and Holmes that Meiklejohn sees as the source of intellectual irresponsibility among self-governing citizens.

[23] An interesting analogue to the problem of hate speech, though, may exist in the legal system of ancient Athens with the *graphê hubreos*, a law that allowed for the prosecution of those who suffered from the *hubris* of another. What exactly constituted *hubris*, that is, whether it was only physical harm and actions that demonstrated dishonor or whether it could include disrespectful speech, which would bring dishonor to the victim, remains unclear. See the extensive discussion of this law in Fisher (1992).

serve as a bulwark against a distant and alien force to whom political power had been entrusted.

The tension between the fortress model and the Meiklejohnian self-governing body gives us very different understandings of how free speech may find its place in the life of the political body. Meiklejohn's approach is obviously much closer to that which emerges in ancient Athens. The practice of freedom of speech in Athens was not a protection *against* a government that could tyrannize over the people. Rather, the practice of free speech (as I shall develop in Chapter 4) was entangled in the egalitarian foundations and participatory principles of the democratic regime of the Athenians, a regime that emphasized equality, not rights,[24] and participation, not the evaluation of performance associated with the practice of democratic elections.[25] There is no "government" (a word that, of course, derives from Latin, not Greek) to be protected against. Freedom of speech in Athens is the opportunity for those who are considered equals to say openly whatever they may think in a world of equal citizens.[26] It is, as noted in the Preface, the healing of Thersites' welts as he moves from the periphery (where he is expected to show deference to his leaders) into the center (where he joins in the common deliberations of the Assembly). Freedom of speech accorded the Athenians a release from that reverence for those of a higher social status; it neither protected them nor gave them the tools to "check" the power of an overwhelming government – or the tyranny of popular opinion. The fate of Socrates (to be discussed in Chapter 5) makes that evident. Freedom of speech, then, simply marked the citizen allowed to speak without deference grabbing that opportunity. This practice separated the citizen as an equal among equals from the slave and from the female who remained enmeshed in a hierarchical world of free and unfree, of better and worse.

---

[24] Graber (1991) and others try to associate First Amendment jurisprudence with the Fourteenth Amendment in an effort to connect it with equality and thus address the inequalities of access to speech, inequalities that derive from the unequal distribution of wealth. Contemporary issues concerning equal access flood the discussions of free speech – as in considerations of election finance reforms, but also in considerations of gender and racial inequalities resulting from ingrained hierarchical biases. (See e.g., Post [1998] who sees these inequalities as comparable to censorship.) There has been an effort of late to find in ancient Athens hints of "rights" as individual protections (see, e.g., Ober 2000).

[25] Manin (1997) is excellent at developing the significance of these differences.

[26] The reference to the "equal" citizens of ancient Athens must always be qualified by the recognition of the many excluded from citizenship: women, slaves, foreign merchants. One cannot bring back to Athens visions of universal citizenship. Out of a population of approximately 120,000, only somewhere between 5,000 and 7,000 would have attended the Assembly where they would have participated in the processes of self-government (Thucydides 8.72; Hansen 1991: 130–1; Stockton 1990: 71–2). Hansen estimates the adult male population of those eligible to attend at around 30,000 (1991: 132). Any discussion of Athenian self-government always entails this tension about those who are excluded from participation.

Though the Athenians took pride in their practice of *parrhêsia*, they did not offer justifications for this practice. It was emblematic of the freedom they enjoyed as a democracy. Herodotus perhaps addresses this most powerfully in his famous paragraph describing the transformation of Athens after the overthrow of the tyrants at the end of the sixth century BCE:

The Athenians now increased in strength. It is clear that not only in one thing but in every way equality of speech (*isêgoriê*) is a worthy thing. While they were under the rule of the tyranny, the Athenians were in no way better (*ameinones*) than those who lived around her in the affairs of war; after they cast off the tyranny, they were by far the foremost. It is clear that when they were held down they were unwilling, as working for a master, but when they were freed (*eleutherôthentôn*) each one was eager to work for himself. (5.78)

Their equality of speech made the Athenians "better," but what "better" means exactly is unclear. The Socrates of Plato adopted the political language of the Athenians for the purposes of philosophy when he urged his interlocutors to practice freedom of speech so that they may all discover their errors and move forward toward understanding what is true. But, as has often been remarked, nowhere in the great literature of the first democracy do we find the justificatory expositions of their practices of democracy.[27] Rather, we must look to their practices to appreciate (insofar as we can) their understanding of the democratic model of political organization. And we find in the practice of free speech a vivid expression of the rejection of respect or reverence for ancient hierarchies and patterns of social organization. For the Athenians freedom of speech entailed the daring not to revere a limiting past that might hover over them. They prided themselves on free speech as an aspect of their own capacity to rule themselves in a regime of equal citizens without hierarchy. They lived in a city where there was no external government – no "other" – with the potential to oppress them. Freedom of speech was the tool of self-government, not a bulwark. Freedom of speech was the practice of men in public, not a protection for self-development.

As I will suggest in the later portions of this book, the playwrights and Thucydides writing in the fifth and Plato writing in the fourth centuries BCE recognized the centrality of this peculiar freedom, this *parrhêsia*, to the practices of self-government in Athenian democracy, but they also worried about the potentially tragic and destructive consequences of this practice when it was taken out of the context of the Assembly. These authors explored the ambiguous impact of what was spoken freely, and while acknowledging its

[27] Aristotle, *Politics* 3.11, where he considers the issue of the wisdom of the majority is perhaps the most important effort to defend democratic practices in the literature of ancient Athens. See Waldron (1995). I discuss the absence of justifications for Athenian democracy in Saxonhouse (1996: chap. 1).

relation to a freedom that was treasured, they also saw the inherent complexity of a practice that encouraged the casting off of shame and of the reverence for what was ancient in favor of an unveiling practice of truth telling. *Parrhêsia* was double edged, not as in Post's public and private speech, but in terms of whether the community benefited or suffered from it.

Curiously, Machiavelli at the dawn of the modern era offers a suggestive way to think about the practice of freedom of speech in a republic that blends the government as potential ogre and self-government models. Writing well before Locke and the whole development of liberal theory and before more recent investigations into democratic theory, Machiavelli proposes what I shall call the safety-valve theory of free speech.[28] In his *Discourses on the First Ten Books of Livy*, Machiavelli studies the founding and early years of the ancient Roman republic, looking to that period of Roman history as a guide for identifying the institutions and practices of the successful regime, one that lasts over time and earns glory for itself and its citizens through military expansion. The Rome that Machiavelli describes is marked by frequent conflict between the nobles and the plebs and in the First Book of the *Discourses* Machiavelli recounts many of those disputes. A chapter entitled "How Far Accusations May Be Necessary in a Republic to Maintain It in Freedom" finds Machiavelli advising: "To those who are posted in a city as guard of its freedom one cannot give a more useful and necessary authority than that of being able to accuse citizens to the people, or to some magistrate or council, when they sin in anything against the free state" (I.7: 23).[29] Citizens in a flourishing regime, Machiavelli tells us, must be able to give vent to their dissatisfactions with those who rule over them. Deference destroys the regime. The tale of Thersites looms large in the shadows here.

Sounding somewhat more like Locke than the author of *The Prince*, Machiavelli suggests that the opportunity to criticize one's leaders serves as a restraint on the actions of leaders, thus protecting the liberty of a people. The understanding of freedom of speech here is not as a protected right, but as a tool of liberty. Yet, more important for Machiavelli than fashioning this freedom to criticize into a tool is the psychological significance he ascribes to allowing the people to speak their mind. Sanctioning the open expression of anger provides "an outlet . . . by which to vent, in some mode against some citizen, those humors that grow up in cities; and when these humors do not have an outlet by which they may be vented ordinarily, they have recourse to extraordinary modes that bring a whole republic to ruin." He concludes: "So there is nothing that makes a republic so stable and steady as to order it in a mode so that those alternating humors that agitate it can be vented in a way ordered by the laws" (I.7: 23–4).

[28] Blasi uses the same term in his review of Bollinger's books (1987: 408).
[29] Mansfield and Tarcov translation (1996). Subsequent quotations from Machiavelli will come from this translation, cited by book and chapter and by page number in the translation.

Machiavelli finds support in examples from both ancient Rome and from modern Florence for his claim about the benefits of enabling a population to express its anger, unleash its views, and speak daringly about the failings of its political leaders. In this particular chapter of *The Discourses*, Machiavelli develops a theory of free speech based on his analysis of the dangers of repression.[30] Human nature, Machiavelli contends, longs for the chance to criticize those who have power and founders of republics need to acknowledge that need – or else, Machiavelli warns, they will found states that will quickly be lost to memory, bringing glory neither to themselves nor to their people. Insofar as republics depend on the mutual participation of both the wealthy and the poor (or the nobles and the plebs), a regime that builds into its structure these guards against rebellion preserves itself and its liberty.

Machiavelli's concern here is not freedom as we know it in the liberal state; it is not the autonomy of the individual; it is not the pursuit of truth in any free market of ideas; and it is certainly not the moral improvement of a self-governing citizen population. Machiavelli instead burrows into human psychology and offers a political (some might say cynical) argument; free speech – or at least the opportunity to criticize the political leaders – is essential for a regime's political stability. Great strength bubbles up from the conflicts between the plebs and patricians. Those necessary conflicts can be constructive, but only insofar as the liberty to criticize one's superiors remains. Thus, with no real attention to the benefits for the individual nor with a vision of legal protection nor with a view to self-government as a goal in itself, Machiavelli recommends that polities practice freedom of speech as a matter of prudence and of political self-preservation. Machiavelli's psychological reading of the freedom, while focused on the needs of a people, cares not for the self-improvement of the citizens in a republic – just for their participation in a glorious and resilient political body.

Meiklejohn had disdained efforts to understand the centrality of freedom of speech in a democratic regime as directed toward self-development and he had not cared about individual group psychology. He thought attention to the individual would dilute the intent of the First Amendment by turning the focus away from the fundamental principle of a self-governing people to an unregulated individualism. And yet, justifications for freedom of speech over the last century and a half have often followed John Stuart Mill's appreciation in *On Liberty* of this freedom's capacity to inspire individual intellectual and moral development. Without the constant questioning of received opinion

---

[30] Schwartz (1986) investigates how in Freud's psychoanalytic theory the freedom of speech is also linked to the need to vent aggression constructively rather than destructively. But Schwartz's argument is specifically concerned with how Freud's interest in "venting" does not concern itself with the *quality* of the speech that is expressed, but simply with the release of aggressive passions.

made possible by a freedom of speech "[b]oth teachers and learners go to sleep at their posts...A contemporary author has well spoken of the 'deep slumber of decided opinion'" ([1859] 1978: 41).[31] Mill, concerned with correcting the defects of democracy, insists on the individual's independence from "decided opinion" both for the individual and for the practices of self-government. *Considerations on Representative Government* is a storehouse of proposals intended to improve self-government by preserving the capacity for citizens to think independently. While Mill is certainly known for his multiple defenses of freedom of speech and protections from the intrusive arm of any government, we cannot ignore the importance of that independence for the practices of self-rule as well as self-improvement.

The concern with the educative role of freedom of speech in producing moral citizens surfaces already in Milton's *Areopagitica* where freedom of expression allowed for the development of intellectual autonomy, the individual who could think for himself, for whom reason is the art of choice. Mockingly he asks about all those who accept without questioning the sanctioned and unquestioned doctrine: "What need they torture their heads with that which others have tak'n so strictly, and so unalterably into their own pourveying. These are the fruits which a dull ease and cessation of our knowledge will bring forth among the people. How goodly, and how to be wisht were such an obedient unanimity as this, what a fine conformity would it starch us all into? doubtless a stanch and solid peece of frame-work, as any January could freeze together" ([1644] 1999: 35–6). The repression of free speech leaves all with that "dull ease" that dims our moral character and our thirst for knowledge. We find a similar concern with the educative capacity of this freedom surfacing frequently today. Despite Meiklejohn's disdain for this aspect of freedom of speech in favor of the discursive orientation of democracy, authors identify free speech specifically with the education of the democratic citizens who are to participate in democratic institutions. Bollinger (1986), for example, explicitly dismisses the truth-seeking marketplace of ideas justification for free speech so often associated with Mill and so powerfully articulated by Justice Holmes in his dissent in *Abrams v. United States*. Instead, he defends the freedom as a practice that teaches citizens toleration, a virtue he judges essential for the democratic citizen. The claim that free speech facilitates the search for truth would be an inadequate

---

[31] O'Rourke (2001) has recently offered a reading of John Stuart Mill that follows this same line suggesting that Mill is far less concerned with uncovering the Truth through the titanic clashing of differing opinions (with which his work is so often associated) than with the development of individual autonomy that comes through the practice of freedom of speech: "To construe it otherwise is to rob Mill's argument of its richest ingredient" (2001: 163). This reading of Mill conforms to the proposal for a "liberty model" of free speech offered by Baker (1989) who still reads Mill as the major exponent of the "marketplace of ideas" proposal, a model Baker rejects largely because it relies on the acceptance of an objective truth that awaits discovery.

justification for protecting extremist speech. Such speech does not and cannot assist in any such search, but protecting extremist, detestable speech serves the goal of nurturing a tolerant population – one educated to accept the diversity of views among the multitude of fellow citizens. The educative goal with a view toward developing those qualities essential for a self-governing people trumps the truth-seeking goal. Shiffrin, in his turn, finds Emersonian romance in free speech, which nurtures individuals who develop a spontaneous commitment to a nation that is dedicated to "preserving dissent, encouraging free minds, and basking in the rich cultural diversity that follows from such preservation and encouragement" (1990: 161). Though it is not always phrased in this language, freedom of speech in such stories as these cultivates a democratic citizenry, intellectually alive, tolerant of diversity, and devoted to the principles of self-government and at the same time enjoying an independence of thought whenever they venture into the political world.

Current debates about free speech begin from the assumption that this freedom is part of our social and political world, that it is essential to the flourishing of our modern democracies and the flourishing of the individuals who live in those democracies, whether we focus on the practice of self-government in deliberative assemblies or on the education of a citizenry. Any restraints on freedom of speech – not the practice itself – must be justified now as when issues about hate speech or pornography surface. There are certainly those who recognize the harms that freedom of speech may bring, but these harms affect individuals or groups within the polity, not the polity at large.[32] Despite the occasional power of such arguments, the dominant assumption remains that freedom of speech no longer is in need of defense itself. It is rather the expectation. Not freedom of speech, but the exceptions require the justificatory arguments.

3. PERSECUTION AND TEXTS

Leo Strauss in his famous essay, "Persecution and the Art of Writing," first published in 1941 and then reprinted in a book of the same name in 1952, reminds his readers of this change and that the freedom of speech we so casually assume has not always enjoyed the status of being the "given" that it largely enjoys today in liberal democracies. In his essay, Strauss succinctly introduces his theory of "esoteric" writing and offers in the other essays in the book an education in reading between the lines that such an

---

[32] Arguments for the control of speech often come from the concern that "access" to speech resides in the powerful and thus subverts democratic principles of equality. For the most powerful of such arguments: MacKinnon (1993); Butler (1997); Brown (1998). Brown, for instance, writes (and worries) about the "regulatory potential of speaking ourselves, its capacity to bind rather than emancipate us" (1998: 315).

esoteric reading requires. It is a style of writing and reading brought into being by societies – whether ancient or modern – that inhibit the publication and expression of thoughts, that deny free speech. Strauss first publishes this essay during years when Europe suffered under the totalitarian regimes of fascist states and then republishes it during the height of the McCarthy years in the United States. He begins the essay by noting in general terms that a freedom of speech once enjoyed "in a considerable number of countries," which he markedly refuses to name, "is now suppressed and replaced by a compulsion to coordinate speech with such views as the government believes to be expedient" (1952: 22). It is for this reason, Strauss believes, that we must relearn the art of writing and especially of reading "between the lines." For Strauss, the legacy of freedom of speech has dulled our critical faculties hindering us from appreciating the beauties of the philosophic texts written in polities that lacked that freedom. It is the failure to understand the absence of that freedom that limits, he implies, our capacities to address the threats to our own liberties in the contemporary world.

Strauss, though, speaks not of freedom of speech in the political practices of town meetings or the Senate or on street corners. He calls on his readers to create a world of freedom of speech for themselves that allows for the uncovering of truths in the books they read. The freedom of speech he applauds is the conversation with the texts and here he holds forth the model of the Platonic dialogue. By becoming participants in the dialogues with those who spoke through their writings, one enjoys both the uncovering of truths and the moral development of the liberal soul that a number of contemporary scholars attribute to the practice of free speech. Strauss takes the practice out of the political world in which we live and puts it into the reader's engagement with the text, precisely so that he or she may understand the political world.

My goal in the rest of this book is, in part, to attend to Strauss' admonitions and advice about the conversations with texts, in particular a select group of texts from the world of ancient Athens. I engage in this conversation not to address the multitude of justificatory claims that have surfaced over the past century or so defending freedom of speech, nor will I address those that specifically suggest the dependence of democracy on freedom of speech. Rather, by engaging with the texts, and drawing on the historical practices of ancient Athens, I want to suggest the intersection and congruence between free speech as practiced by the Athenians living in the first democratic regime and democracy itself.[33] Ultimately, I want to develop the association of both

[33] I am avoiding here the currently popular conundrum of the "strangeness and otherness of the Greeks" (Hesk 2000: 17 and the helpful and insightful discussion there) and the degree to which that limits any analysis. I make no claim to "understand" the Athenians, only to draw on their practices and their literature to reflect on the themes of this book.

freedom of speech and democracy with the practice of philosophy as understood in the world of the Socratic dialogue. I see a congruence between the Athenian version of freedom of speech, of philosophy, and democracy, all exhibiting a common hostility to hierarchy and to history or the past. They all share a need to break through and against a past protected by the emotion of shame, and move us toward both the benefits and dangers of a certain form of amnesia that I associate in the next chapter with democracy. It is this amnesia that lies at the beginning point of Socratic investigations, democracy, and freedom of speech as practiced in ancient Athens. All entail a focus on the future, on a willingness to discard an enslaving past in the eagerness to confront the new. To illustrate this, though, I need in the next chapter to explain how I understand that much contested and yet widely appropriated word, democracy, and its relation to memory. The discussion of shame (or *aidôs* in the Greek) will have to wait until Chapter 3.

2

Democratic Amnesia

Self-assured Meno, so certain that he understands what virtue is, admits to Socrates: "Truly my soul and my lips are numb, and I am not able to answer you. Yet, I have given many speeches about virtue hundreds of times before many people, and good ones too, as they seemed to me. But now I am unable to say anything at all" (80b). Euthyphro, ready to assure Socrates that he, Euthyphro, and not the Athenians, knows what piety is, finds himself admitting to Socrates: "I do not know how to say what I think: Somehow whatever we put forward keeps us moving about in a circle and is not willing to remain where we put it" (11b). Euthyphro blames Socrates for these wandering opinions: "You seem to me to be the Daedalus, since for me, they would have remained just so" (11d). Polemarchus, inheriting the argument from his father in the *Republic*, defines justice as helping your friends and harming your enemies, but after Socrates manipulates him into admitting that then the thief might be a just man, Polemarchus confesses: "I no longer know what I did mean. Yet this I still believe, that justice benefits friends and harms enemies" (334bc).

Socrates' challenge in each case is to bring about in his interlocutors that state of confusion, of *aporia*, that causes them to question the legacy of opinions that have guided their claims to knowledge. His interlocutors each reach that state of so-called *aporia* when the past is no longer a guide and they, sometimes willingly, sometimes not, must follow Socrates in the dismissal of the old and in the search for a new grounding, a truth that lies far away from what they previously believed. The old grounding based in traditional beliefs has been taken away and the eternal question in Platonic scholarship is whether Socrates or Plato ever provides an adequate replacement for past beliefs and tradition as the source of knowledge. Yet, the initial step in the pursuit of knowledge for the Socratic philosopher is always this act of moving beyond a reliance on what has been, thereby liberating oneself from one's past. The past in the Platonic dialogues is a chain on the present; the escape from it becomes a condition for any claim to knowledge.

It is this escape from the legacy of the past, what we might call amnesia or an enforced forgetfulness,[1] that marks Socratic philosophy – and, I would suggest, the democratic regime of self-rule as well. For both, the Socratic philosopher and the democratic regime, the past must initially be shed in the move to a new order. The democratic regime may discover the need to construct for itself a "new past" or what M. I. Finley in his lecture on the "ancient constitution" in Athens has called a "bogus history" (1971). In Socratic philosophy there is the search to replace the lost opinion or *doxa* with a new-found knowledge or *epistemê*. For a democracy, dependence on history would limit the freedom of self-rule. For Socrates it is the journey of questioning past beliefs that defines his humanity, not the achievement of an unclear conclusion (Nehamas 1998). Respectful reverence (or in the Greek *aidôs*) for what has been or what has been opined counteracts in both cases the fundamental principle of an escape from a limiting past. It is the refusal to revere that which is old that, in my argument, unites democracy and philosophy; both defy the stranglehold of earlier forms of rule and earlier beliefs in order to look toward a future, in order to set out on one's own journey. In the previous chapter, I presented an abbreviated version of the legacy of free speech in the modern mind and urged a willingness to understand how that legacy can color our picture of the Athenian *parrhêsia*, thereby inhibiting an appreciation of the practice in Athens. In this chapter, I want to assert the place of amnesia in democratic regimes to suggest how a willingness to forget, to shed the *aidôs* that inspires a reverence for what has been, is key to democratic practice and to philosophic enlightenment as well. As the Socratic endeavor to force his interlocutors into a state of *aporia* is familiar to any reader of a Platonic dialogue and will resurface later in my discussion of the *Protagoras*, I will focus my attention in this section on the meaning of democratic amnesia. *Aidôs*, often translated as shame, enters in the next chapter as the foundation for the resistance to this amnesia.

Today, democratic theory wanders across a broad range of issues from participation to deliberation to rights to majority rule to civic equality and so on. Furthermore democracy, while enjoying the status of almost universal praise and appropriation,[2] nevertheless boasts a multitude of meanings with little agreement or precision about what the preconditions of a democratic system are. Broadly, we can take democracy to entail self-rule; we can take it to entail certain individual freedoms (confusing it, I would suggest, with "liberal" theories of rights); we can take it to mean constitutionalism creating what Sheldon Wolin (1994) has suggested is the oxymoronic phrase

---

[1] The key Platonic dialogue on memory and amnesia is, of course, the *Meno*, but the "memory" toward which Socrates exhorts the slave in that dialogue and the reader is not of past historical events or beliefs, but of an unchanging world seen before one's birth. See Klein (1965) and for a somewhat different take on the status of memory Weiss (2001: 68–9, 135–6).

[2] Though we must note the recent emergence of cautionary authors such as Zakaria (2003).

"constitutional democracy" (of which more to follow) or the rule of law; we can use democracy as a normative appeal for equality; we can accept Pericles' definition when he calls Athens a *dêmocratia* in his Funeral Oration because "it is a government attending to the interest of the many rather than the few" (Thucydides 2.37). All these meanings and many, many more come to play in their particular ways to satisfy the distinctive agendas of those who employ them.[3]

My agenda in this volume is to understand democracy not in the contemporary language of *liberal* democracy but as practiced among the Athenians where the principle of self-rule dominated the political culture. Within the practice of self-rule a host of other principles flourished. This was a regime that emphasized equality, albeit only among those it deemed citizens; it was free of rule by other cities or empires. Its citizens assembled in the ecclesia to make their decisions *en meson*, in the middle, and they served in a multitude of administrative posts and sat as judges, sharing in the processes of self-rule and in the "offices and judgments"[4] of the city without regard to the social and economic background of its citizens.[5] It was a regime so dependent on the self-rule of a people that decisions made one day by the people in the Assembly could be revoked by a vote of the people attending the Assembly the next day.[6] In the fourth century Plato and Aristotle draw from Athens abstracted portraits of the democratic regime as a way of uncovering its fundamental principles. Socrates in the *Republic* worries about a regime in which the young will be molded by the praise and blame they hear echoing throughout the city, but in Book 8 he portrays democracy as a regime enjoying the absence of constraints that any particular form might impose on it (557a–564a).[7] In Aristotle's formulation democracy is a regime where "whatever seems best to the many, this is what is final and this is what is just" and where a key measure of the regime is "to live as one wishes" (*to zên hôs bouletai tis, Politics* 1317b12). Aristotle writes at length of the variations of democracy, of those where farmers are the majority, of those where fishermen are the majority, of those governed by the rule of the law (the *nomoi*),

---

[3] The POLITY scale developed by the Polity Project under the guidance of Ted Robert Gurr identifies a set of conditions to allow social scientists to rank the degree of democracy achieved by various political regimes. The conditions identified give a very good sense of the wide range of (and often contradictory) criteria that tend to be associated today with the democracies of today. See http://www.cidcm.umd.edu/inscr/polity/.

[4] This phrase comes from Aristotle, *Politics* 1275a23.

[5] Ober (2001: 177) would add to this list the security that Athenian citizens would feel in the protection of their bodies and their self-esteem in the city. Such a reading might be guilty of bringing certain liberal principles back to the ancient regime of self-rule.

[6] See Thucydides' descriptions of the Mytilenian Debate (3.37–49) and the debate at Athens about the decision to send the expedition to Sicily (6.8–24) discussed in Chapter 7. Also see Saxonhouse (1996: chap. 3).

[7] See further pages 47–9 and Saxonhouse (1998).

and of those which are ruled by decree (*Politics* 1292a). In the discussion that follows, I have in mind only the most radical or extreme democracy, the "complete" democracy uncurbed by the moderating principles Aristotle envisions for his more restrained versions of the democratic regime, enjoying the freedom of form that Socrates envisions in Book 8 and that the Athenians practice when they change their minds and when they actually even vote to restructure themselves briefly in 411 BCE.

For my argument in this book, the moment of democratic foundation for Athens is the moment when the Athenians acquire the authority to rule over themselves. That authority comes at the expense of history, of the past. To rule themselves, the people must liberate themselves from what has been, just as the interlocutors in the Platonic dialogues must shed the chains of past opinions to engage in the pursuit of what is true. For the political development of Athens, the key moment for this way of understanding democracy occurs in 508 BCE when the past, especially the hierarchy of the aristocratic past, was overturned by Cleisthenes in order to create the egalitarianism that governed this peculiar political regime, the one that came to be called a democracy many years later.[8] We do not know all the details of how Cleisthenes, the Athenian credited with "founding" democracy in Athens,[9] instituted the beginnings of the democratic regime. Herodotus simply says that Cleisthenes "established for the Athenians the tribes and the democracy" (6.131) without further detail. Aristotle's *Constitution of Athens* provides some more detail indicating that the rejection of the old familial and tribal ties lay at the core of this so-called founding, and he offers a lengthy – if not always lucid – description of the innovations introduced by Cleisthenes. I quote the passage at length since it suggests Cleisthenes' efforts to eradicate the old and to refashion the relationships among the members of the polity through a deep restructuring of the social organization of Athens.

First he distributed all into ten tribes instead of four, wishing to mix them up so that a greater number might take part in the political regime (*politeia*). From this it is said not to judge by the tribe to those who want to investigate [people's] clan (*genos*). Then he set up the Boulê with 500 members with fifty from each tribe. At that time

---

[8] For a discussion of the early use of the word *dêmokratia* and the scholarly debates surrounding its first usage see Saxonhouse (1996: 32–5).

[9] Aristotle, *Constitution of Athens* 29.3. Aristotle attributes to Cleitophon the proposal that the committee set up in 410 BCE to "write down together what they think to be best for the city" investigate "the ancestral laws (*patrious nomous*) that Cleisthenes laid down by when he set up the democracy." Finley, however, notes the curiosity that by the end of the fifth century "[e]veryone now agreed that it was Solon who founded the modern Athenian state . . . whereas Cleisthenes gradually dropped from sight" (1971: 36). For our purposes, it is Cleisthenes, not Solon, who is responsible for the introduction of the egalitarianism that remained at the heart of Athenian democracy, transforming a society dominated by aristocratic principles that referred to the past, and for the democratic principles that turned the city toward the future.

there were 100 members of the Boulê. On account of this, he did not set them up as twelve tribes, so that he might not have to use the previously existing divisions into trittyes [the administrative units established initially by Solon out of which the tribes were structured]; out of the four tribes there were twelve trittyes, so that it would not have turned out to have mixed up the multitude (*plêthos*). Further he distributed the countryside into thirty groups of demes . . . And he made those living in each of the demes demesmen of each other so that the new citizens [*neopolitas*] might not be noticed when they were not identified in terms of their family names, but that all might be identified by their demes. And thus, Athenians refer to themselves according to their deme . . . He named some of the demes from their location, some from their founders, since they were not all connected with their [old] locations. But the clans and brotherhoods and the religious associations he allowed each one to keep according to ancestral custom (*patria*) . . . With these things being done, the regime (*politeia*) became by far more democratic than that of Solon. (21.2–22.1)[10]

The earlier administrative structure built out of four traditional aristocratic tribes was replaced by one based on ten newly created tribes. These new tribes with ties to neither the patriarchal aristocratic past nor to any traditional territorial configuration were artificially constructed and not grounded in nature or in history. As such, they could always be subject to further transformation by individual or collective human craft and choice.[11] In other words, breaking away from the limits of the patriarchal past was at the heart of the founding of Athenian democracy.[12] It was a break that came from the calculations of those involved in the life of the polity, not from external forces be they human or divine.

The naming of citizens according to their *deme* that Aristotle describes allowed for the introduction of "new citizens" who did not necessarily find their ancestry in the ancient tribal units; to identify oneself by *deme* within the new regime signaled devotion to the democracy. The *deme*, the local administrative territorial unit comprising these new tribes, replaced the connections to the city through one's father's name or lineage, connections that

---

[10] The passage is rife with ambiguity. Why does intermixing lead to an increase in the numbers eligible to vote? Who were the "new citizens"? For some attempts at understanding the passage in addition to the discussion that follows see Ostwald (1986: 15–28), Manville (1990: 185–94), and the references cited there.

[11] For an excellent discussion of the complex issues raised by the creation of a new body of citizens see Manville (1990).

[12] For my discussion here see especially Lévêque and Vidal-Naquet (1996) who comment, for example, "In order to construct this new territorial framework, however, the traditional geographical and social context, which had given disproportionate influence to the Eupatrid families, first had to be destroyed" (1996: 12). Lévêque and Vidal-Naquet's focus on the person of Cleisthenes as the "founder" of democracy raises some hackles in its suggestion of the "great man theory" of history. Ober especially resists this understanding of the founding of Athenian democracy (1996: chap. 4) and argues for the "decentering of Cleisthenes," though he nevertheless still writes of "moments of rupture" (1996: 32–3). Along similar lines, but with some qualifications as well, see David Curtis' "Translator's Foreword" in Lévêque and Vidal-Naquet (1996: xii).

depended on looking back in time.[13] The past was no longer to be a limit; the new democracy lives in the present and, as we shall see, even in the future. With the past cast out, as it were, one was not bound to respect the old, to esteem what had been. As Lévêque and Vidal-Naquet phrase it: "[Athens'] past was thenceforth to coincide with its present" (1996: 33). Speech, the focus of my discussion, likewise, in the development of democratic practices sheds the respect for what has been and is released from the bonds of an *aidôs* that entails a reverence for the old. *Parrhêsia* deriving from and fostering the new egalitarianism enters the political life of Athens with this escape from what had been the hierarchies of the past.

The same impulse that lay behind the democratic rejection of the past visible in Cleisthenes' reforms in 508 BCE reappears with rhetorical boldness in Pericles' oft-quoted Funeral Oration from Thucydides' *History*. Thucydides' introduction to the Funeral Oration emphasizes the traditional character of the burial and the speeches that accompany such public funerals. Thucydides refers to the ceremony as a *patrios nomos*, a custom that comes down from the ancestors (2.34.1)[14] and he proceeds to detail the precise nature of the burial, what is done with the bones, how the cypress coffins are carried through the city, and how the relatives participate in the ceremony. Though no further mention of such a ceremony appears in the *History*, Thucydides mentions that this *nomos* was observed throughout the war. Pericles echoes Thucydides' emphasis on the *nomoi* in the first sentence of his speech by himself referring to the *nomos* that had been established for those who die in battle (2.35.1). Yet he, the leader of the Athenian democracy, immediately questions the wisdom of the ancestors who thought that words could adequately describe the deeds of the city's heroes. He seems at first to respect their tradition, proceeding to give the speech according to the *nomos* since that is what is expected of him. Yet, in so doing he undermines that past, moving his audience very quickly and very powerfully from a focus on the past to a focus on the future – leaving the ancestors and their customs far behind in the turn to the glorious present and the even more monumental future that awaits them.

Pericles initially makes the obligatory (but so brief) mention of the ancestors. "For it is just and proper on such an occasion to give them such honor of remembrance," he says. They are remembered, though, not for any glorious actions, but simply for having inhabited the same land and handing it over to their offspring (2.36.1). He then turns to those even more worthy of praise, "our fathers" (who nevertheless receive even briefer mention than

---

[13] Just as important as the rejection of the hierarchy of the aristocratic past was the rejection of the economic ordering of society. Cleisthenes' reforms ended the level of participation in political affairs according to wealth that had been introduced by Solon.

[14] Whether the burial and the oration were in fact old customs has been questioned: Gomme (1945–81: 2.94–101) and Jacoby (1944).

the ancestors), before he hastens toward the regime that raised Athens to its heights. Pericles races to the present as he chooses not to make a long speech about the battles and successes of the past; instead, he lingers for many paragraphs over the qualities of the city in which they currently live.[15] Within this rich description of the Athenian polity is a remark, embedded in the most convoluted language, suggesting that worth and renown within the democracy that is Athens derives from the ability "to do good for the city," not from chance (*meros*), that is, presumably inheritance; even more remarkable is the affirmation that the poor who serve well are not denied renown (2.37.1). The present replaces the past. Qualities of soul replace ancestry – and Thersites enters the deliberative circle.[16]

The old hierarchies of aristocratic family and of Solonic wealth disappear in the social and economic egalitarianism of Pericles' vision of his democracy. It is the citizens of the present, those lovers of the city, not the legacy or the wealth they have inherited, who matter for Pericles in this eulogy of democracy. And then, as the speech proceeds, not only does the present dominate the past, but the future dominates the present.[17] Events in the present become only markers on the way to the future. The praise of the city in which they live is followed by Pericles' praise of those who died for the city. Though death has overtaken them, they will forever be memorialized (*aieimnêstos*, 2.43.2) in word and deed. The manner of their death allowed them to escape their past. Even if they had been bad men before, doing harm, their past deeds, Pericles says, are effaced by their valor (2.42.3). Defense of the democratic city erases their individual pasts. Pericles has taken them out of the past and flung them into an eternal future. The "always to be remembered" deeds of those whose public funeral the Athenians are now attending slip into the future. And so, Pericles tells those who remain, they too must turn to the future, not the past; they too must sacrifice themselves for the city and live on into its future, replacing the ancestors and the fathers with whom Pericles had begun the speech and even the fallen warriors for whom he gives the speech.[18] Parents young enough to bear

---

[15] Contrast this with the speech Socrates attributes to Aspasia in the *Menexenus*. She emphasizes the autochthony theme and the past, not the future (Saxonhouse 1992: 118).

[16] Loraux remarks on how Thucydides' introductory comments to the oration reinforce the democratic themes of the speech to follow, in particular how the selection of the speaker "must not be seen as mere chance: by this choice, an act of homage to a man's merit, the city honored the most valorous of its members" (1986: 19).

[17] See also Ober (2003a: 26–7).

[18] Thucydides the Athenian (as he describes himself in the first words of what we have come to call his *History*) is a product of the democratic regime that Pericles so praises and writes not to investigate the past and make it a chain upon the present, but to record the present, the greatest movement ever, so that men in the future might "see clearly" (1.22). The insights he offers come not because we need to learn about "our" past as determining the relations of the present, but because events repeat themselves, given the unchanging nature of the human being.

more children must do so: "Those still to be born will make them forget those who are no more" (2.44.3).[19] And those younger brothers, they who must deal with the halo that memory puts around the men who have sacrificed their lives for the city, must vie for a place too in the minds of future generations.

The very fact of a public burial such as the one at which Pericles speaks, as several scholars have pointed out, indicates the democratic breaking down of the aristocratic connections that would tie the soldier to his family and his personal history rather than to the unity of the city. As Nicole Loraux writes: "In burying its dead, then, the Athenian community appropriated them forever, and at the demosion sema [public tomb] all distinctions, individual or familial, economic or social, that might divide Athenians even in their graves were abolished" (1986: 23). The past divided and hierarchicalized them. Archaeological studies of grave stele set up by families for individuals – or rather the sudden disappearance of such stele – associate the decline in the numbers of these burial stele to the time period of the founding of democracy.[20] The chains of the past dissolve as the private burial sites become less common.

While the founding of democracy entailed the breaking down of the stranglehold of the aristocracy and the aristocratic focus on the past, the security of democracy – any democracy, a regime based on the openness of choice, not on the guiding principles of an assumed directive nature that assigns us to hierarchical relations – becomes problematic; there is in such a regime where the Assembly is the originator of policy decisions the potential for constant refoundings. The Athenians, living long before the concept of a written constitution came to lie at the core of principles of political liberty, did have laws such as the *graphê paranomôn* to provide a reverential glance at a limiting past, but how controlling this law may have been is unclear. According to the *graphê paranomôn*, those who proposed laws in the Assembly contrary to laws previously passed could be prosecuted. Though much is made of this *graphê* and its role in foreshadowing a sort of constitutionalism at Athens, the first attested example of the *graphê paranomôn* is in 415 BCE, almost a century after Cleisthenes reorganized the Athenian city (Munn 2000: 102). Further, several scholars regard the *graphê paranomôn* not as a law to provide constitutional stability to a potentially ungrounded regime, but as a device invoked in an effort to limit the excesses of the "radical democracy" present

---

[19] Note the irony of the eternal memory that is supposed to surround those who died – but who will nevertheless be forgotten by their own parents.

[20] The case has been made for legislation under Cleisthenes to forbid such stele, but H. A. Shapiro writes that if this were accurate it would have taken a while for such legislation to take effect. Shapiro finds the theory that the public burials might have been introduced by Themistocles "a further blow against the prerogatives of the aristocracy more appealing." He continues, the "stately but modest tombs were not to be outshone by the ostentatious memorials to wealthy aristocrats" (1991: 647, 655).

at Athens at the end of the Peloponnesian War (Munn 2000: 382n17).[21] The
effect, like the "bogus history" of which Finley writes, was to introduce an
alien concept to restrain the democratic regime from enjoying the freedom
that would match the principles of its founding moment and that some found
excessive.

Long after Pericles had given his glorious Funeral Oration exalting the free
city of the Athenians, Thucydides describes toward the end of his *History*,
at a point in time when the *graphê paranomôn* would have been relevant,
an Athens quite different from the one existing when the war began under
Pericles' leadership. Now, it is no longer led by a general with a focus on the
future. Now, it is an Athens that is suffering from the ravages of the war she
has brought upon herself. During brief periods, it is no longer even a democracy. In the oligarchic coup of 411 BCE, the Assembly is persuaded to turn all
power over to the so-called Four Hundred. Thucydides' description of this
coup captures the loss of *parrhêsia* in the transformation from the freedom
of the democracy to the restraints of the oligarchy. As the conspirators plotting the overthrow of democracy gain power, those sitting in the Assembly,
according to Thucydides' report, "deliberated about nothing except what
seemed best to the conspirators, and further those who spoke were from
among them and what was to be said was first reviewed by them. And no
one of the others still spoke against them, since they were fearful and saw
the number of the conspirators. If anyone did speak against them, straight
away in some convenient fashion, he was dead ... For the same reason, it
was impossible for anyone who was angered to express his grief to another
so as to plot his defense, for he would not know the one to whom he would
be speaking, or if he knew him, he would not be trusted" (8.66.1–4). The
destruction of democracy was marked by the absence of the *parrhêsia* that
we shall see Athens prided itself on.

The oligarchs pervert the practice of *parrhêsia* for their own purposes. It
is unclear how, but they get the Assembly to meet at Kolonos where "the
commissioners introduced no measures apart from this, that it was permitted
for any Athenian to make any proposal he wished with impunity; in case
anyone should indict the speaker for illegal procedure (*graspêtai paranomôn*)
or in any other way hinder him, they imposed severe penalties." With this
protection for their proposals, the oligarchs recommend "that no one any
longer hold any office belonging to the present system or receive pay" and
that henceforth the Four Hundred will in effect rule over Athens (8.67–8).
In this way, the freedom of speech enjoyed by the democracy leads to the
freedom to completely transform the democracy – even into an oligarchy.
The Four Hundred ruled briefly before being replaced by the Five Thousand,
considered by Thucydides "the best form of government that the Athenians

---

[21] See also the discussion in Ostwald (1986: 135–6).

had known, at least in my time" (8.97.2), but with its property qualifications and other restrictions it was hardly the free and egalitarian democracy of earlier times. By 410 BCE, the full democracy of the earlier period reemerged, although in 404–403 BCE it was put on hold as the Athenians suffered under the rule of the Thirty Tyrants. This time it was not the Athenians who had transformed themselves; rather, the victorious Spartans put the Thirty into power after they defeated Athens. Eight months later, democratic resistance to the Tyrants brought about the restoration of democracy in Athens.

In the curious inversions that appear at times of such crises, reaction to these assaults on the freedoms of a democratic regime evoked the past, the *patrios nomos*, the traditions of the ancestors, or in the frequent (but less accurate) translation the "ancient constitution." Appeals to the *patrios nomos* suggested the effort to recover a regime that depended on the time-honored customs from long ago rather than – as Pericles had seen it – on what was new and creative. Athens at the end of the fifth century, instead of looking forward as Pericles had urged, now turned backward to its ancient customs and tried to recall (or create?) for itself a past, bringing reverence for that past (imagined or otherwise) as a restraint into its present so that the laws creating the democracy could not be voted out of effect. The Athenian democracy that had dismissed its aristocratic history at its very founding now tried to recover a history that claimed an ancestry for its laws. This would give to the Athenians as a city the legitimacy to withstand the assaults of a variable Assembly of the people who themselves had been created by those laws.

The Assembly of the people had voted for a complete regime transformation when they handed power over to the Four Hundred. Lest they display such freedom to change again, the Assembly voted after the fall of both the Four Hundred, and again after the fall of the Thirty Tyrants, to establish commissions with the express mandate of codifying the laws, setting them down as fixed rules that would not be subject to constant revision. Instead, engraved on stele and visible to all, these laws would, it was hoped, ensure the grounding by which democracy could preserve itself. Rather than leap into the future and establish the unseen memorials in the hearts of all as Pericles had envisioned, there is the sudden desire to put on restraints etched in stone and drawn from the past – even if that entailed making up that past. It is after a period of such political instability in Athens at the end of the fifth century that the language of the *patrios nomos* surfaces as a rhetorical tool to recall a stable, but no doubt mythic past.[22] The crises of a city

---

[22] As is clear from Munn's discussion, such recollections of an ancient constitution could also be used by the oligarchs whose researches into the "ancestral laws that Cleisthenes enacted when he established the democracy" (Munn quoting from the decrees commissioning the thirty *syngrapheis* who were to draw up "proposals for the security of the state") could find a regime in which there was no pay for attendance at the Assembly or for officeholders (2000: 137, 389n20). Pay for public service had certainly worked to expand political participation.

facing defeat brought forth appeals to this "ancient constitution"; humility before its traditions would ensure, it was hoped, the safety of a democratic Athens.

No sooner was the democracy restored in 403 than the Assembly decided to complete the codification of the laws begun in 410. That decree in Finley's translation began as follows: "The Athenians shall be governed in the ancestral ways (*patrios* is here converted into a plural noun, *ta patria*), using the laws, weights and measures of Solon and also the regulations of Draco which had previously been in force" (Finley 1971: 11–12). As Finley writes: "Clearly *patrios* here is [used] . . . to mean merely the way Athens was governed before the Thirty Tyrants took charge . . . not in any archaic sense. . . . By the 'laws of Solon and Draco' the decree meant the law of Athens as it stood in 401, some of it indeed going back to the ancient lawgivers but much of it either revised or wholly new legislation promulgated in the two centuries since Solon" (1971: 12). The freedom of democracy in this instance becomes the freedom to create its own history – be it the mythic image of a democratic Solon or even Theseus or of the tyrannicides who now would be portrayed not as acting because of personal slights and homoerotic attachments, but to free the city from an oppressive tyranny.[23]

The rhetoric appealing to this history, whether "bogus" or not, continues throughout the fourth century, especially, for example, in the speeches of Isocrates. Admonishing the Athenians for their loss of civic virtues, Isocrates stirs up memories of the good old democratic regime of Solon (as if there were one),[24] a democracy that supposedly was *reestablished* by Cleisthenes after the interlude of the tyrants in 508 BCE. Isocrates' history bears little resemblance to what had happened two centuries earlier. Isocrates' (and others') appeals to reincarnate that mythic past sit uneasily in the world of Athenian democracy envisioned by, let us say, the future-oriented Pericles.

Socrates in the eighth book of the *Republic* captures the tensions created by introducing an ideology of a *patrios nomos* into the democracy that is Athens. In that book of the *Republic*, Socrates offers a portrait of the democratic man and the democratic regime as marked by freedom, gentle at first and then shading into excess before becoming tyrannical. Recalling

---

[23] Thucydides in particular is especially disturbed by this misreading of the past by the Athenians and the dangers such a misreading poses for the ability to "see clearly." See especially 1.20 and 6.54–9.

[24] From what we know of Solon's proposed innovations to the Athenian political system, in its efforts to steer a "middle course" it was certainly not the radical democracy of the fifth century, though it did open political participation through his efforts to undermine the exclusive power of the nobility by changing the grounds of office holding from birth to wealth (Solon, especially Fragments 5, 6 where he says that he gave to the *dêmos* just so much privilege and honor as was adequate for them and that it would be best for the *dêmos* to follow those who are leaders; Aristotle, *Politics* 1273b–1274a; Sinclair 1988: 1–2; Manville 1990: chap. 6; Martin 1996: 84–6).

Pericles' emphasis on the freedom of daily life in Athens, Socrates introduces the discussion of democracy by defining it for Glaucon as the regime where the citizens are free (*eleutheroi*) and "the city is full of freedom and free speech (*parrhêsia*) and there is license (*exousia*) to do whatever one wants" (557b).[25] That license comes from the denial of any restraints, of any laws that may limit individual choices. He describes a strange world marked especially by the absence of hierarchy: "The greatest point of liberty . . . however much it comes to be in such a city is when the slaves, male and female, are not less free than those who bought them. Among the women toward the men and among the men toward the women how much equality is there before the law (*isonomia*) I almost forgot to say" (563b). It gets even more extreme than equality between slaves and masters, male and female; animals, Socrates tells us, are freer in a democracy than anywhere else and horses and asses are accustomed to journey freely and haughtily, bumping into whomever they encounter on the road if they do not stand aside (563c).

It is in this section of the *Republic* that Adeimantus asks: "Won't we with Aeschylus say whatever comes to our lips?" (563c), an allusion to the *parrhêsia* that shall be the focus of so much of the following chapters, but it is also an allusion to the potential for blasphemy that comes with the freedom of democracy, its freedom to exclude hierarchy and reverence from its practices. The democratic man of Socrates' story shows complete indifference to hierarchy. Socrates' portrait transforms democracy into anarchy such that "the father habituates himself to be similar to the child and fears his sons, and the son is like the father and displays neither shame nor fear before those who bore him in order that he might be free, and the metic makes himself equal to the townsman and the townsman to the metic, and likewise with the stranger" (562e–563a). Socrates summarizes this portrait of democracy and the democratic man by commenting that "they do not care for the *nomoi*, whether they are written or unwritten, in order that in no way can there be any despot for them" (563de).

Of course, no regime enjoys the freedom of Socrates' caricature, and a curiosity about Socrates' description of democracy is how little resemblance it bears to the Athenian democracy we know from historical and literary sources.[26] It has none of the institutions of Athenian democracy – the Assembly, sharing of political offices, and juries. There is no reference to the participatory ideals expressed in Pericles' Funeral Oration, and the image Socrates introduces of the condemned man walking freely through the city lies in

---

[25] Aristotle, who describes a multitude of democratic regimes based on his researches of the varied constitutions in the Greece of his time, also remarks at one point that while the particular groups making the decisions in a democracy may vary from regime to regime, a democracy is a regime in which one does what one wishes to do (*ho ti an boulêtai tis poiein*, 1310a32). See also the reference to 1317b12 cited on page 39.

[26] Roberts (1995: 263–5) details these differences point by point.

striking contrast to his own execution. And yet, this portrait of democracy by Socrates captures the theoretical foundations of democracy in its emphasis on equality, the resistance to hierarchy, especially a hierarchy that depends on respect for what has been, a hierarchy where sons revere their fathers and the young their teachers. When the Athenian democracy reestablished itself after the oligarchic coup of 411 BCE, it formed, as noted previously, a commission to write down the laws. These written laws were to structure the regime, to give it a form so that it would not be subject to constant transformation as the people changed their minds. By inscribing these laws on the stele, by creating in Wolin's terms the oxymoron of a "constitutional democracy," the Athenians moderated the democracy that allowed for the constant self-recreation of the democratic man such as Socrates describes in the *Republic*.

The instability of the life of the democracy, so evident in Socrates' portrait of the democratic man, ensures that no democratic regime can ever achieve its full expression, and as with every regime, democracy becomes a balancing act between those foundational principles of freedom and equality and the excessive expression of those principles. Thus, the appeal to the *patrios nomos* surfaces in the rhetoric of Athens to counteract and balance the opposing tendencies. It is an appeal that fits uneasily into a political system that had been founded by the breaking down of the patriarchal and hierarchical world of the sixth century with Cleisthenes' reforms, but it captures as well the essential balancing that is entailed in the relation of *parrhêsia* and *aidôs*, free speech and shame, uttering all without respect for hierarchy and a reverence for the past and its traditions. Democratic amnesia may be an unattainable goal. The Athenians, for sure, beyond the inscribed stele, appealed to Delphi, to the gods. *Parrhêsia* is an expression of the amnesiac aspirations – but it is also a threat that undermines the polity that demands structure as well as freedom. Thus *aidôs* keeps intruding.[27]

The challenge of the relationship between democracy and the past or the bonds of tradition faced not only the ancient Athenians between Cleisthenes' dramatic restructuring of Athens and its conquest by Philip of Macedon in 338 BCE. It is a challenge that faces democracies and republics of the modern world, a challenge captured vividly in Sheldon Wolin's focus on the problematic status of the language of constitutional democracies. Wolin asks the question: "When a democratic revolution leads to a constitution, does that mark the fulfillment of democracy, or the beginning of its attenuation?" (1994: 30). The answer for Wolin is the latter, for once a constitution is established and accepted, once there is an appeal to the *patrios nomos*, the past comes to control the present and the choices of the people are no longer

---

[27] Though Ostwald does not use the language of *aidôs* as I do, his great volume (1986) is built around the transformation of Athens at the end of the fifth century into a regime governed by law, not the popular sovereignty of what I am calling democratic amnesia.

free. Self-rule disappears into the maw of constitutional structure. Respect for the constitution itself (often expressed in the United States in the language of "original intent") constitutes a deference before others, those who lived before and made the decisions that limit the choices of the present. It denies the individuals of the present the freedom to decide for themselves. The condition Wolin describes is put into a powerful metaphor when Elster (1979; 2000: chap. 2) writes of Ulysses and the sirens as a way of understanding the meaning of constitutionalism. Whereas Elster and others writing on constitutionalism explore the positive effects that such restraints put on democratic decision making, Wolin is more prone to raise the concerns of the people's lost freedom. "Constitutional democracy is an ideological construct designed not to realize democracy but to reconstitute it and, as a consequence, repress it" (1994: 32).[28]

While the current volume addresses the tension between democracy's resistance to the burdens of past decisions and its need to respect the past by looking back to the classical world of ancient Athens and its language of *democratia, parrhêsia,* and *aidôs,* the challenge of constituting a regime on the basis of democratic amnesia has confronted the American political regime from its very founding. Virginia Woolf observed, albeit with a certain degree of exaggeration: "[W]hile we [the English] have shadows that stalk

---

[28] The contradictory language of constitutional democracy regularly plagues democratic theorists. Habermas, for instance, has recently written an article entitled "Constitutional Democracy: A Paradoxical Union of Contradictory Principles?" in which he recognizes that the "principle of the constitutional exercise of power... appears to set limits on the people's sovereign self-determination" (2001: 766). Habermas places this conundrum in the modern language of human rights and popular sovereignty and tries to resolve it by introducing the notion of "cooriginality" contending: "Citizens can make an *appropriate* use of their public autonomy, as guaranteed by political rights, only if they are sufficiently independent in virtue of an equally protected private autonomy in their life conduct" (2001: 767). Rejecting the solutions offered by Rousseau and Kant as inadequate for finding "an unambiguous way of using the concept of autonomy for the justification of constitutional democracy," he turns to a time dimension or a "self-correcting historical process" (2001: 768). In Chapter 7 on Thucydides I will discuss the advantages of changeability of the assembly and its relation to democratic principles. See also Saxonhouse (1996: chap. 3).

Habermas develops an argument from Frank Michelman and claims to resolve Michelman's paradox "in the dimension of historical time, provided one conceives the constitution as a project that makes the founding act into an ongoing process of constitution-making that continues across generations" (768); in other words, Habermas sees the resolution lying in "the self-correcting learning process" of continual constitutional change. Others have responded with critiques aplenty to this theory of "cooriginality" for far too simply cutting through the Gordian knot of democratic constitutionalism and ignoring such difficulties as explaining why "a situated learning process, taking place in a political community at a given time and originating from one specific constitutional project, [should] bear any significance for any other political community differently situated" (Ferrara 2001: 789) or how we can get beyond a series of "as if's" in imagining that "the constitution is the same over time, *as if* our perspective is the same as that of our forebears" (Honig 2001: 795). One might also remark upon the continued instability implicit in a model that tries precisely to escape that problem.

behind us, they [the Americans] have a light that dances in front of them. That is what makes them the most interesting people in the world – they face the future, not the past."[29] Hyperbolic as this statement may be, it nevertheless distills the language and the conceptual framework that captures the founding moment of the American regime. Tom Paine, that Englishman who became the spokesperson of the American Revolution, wrote with passion and assurance: "A situation similar to the present has not happened since the days of Noah until now. The birthday of a new world is at hand" ([1776] 1995: 52).[30] And in *The Rights of Man* he would write in his response to Edmund Burke: "If any generation of men ever possessed the right of dictating the mode by which the world should be governed for ever, it was the first generation that existed; and if that generation did it not, no succeeding generation can show any authority for doing it, nor set any up. The illuminating and divine principle of the equal rights of man, (for it has its origin from the Maker of man) relates, not only to the living individuals, but to generations of men succeeding each other. Every generation is equal in rights to generations which preceded it, by the same rule that every individual is born equal in rights with his contemporary" ([1791–92] 1995: 462–3). With his powerful rhetoric, Paine remarks in an often quoted phrase: "The vanity and presumption of governing beyond the grave is the most ridiculous and insolent of all tyrannies" and warns his readers about the "manuscript assumed authority of the dead" ([1791–92] 1995: 438–9). The language of rights, of course, is alien to the ancient world, but the democratic resistance to the control of current generations by those long dead defines the political independence of democracy.

James Madison in the *Federalist Papers*, even as he argues for ratification of a constitution that will limit the new regime, marvels:

> Is it not the glory of the people of America, that whilst they have paid a decent regard to the opinions of former times and other nations, they have not suffered a blind veneration for antiquity, for custom, or for names, to overrule the suggestions of their own good sense, the knowledge of their own situation, and the lessons of their own experience? To this manly spirit, posterity will be indebted for the possession, and the world for the example, of the numerous innovations displayed on the American theatre.... Happily for America, happily we trust for the whole human race, they pursued a new and more noble course. They accomplished a revolution which has no parallel in the annals of human society: They reared the fabrics of governments which have no model on the face of the globe... This is the work which has been new modelled by the act of your convention.   (*Federalist Paper* 14)

Nevertheless, while Madison wonders at the willingness of the American people to forge new roads, to innovate and not let themselves be chained by the past, the Constitution he supports goes only so far in allowing for such

---

[29] Quoted by McGrath (2002).
[30] This comes from the Appendix to *Common Sense*.

innovations and acknowledges that in order to establish its own authority it must limit the degree of amnesia allowed in the new regime. Thus,
Madison faults Jefferson's proposal in *Notes on Virginia* for the calling of
regular conventions for the purpose of amending the Constitution. Though,
like Jefferson, he is ready to affirm that "the people are the only legitimate
fountain of power," Madison resists the regular recurrence to "the people,"
for such appeals "would in great measure deprive the government of that
veneration, which time bestows on every thing, and without which perhaps
the wisest and freest governments would not possess the requisite stability." Like Burke in his *Reflections*, Madison sees the advantages for the
nation of having "the prejudices of the community on its side" (*Federalist* 49). The Socratic philosopher who brings citizens into a state of *aporia*
about the certainty of previous opinions is not welcome in Madison's well-
functioning republic.[31] Jefferson, far closer in sentiments to the principles
of democratic amnesia, imagines a regime in which one can escape from
the past, and his dreams of regularly assembled constitutional conventions
attest to his worry about the chains that past generations can place on present
ones.

Commenting on Jefferson's vision of democracy, Judith Shklar remarks
that for him majority rule "meant first of all a rejection of the European
past, America's future depended on forgetting all traces of that past." She
imagines him thinking that "a democratic people did not need a past of
any kind; it must live entirely in the present... Every generation was new
and unburdened with obligations to the past. Jefferson wanted no merely
new politics, but a politics of perpetual *newness*, as implicit in democratic
principles" (1998: 174–5). Though she may exaggerate as much as Virginia
Woolf in the quotation cited previously, Shklar's description of Jefferson
captures the underlying perspective of democracy as I will use it throughout this volume. In Jefferson's thinking, according to Shklar: "Reverence
was simply not a democratic feeling, and the authority of political tradition
might be meaningless without the myth of the superiority of the first men,
of the heroic demigods who created cities" (1998: 175). What Shklar calls
reverence here is *aidôs* in the Greek, and for the Greeks as for Jefferson
it "was simply not a democratic feeling."[32] Shklar attributes a similar perspective to Madison when she writes that such reverence for tradition was
"the story Madison had already laughed out of court in the *Federalist*." For
Madison, "the new government did not need traditions, just social science"
(1998: 175). The difference between Jefferson and Madison, in Shklar's story,
then becomes the difference between relying on the choice of the people or
the social science of the *Federalist*. They both, however, triumph over the
past.

---

[31] See especially *Federalist Paper* 49 for the importance of "prejudice" supported by its antiquity.
[32] Similar views are voiced today by writers such as Barber (e.g., 1984; 1996: 368–9).

The Athenians in their democratic founding made a grander leap than either Jefferson or Madison did in their willingness to question the authority of the past. For Jefferson and Madison the new world that was opening up to them entailed the rejection of a past bound by the unwise decisions of those who lived before, decisions that arose from mistakes in their understanding of universal principles of individual rights and of the meaning and purposes of government. For the Athenians, it was not the foolish mistakes of the ancestors that they rejected when they turned to themselves and released themselves from that undemocratic "reverence"; they were far braver in going beyond what they had understood as Nature (with a capital "N") – the natural order. In replacing the hierarchies of the past corresponding to the natural order of things, they exalted human choice over Nature. This was the true radicalness of Athenian democracy that gave to the people their power to rule themselves.

Herodotus in Book 3 of his *History* includes a debate among three conspirators in Persia. The conspirators have overthrown the usurper and they deliberate about which regime to institute. One argues for monarchy, another for oligarchy, and the third for a regime he calls *isonomia* where the institutions resemble those found in the Athens of Herodotus' own time. The significance of this debate is less the rather puerile justifications each one offers in support of his preferred regime than the fact that they believe they have a choice as to which regime they will institute. Though they conclude that monarchy is the regime of choice, the decision rests on the persuasiveness of their arguments, not on an appeal to what has been. It is not history that determines their regime, nor is it Nature. It is what they conclude in their consideration of what is the best regime (3.80).[33]

Parrhêsia, a freedom of speech ready to explore and question history and Nature, ready to suggest that the world is open to choices that can be investigated through speech, ready to resist shame and reverence before traditional hierarchies and beliefs, is emblematic of the democratic accomplishments of the Athenians. In the discussion about the legacy of free speech in Chapter 1, I noted how Meiklejohn in particular, but also more recent authors, connect the practice of free speech to the needs of a democratic regime of self-rule where citizens deliberate together in the active life of the polity. I want to suggest that the connections between free speech and the democratic polity run much deeper than that and that freedom of speech lauds the potential of democracy as a grand and exalted realm of human choice, but that it also introduces a dark specter of groundlessness that accompanies the abstraction from historical structures essential to the questioning of all.

The opposition between a practice of freedom of speech and a reverence for the past (often understood as what is according to Nature) is the

---

[33] See further Saxonhouse (1996: 49–56).

crucible out of which emerges the formless/free democracy of Athens. As a regime always capable of re-creation, it confronts the dangers of casting off a constricting tradition in order to create new traditions. The crises at the end of the fifth century in Athens brought Athenian democracy face to face with that challenge when they chose to inscribe their laws in stone stele, just as Madison and Jefferson faced each other across the divide of self-perpetuating novelty. Cleisthenes' "founding" of Athenian democracy extolled the dismissal of the old, but the progress of the Athenian polity harshly tested efforts to make such breaks total, giving rise to a clear need to reintroduce into the Athenian democratic polity a reverence for a past. Yet, whatever limits do come into play in the political arena of Athens emerge from a residual respect for the old (be it for the ancestors or for the gods); they are aberrations from democracy's fundamental principles and they – not the democracy itself – are the source of Socrates' execution. When I. F. Stone in his book on Socrates' trial complained that Athenian democracy was not true to its principles when it executed Socrates (1988), he was in a sense right. When he says, though, that Socrates' antidemocratic bias prevented him from reminding the judges of this, he was not. Stone failed to recognize how consistent Socratic philosophy is with the basic principles of democracy in its deep dependence on the freedom of an unrestrained speech that breaks forth from the chains of the past. The regime that executed Socrates violated its own democratic foundations. Threatened as it was by the dangers inherent in democratic amnesia, it had brought *aidôs* back into the regime. Socrates' execution marks that unbridgeable divide between the freedom of *parrhêsia* and the polity's need for *aidôs*.

PART II

AIDÔS

3

The Tale of Two Gyges

Shame, Community, and the Public/Private Self

Gyges the Lydian warrants two stories in the ancient corpus. In one he is a shepherd; in the other he is the bodyguard to a king. In both he kills the king and marries the queen. Plato has Glaucon in the *Republic* introduce the myth of the shepherd Gyges (or, to be more precise, an ancestor of Gyges), giving the shepherd a magical ring that grants him invisibility. Glaucon thus challenges Socrates to explore the question of why the shepherd in possession of this magical ring should not kill the king and marry the queen, that is, take what is not his and be unjust. In Herodotus' tale the queen commands the king's bodyguard Gyges to kill the king and marry her or be killed himself. It is Herodotus' tale that will help me introduce the concept of shame in this chapter and it is Plato's Gyges who will conclude the chapter.

I. HERODOTUS' GYGES

Candaules, the king of the Lydians, enthralled by and clearly proud of the beauty of his own wife, does not believe that his bodyguard Gyges fully appreciates the extent of that beauty, though the king has spoken to him of it often and with great enthusiasm. To convince Gyges, Candaules insists that Gyges see his wife naked. Gyges resists: "Master, why do you speak such unhealthy words, commanding me to see my mistress naked? When her clothes are set aside, a woman sheds also her shame (*tên aidô*). Beautiful things (*ta kala*) have been discovered (*exeurêtai*) by humans long ago, from which it is necessary to learn. Among them is this one: to look upon what is one's own ... I beg you not to demand what is unlawful (*anomôn*)" (1.8). Candaules persists, but assures Gyges he will arrange it so that his wife will not know that she has been seen naked. The queen, of course, does see Gyges slipping out the bedroom door after she shed her clothes and, though "shamed (*aischuntheisa*)," she does not cry out at once. Rather, she plots how to make Candaules pay, for "among the Lydians and among nearly all the other barbarians it is a great shame (*aischunên megalên*) to be seen

naked" (1.10). The queen sends for Gyges and says he will be executed if
he does not kill his king, for Gyges did "that which was not lawful (*ou
nomizomena*) by looking on her naked" (1.11).[1]

Aidôs is the word Gyges uses to express a woman's respectability, a
woman's sense of shame, of what may be seen and what not.[2] Etymolog-
ically, *aidôs* takes us back to the *aidoion*, the Greek word for genitals or
what we have come to call "the private parts," that which is to be covered.
Immediately, shame/*aidôs* is connected with a concern for hiding and with
the gaze of others.[3] As such, it also sets us immediately into a social context,
one where we are aware of others who can gaze upon us, and where we are
furthermore dependent on the community for our understanding of what is
to be hidden and what revealed.[4]

The story of Gyges and his dilemma alerts us to shame's relationship to
the boundary between public and private.[5] To view the queen dressed and in
public is acceptable; to view her without her clothes, uncovered, in the king's
bedroom, is to transgress the boundaries of the private and observe what is
not his. Where, however, do those boundaries between public and private
come from? In Herodotus' tale they do not come from nature, but from a
reverence for laws discovered by men long ago. The longevity of the laws
may make them appear natural, but Herodotus does not claim that nature
defines what is shameful and must be hidden. It is rather the knowledge
gleaned from life in Lydia, from exposure to the values of the particular
society in which one lives, that defines those boundaries. Herodotus at first
says that to be seen naked is a great source of shame among the Lydians
and then amends this statement to say that it is a "great shame" among
most of the barbarians; he does not say that it is a great shame among
all men.

---

[1] The queen may be responding to the demands of the laws of the Lydians that only her husband
see her naked. To leave Gyges, who has seen her naked, alive and not kill her husband would
be to violate those laws. I thank Roslyn Weiss for this point.

[2] The word appears only here in Herodotus' history (Benardete 1969: 12).

[3] According to Riezler, but unfortunately without supporting footnotes: "In the courts of Attica
the defendant had his place beside a stone dedicated to *Aidôs*; the stone on the opposite side,
the place of the prosecutor, was dedicated to *Anaideia*, shamelessness. The one is entitled to
conceal, the other obliged to unmask" (1943: 463).

[4] Robert Kaster has turned attention to shame as it occurs in ancient Rome and studied the
meaning of the Latin *pudor* and its cognates, which are "counterparts – though certainly not
the exact counterparts – of such terms as *aidôs* in Greek and 'shame' in English" (1997: 3).

[5] See also Nichols (1987: 61–2) on the issue of privacy in Herodotus' story and its absence in
Glaucon's tale. There are many more provocative issues that surface in this story, for example,
the woman who is called only by the generic *gunê* and yet controls the situation – killing her
husband and choosing her own mate, a softened version of Clytemnestra; the king whose
vanity makes him want to show others what he has, but understands beauty only in terms
of shape (*eidos*), what is visible. For the purposes of developing the conceptual grounding of
shame, I focus on only one aspect of this evocative tale.

The word *aidôs* incorporates within it as well a sense of awe or reverence for that which is old, for the laws and traditions, the *nomoi*, of one's society, which teach what is public and to be seen by all and what is private and to remain hidden. Reverence means we do not question the laws or believe – like Candaules – that the laws can be disregarded, because they derive from the opinions of men that have been passed down through the ages, even if it is to show what is beautiful to someone else. Completely shameless in his eagerness to display his wife's beauty, Candaules sees himself as free from submission to the laws, thus showing no reverence for the laws' lessons about what must be hidden from view. In Herodotus' tale, though, it is he who suffers at the end when he is killed for showing beauty to another rather than shame before the laws. In many ways I see him as a precursor to Socrates, who also dies for showing what perhaps should have remained hidden, at least from the perspective of the truths assumed to be discovered long ago. Gyges, who acknowledges shame and reveres the laws of old at least at the beginning of the story, kills Candaules, marries his queen, rules over his kingdom, and founds a new dynasty.

The story of Gyges relates the understanding of shame to what is private, what may not be uncovered before others. The question, nevertheless, remains: what is to be uncovered and shared with others? What establishes the boundary between the private and the shared? And how do we know the boundaries? In Herodotus' story, Gyges says that long ago *ta kala*, beautiful things, were found out. The beautiful for him resides in what survives from ancient times; for Candaules the beautiful is in the body[6] of the woman who is his wife, which must be hidden from the gaze of others because of the "beautiful things" discovered long ago. Gyges' "beautiful things" are open to all through the *nomoi*; for Candaules beauty lies in nature itself, not in the laws. Indeed, for Candaules the laws hide that which is beautiful by separating the spheres of public and private.

Gyges does not tell us *where* the men of old found the beautiful things that became the *nomoi* – in nature or themselves. This ambiguity is emphasized by the fact that the beautiful things found out by the Lydians (and even most of the barbarians) may not be (indeed, are not) the same as the beautiful things found out by others. Age does not confer universality; it simply identifies the opinion of men in society from long ago as setting the boundaries. But what are the consequences of relying on boundaries set up long ago? Would not Gyges have been prevented from viewing that which is beautiful had the laws of old been obeyed, if the concern with shame and reverence for the traditions kept him out of his king's bedroom? Does awe/shame/*aidôs* prevent us from seeing the beautiful?

---

[6] *Eidos* is the word used here for body; while a woman may shed her *aidôs* when she takes off her clothes, she retains her *eidos*, which can mean form or shape – that which is seen. The word play here is suggestive of the ambiguities inherent in this tale.

In Greek, the word for truth is *alêtheia*, a word with a double meaning, one of which entails uncovering, the other of which entails "unforgetting" (or remembering). It is the former meaning that I will focus on in this chapter.[7] The customs of Lydia keep covered that which is beautiful by creating those boundaries between public and private. Only the shameless get a vision of the beautiful. The story of Gyges raises questions about these laws of covering and of shame. Herodotus has Gyges, the one governed by shame, say that one should uncover only that which is one's own. Yet, Herodotus' history is a volume filled with its author's reports of viewing that which is not his own, from the bedroom of the Lydian king, to the councils of the Persian royalty, to the customs of the Babylonians and so forth. Seth Benardete writes in reference to this story: "[Herodotus] has lost his shame" (1969: 12–13). But this is not entirely accurate. What he has lost is the shame specific to the men of Lydia and "most of the barbarians" who forbid looking on that which is not one's own. Perhaps Herodotus' history offers a Greek response to the shame of the barbarians. The Greeks do not hide, but open up the beautiful for all, precisely by looking at what is not their own. The challenge Herodotus sets before us in this tale is the challenge that governs this book – does shame as the inhibiting and (as I shall suggest in a moment) civilizing emotion limit the philosophic pursuit of the good and the beautiful? Does freedom of speech in its role of uncovering resist the boundaries of the private, and yet in the process make it possible to reveal the beautiful?

2. PROTAGORAS' TALE

So well known for the maxim "Man is the measure of all things – of those that are that they are and of those that are not that they are not," Protagoras the Sophist warrants a Platonic dialogue bearing his name. Socrates narrates most of this dialogue but includes a myth told by Protagoras to justify the claim that politics is a craft that can be taught like medicine or astronomy or carpentry.

Protagoras begins what is essentially a creation myth in classic fairy tale fashion. Once upon a time there were gods, but no mortals. When mortals fashioned out of earth and fire appear, Epimetheus, the brother of Prometheus, takes on the task of distributing assorted powers (*dunaneis*) to all the animals. As often happens in these tales, the human species is forgotten until all the qualities such as speed, feathers, a hard protective skin, claws, and strength have been given away to other animals. Now the human stands naked. Since Epimetheus has bungled his task, Prometheus takes over. Concerned about the safety of the human species, he steals wisdom from Athene

---

[7] This reading of *alêtheia* draws on Heidegger's reading of the term (1997: 1–26). This reading has been subjected to its share of criticism. See, for example, Lane (2001: 62) for some of the concerns.

and fire from Hephaestus to give to mankind. "In this way man possessed wisdom (*sophian*) concerning life, but he did not have *politikê*, the political craft" (321d). Zeus keeps that craft secure in his citadel, protected by fear-inspiring guards. Mortals are able to develop speech, build houses, weave clothing, and cultivate the earth with the skills Prometheus did manage to steal, but they are still attacked by wild animals. When they come together and found cities for their own protection, they are unjust toward one another (*êdikoun*) for they do not yet have the political craft (*tên politikên technên*, 322b). Zeus finally steps in lest the entire human race be destroyed and sends Hermes to deliver to humans two qualities: a sense of justice, *dikê*, and shame or respect, *aidôs*. When Hermes asks Zeus in what fashion he should give *aidôs* and *dikê* to men, that is, whether he should deliver them like the crafts (*technai*) to some and not to others, or if he should distribute *dikê* and *aidôs* to all, Zeus responds that all should share in them since "there would not be cities if only a few partook of them as with the other crafts" (322d). Indeed, Zeus goes so far as to legislate that whoever is not able to share in *aidôs* and *dikê* is to be killed "as a disease of the city" (322d).[8] The curious word in this tale for my purposes is again *aidôs*, used only once by Herodotus writing in the mid-fifth century BCE and considered archaic by the time Plato in the fourth century puts it into the speech of Protagoras in this dialogue. Most often translated, as in the Gyges tale, by the English word "shame," it takes on here the connotations of reverence and respect.[9]

Why does Protagoras consider *aidôs* (together with *dikê*) *the* quality of soul that enables the political world to come into being?[10] In the *Laws*

---

[8] Fisher (1992: 191) suggests that this might be a reference to Hesiod's men of bronze who lacked *aidôs* and *dikê* and were the race of men devoted to war as a way of life.

[9] Guthrie translates it as "respect for others" and "respect for their fellows" (1956: 54), C. C. W. Taylor as "conscience" (1976: 14–15), Sinclair (1952: 58) as "decency." Cropsey describes it as a "complex amalgam of respect and susceptibility to shame or disgrace" (1995: 9). Bartlett translates it as "shame" and footnotes it as "awe" and "reverence" (2004: 19, 19n67). There has been much debate about the relation between *aidôs* and another word that is often translated as "shame," *aischron*. Assorted efforts have been made to distinguish them, for example, Riezler, "The origin of *Aischyne* is dishonor, of *Aidôs*, awe. Dishonor puts the emphasis on man-made codes" (1943: 463). In contrast, see Cairns' book with the simple title *Aidôs*: "The code of honour studied in this book is also a code of appropriateness, and thus the concept of *to aischron* ... is as central to *aidôs* as is that of *timê*" (1993: 433). Williams (1993: 194n9) uses numerous examples to suggest that there is no difference between the words, though *aidôs* tends to be used in more ancient texts and then replaced by words derivative of *aischun-*. Konstan (2003) now questions Williams' conclusions and offers an extensive discussion of the differences with a primary focus on the usage of the terms in Aristotle.

[10] As numerous commentators have noticed, *aidôs* seems to be subsumed under *sôphrosunê* in subsequent parts of the dialogue, but it is my contention that this is not mere slippage. Its appearance here is to be noted; the emotion it captures is quite distinct from *sôphrosunê* and has different roots. *Sôphrosunê* is often understood as self-control or moderation, the setting of limits to one's desires because of an understanding of what those limits ought to

we again find Plato introducing *aidôs*, this time according to the Athenian Stranger as a despot (*despotis*) that enslaves the Athenians to the law. It is the bondage to the laws, he claims, "which often in the above arguments we have spoken of as *aidôs*" that facilitates a friendship toward one another (698b–699c). Shades of Protagoras' argument resurface here. What is this *aidôs*, and what does it accomplish that makes modern as well as ancient authors define it as the truly human emotion, one not shared by any other species? Many, like Cairns in his massive volume, *Aidôs*, have called shame the "inhibiting" emotion, that which holds us back from actions and from sights. Affirming the distinction between *aidôs* and the English "shame," Cairns writes: "*aidôs* words in Greek will bear a set of connotations different from those of shame in English" (1993: 2). This is certainly true, though when he footnotes this claim by noting that since *aidôs* relates to others as well as to oneself and that it is therefore commonly more positive than shame and often recommended as a virtue (1993: 14n29), he misses much contemporary writing about the positive influence of shame in creating conditions under which humans can construct and live in their polities. Indeed, Protagoras' view of shame's civilizing effects travels surprisingly well in the contemporary world. Agnes Heller, for example, suggests that shame and culture are "coeval." According to Heller, "it is the very affect [a few lines later she will call it an "emotion"] that makes us conform to our cultural environment" (1985: 5). Soon thereafter she describes shame as "the primary regulator of socialization" (1985: 7). Carl Schneider writes: "Shame raises consciousness. Shame is the partner of value awareness; its very occurrence arises from the fact that we are *valuing* animals... To extirpate shame is to cripple our humanity" (1977: xv). For the philosopher Richard Wollheim shame (along with guilt, remorse, and regret) is one of the "so-called moral emotions" (1999: Lecture 3).[11]

Shame plays this positive role by controlling our actions when it forces us to imagine ourselves as others see us and when it makes us sensitive to

be. *Aidôs*, as I will develop further, entails an experience in front of others, that is, it requires the observer. I must care what others think of me; to do so I must respect those who observe me. *Sôphrosunê* entails a concern with oneself. Attention to the usage of the archaic or the more familiar term allows for a deeper understanding of the meaning of the dialogue (to which I shall return in Chapter 8). On the meaning of *sôphrosunê* in Greek thought see North (1966).

11 In the psychoanalytic literature shame serves as an agent essential for the establishment of an identity (Seidler 2000; Tajfel 1981). Within the world of literary scholarship, see Fernie (2002: 8), who examines shame in Shakespeare because it "opens a door, pointing to the spiritual health and realisation of the world beyond egoism." There are also contemporary authors who propose the reintroduction of "shame punishments" as an important alternative to the modern punitive system. They argue, for example, that shame "deters criminal behavior because social approval of significant others is something we do not like to lose... both shaming and repentance build consciences which internally deter criminal behavior" (Braithwaite 1989: 75).

what others value as a normative standard. In the famous passage from the *Iliad* where Hector bids farewell on the battlements of Troy to Andromache and their young child, he reproaches Andromache for her pleas that he not return to battle: "I would feel deep shame (*aideomai*)/ before the Trojans and the Trojan women with trailing garments, if like a coward I were to shrink from the fighting" (6.441–3).[12] His awareness of being on display prevents him from abandoning the battle to satisfy his longing to stay with the wife and child whom he loves and who love him. Shame prevents him from not fighting.[13] But shame is far more than simply, as Cairns calls it, an "inhibiting emotion," like the fear that prevents us from touching a hot stove. It is primarily a social emotion connecting us to those around us. It requires the ability to know and understand what are to be the limits of human behavior as defined by the social community in which we live, limits that are set not by natural capacities but by how we appear in the eyes of others.[14] The mental image of the men and women of Troy seeing him refrain from battle sends Hector down from the battlements and into the thick of the conflict toward his death. To know the disgrace accompanying the transgression of those limits, we must observe and learn through our interactions with others. Shame dissolves if one neither knows nor reveres the customs and if one cares naught for the opinion of those around one. Without reverence for others there could be no shame.[15] One who does not learn these lessons must, in the phrase Protagoras attributed to Zeus, be killed as a disease. The past lives in Protagoras' tale as a restraint in the political world of the present through *aidôs*.

Amidst the literature surviving from ancient Athens, Protagoras' speech serves for many as one of very few, if not the only, serious justificatory argument for democracy. Emblematic of this reading of his speech is Cynthia Farrar's *The Origins of Democratic Thinking* (1988), which returns to ancient Athenian thought in an effort to uncover the fundamental principles of political engagement and the value of including the many in the life of the political regime.[16] For her Plato is the villain, "repelled by the politics of

---

[12] I use here the translation of Homer by Lattimore (1951).

[13] See footnote 20 for a discussion of James Redfield's reading of Hector's *aidôs*.

[14] Shame may take on a very different tone when it is used to diminish individuals for qualities that do not belong to us as agents, but as the result of how we appear before others – for example, a physical handicap or being a racial minority. I am grateful to George Kateb and Anthony Appiah for pointing out this aspect of shame to me. See Dover where he discusses how the Greek language of shame "was sometimes applied to behavior which was not the fault of the agent" (1974: 70, also 240–1).

[15] Those who criticize the use of shaming punishments make precisely this point: such punishments only work if those who are being punished care about the opinions of others and see themselves as part of the community. Usually criminals are precisely the ones who are alienated and therefore not subject to the shame that might be imposed by the creative punishments proposed (see, e.g., Karp 1998).

[16] Others such as Raaflaub (1996: 142) emphasize Protagoras' affirmation that "all citizens shared...in the basic civic qualities needed for successful communal life." Kerferd (1981:

democratic Athens" and "anxious to show that people are not as and what
they think they are" (1988: 77). In her reading of Plato, the "socialization
of the polis is now seen as a destructive influence, and politics is a struggle for power rather than a realization of order." Against Plato, according
to Farrar, stands Protagoras who "sought to demonstrate... that political
action is both collective self-expression and collective self-restraint" (77). As
she interprets the *Protagoras*, Plato has distorted the historical Protagoras,
creating instead a character whom she calls "Platagoras," for this dialogue.
Behind this "Platagoras" lies the real Protagoras whose democratic theory,
Farrar proposes, we can ferret out. Reading the great speech of Protagoras
in the *Protagoras* as especially revealing, she finds in it Protagoras' "defi-
ance of aristocratic tradition" and his affirmation that "political excellence
is a social achievement, not a natural legacy" (84). Participation in society
is "transformational, in the sense that it requires and fosters certain human
qualities, e.g., *aidôs* and *dikê* [justice]" (90).

I note Farrar's democratic reading of Protagoras' speech since she focuses
on Protagoras' use of the word *aidôs*. She recognizes that it "is significant
that Protagoras chose the word *aidôs* to express one of the requisite qualities, for it is an archaic and aristocratic term for other-regarding respect and
corresponding sense of shame or self-respect." This respect, she continues,
"is now owed to all members of the community by all... Protagoras seeks to
show that the highest form of self-realization was to be achieved by means
of the constant interaction of men of all classes, since men of great natural
ability were to be found outside the aristocratic elite as well as within it"
(96). By reducing *aidôs* to "respect" for others, Farrar loses the richness of
the concept, especially its inhibiting connections to a potentially enslaving
(rather than a liberating) force for equality. Thus, Protagoras becomes for
her the democratic hero struggling against a Plato eager to obscure his views
in the persona of "Platagoras." Farrar does not see how it may be Socrates –
not Protagoras – who is the democratic character in this dialogue. My difficulty with Farrar and others who turn to Protagoras as the democratic
hero is that while they note the praise of shared participation in deliberations, they do not attend to what may need to be surrendered in terms
of individuality in order to have this equal participation.[17] Equality, often,

144) writes: "The importance of this doctrine of Protagoras in the history of political thought
can hardly be exaggerated. For Protagoras has produced for the first time in human history
a theoretical basis for participatory democracy." See also Roberts (1994: 40–1 and 1996:
188). See Sinclair (1952: 54–60) for a somewhat more measured reading. Demetriou (1999:
224–5) makes a strong case for this view of Protagoras as strong defender of democracy
by going back to George Grote's writings in the mid-nineteenth century. See also Havelock
(1957: 171).

[17] There is the further issue that a careful reading of this dialogue raises many questions about
the sincerity of Protagoras' speech given the speeches he gives elsewhere in this dialogue. See
Chapter 8 and especially Weiss (2006: chap. 2).

may trump freedom and the sharing of *aidôs* – civilizing an emotion that it may be – may become a source of mutual oppression rather than a meaningful ground of political engagement.[18] By too casually equating political excellence with *aidôs* and *dikê* (for example, p. 82) she does not acknowledge how *aidôs*, as the inhibiting emotion, may surface as antidemocratic rather than democratic.[19]

Before returning to that point more fully in Chapter 8, let us consider – with the stories of Gyges and Protagoras in mind – what this emotion (or "affect") of shame is, how it can be in Heller's words "coeval with civilization," and whether this role fosters or undermines the principles of democratic communities and the free search for truth.

3. SHAME AND GUILT

Any study of shame with a glance back to the world of ancient Greece must acknowledge E.R. Dodds' seminal work, *The Greeks and the Irrational* (1951). Long fascinated by the occult (perhaps, he suggests, from childhood readings of Poe's tales) and by telepathy (1977: 98), and acutely sensitive to the potential of interdisciplinary work as a supplement to philological studies of ancient texts, Dodds appropriated for the study of the classical world theoretical and analytical categories from anthropology and psychology to explore, as he puts it, the "darker and less rational elements in human experience" (1977: 181). These interests served as the foundation for his 1949 Sather Lectures, which became *The Greeks and the Irrational*. Searching for "some understanding of Greek minds, and... not content with describing external behavior or drawing up a list of recorded 'beliefs'" (1951: viii), Dodds probed the inner life of his Greeks and the transformations that took place in this previously unstudied world. In the Homeric epics he found a shame culture where "the highest good is not the enjoyment of a quiet conscience, but the enjoyment of *timê*, public esteem... And the strongest moral force which Homeric man knows is not the fear of god, but respect for public opinion, *aidôs* ... [I]n such a society, anything which exposes a

---

[18] See Euben (1997: chap. 9) for another discussion of Farrar's reading of Protagoras as a democrat.

[19] In this context consider the attitude of the cynic Diogenes. Long (1996: 35) remarks: "[Diogenes] accepted the sobriquet "dog"...as a symbol of his own shamelessness (*anaideia*). The opposite quality, *aidôs*, was hallowed in tradition as a necessary mark of civilized life. As such, it served as a sanction both against antisocial conduct in the strong ethical sense, and as the grounds of modesty in daily life. In the latter sense, *aidôs* covered manners rather than morals – the socially acceptable behavior of men and women in matters of dress, style of eating, conversing, making love, and so on. It is clear that Cynic shamelessness, as publicized by Diogenes, concerns contempt for *aidôs* mainly in this second sense....The positive counterpart of Cynic shamelessness is summed up in the catchword 'freedom of speech' (*parrhêsia*)."

man to contempt or ridicule of his fellows, which causes him to 'lose face'
is felt as unbearable" (1951: 17–18).[20]

Dodds' book, drawing on the anthropological literature that had begun
in the 1930s and flowered in the 1940s (especially with the work of Ruth
Benedict and Margaret Mead), begins with a discussion of the *Iliad*, but then
traces a transition in Greek society away from this shame culture so vivid in
the *Iliad* to that of a guilt culture. The guilt culture acknowledges the universal powers of the gods charged with the execution of justice, independent of
particular social forces and the judgments of one's fellows. Guilt, in contrast
to shame, as Dodds developed his argument, recognized – and demanded –
a cosmic order that went beyond the familiar, narrow world of the family
and community, one that enforced justice and set the individual in relation
to that universal just and divine order. Guilt, unlike shame, did not rely on
the observation of others within one's own culture.[21]

More recently Bernard Williams in *Shame and Necessity* (1993), based on
his own Sather Lectures delivered exactly forty years after Dodds' original
lectures, questions whether such a transition from shame to guilt actually
took place, or more potently whether there is really the sharp distinction
between shame and guilt, which Dodds and others assert. Concerned with
the overwhelming moral universalism bequeathed by Kantian ethical theory,
Williams notes that in the "scheme of Kantian oppositions, shame is on the
bad side of all lines. This is well brought out in its notorious association
with the notion of losing or saving face. 'Face' stands for appearance against
reality and the outer versus the inner" (77). In this sense, shame values the

---

[20] James Redfield (1975: 116) follows Dodds' lead in elaborating this world of *aidôs* in his
powerful reading of the *Iliad* as the story not of Achilles, but of Hector: "*Aidôs* inhibits
action by making the heroes feel that if they acted thus they would be out of place or in
the wrong...The Homeric culture, in other words, is a 'shame culture.' The heroes do not
distinguish personal morality from conformity; in a world where 'what people will say' is
the most reliable guide to right and wrong, the two are practically identical. The feeling of
aidôs is reinforced by the *dêmou phêmis*, the 'voice of the folk.' *Aidôs* is thus nothing like
conscience – a concept which is certainly post-Homeric." Redfield goes further than Dodds:
"*Aidôs* is a vulnerability to the expressed ideal norm of the society; the ideal norm is directly
experienced within the self, as a man internalized the anticipated judgments of others on
himself. As such, *aidôs* is the affective or emotional foundation of virtue" (116). Redfield
reads the *Iliad* as the story of Hector, the man governed by *aidôs*, who belongs to and within
the city, in contrast to the individualistic Achilles who, lacking in *aidôs*, shows contempt
for his superiors and for the guiding principles of the Achaean camp. Achilles, for example,
so focused on his own injuries and sense of justice, rejects of the embassy of Odysseus that
pleads with him to return to battle to save the army of the Achaeans and impiously defiles
the body of Hector. In Redfield's reading, the *Iliad* centers on a contrast between the social
and asocial individual, the one trained by *aidôs*, the other expressing his individual greatness
through the abandonment of *aidôs* and contemptuous of his fellow men and their opinions
of him.

[21] I am greatly simplifying Dodds' argument, which concerns more directly the source of those
actions that bring on shame or guilt, external or internal, to the human being.

heteronomous, but Williams, resisting the apotheosis of the autonomous individual, is not so ready to see only the "bad" side of shame. Williams, like a number of psychoanalysts to be mentioned later in this section, admits that though shame is connected with a certain sense of fear (especially of displays of powerlessness before others), it also "gives a sense of who one is and of what one hopes to be . . . mediat[ing] between act, character, and consequences, and also between ethical demands and the rest of life" (102).

Implicit in Williams' concept of shame is the observer: the "basic experience connected with shame is that of being seen" (78). In his effort to resuscitate shame against the heteronomy accusations of a Kantian perspective, Williams argues that the observer need not be an *actual* Other (82); we can look at ourselves.[22] By focusing on this imagined Other, Williams is able to internalize shame to the degree that he subsumes guilt under shame.[23] It follows for Williams that: "The mere fact that we have two words does not, in itself imply that there is any great psychological difference between shame and guilt" (1993: 89). Williams unites shame and guilt in their dependence on an Other, imaginary or not. The Other according to Williams, though, is not divine. Removing the divine, but retaining an imaginary Other, Williams defends a nonuniversalistic and contextually rich morality.

The peculiar asset of Williams' work for my purposes is his willingness to see in shame the social interactions that underlie it and yet not view shame, as so many do, either as a primitive point from which Western society must "progress" or as an oppressive force that militates against individuality. It is the sensitivity to the opinion of others, as Protagoras suggested in his great speech, that allows cities to come into being. Without it, Williams implies, we would not necessarily be lost in a Hobbesian or a Protagorean war of all against all, but we would rather find ourselves asea in a world of abstract universalism, unable to connect with others.[24]

Actions that are shameful will vary from community to community, but the concern with the opinions (and the gaze of) others is the universal emotion which, implicit in Protagoras and explicit in Williams, is internalized and thus becomes the basis for our communal life. It is foundational of the political craft, but shame functions independently of any fear of punishment meted out by political authorities. It is a source of prepolitical control. Hermes

---

[22] Helen Lynd writing from the perspective of psychology and sociology may also be diminishing the necessity of an actual other when she remarks "The exposure may be to others but, whether others are or are not involved, it is always . . . exposure to one's own eyes" (1958: 27–8).

[23] We see a similar point already in the fragments of Democritus (Fragment # 244 in Diels and Kranz 1961): "Even if you are alone, do not say nor do that which is worthless (*phaulon*). Learn to be ashamed (*aischunesthai*) much more before yourself than another." This would be an example of the move in Dodds' formulation of guilt. Note that Democritus used the less archaic form *aischunê* rather than *aidôs*.

[24] See also Gill's helpful discussion of Williams on shame (1996: 65–78).

delivers both *aidôs* and *dikê* as prerequisites for living in cities. The archaic meaning of *dikê* (which later becomes the root of the more abstract fourth century *dikaiosunê*, justice) is custom or usage that would be the basis for understanding the sources of shame.[25] From "custom" it is an easy journey to a sense of what is right or what ought to be, that which in Protagoras' story needs to be shared by all men if there is to be community among them.[26] If we read *dikê* as punishment (in accord with its most frequent fifth-century meaning), it captures the institutional sources of restraint exercised by the polity while *aidôs* refers to social constraints on actions.

While classical scholarship in the 1950s was rocked in many ways by Dodds' interdisciplinary lectures and attention to the emotions of shame and guilt rather than to reason in discussions of the Greeks, writers in the fields of psychology and psychoanalysis could still write in the mid-1980s about the "neglect of shame" as a subject of study (Wurmser 1981; Nathanson 1987).[27] This may have been a rhetorical trope to justify the significance of their own works since Helen Merrell Lynd's classic work on shame had been published decades earlier in 1958, but among psychologists and psychoanalysts there is the suggestion that once Freud chose to focus more on guilt than shame (perhaps because he considered it "a woman's emotion"), the study of shame suffered an "eclipse" and sat "on the sidelines for more than 30 years after Freud's death" (Lansky 1995: 1076, 1079). Of late, though, shame is no longer neglected.[28] Whether the "moral emotions" of shame and guilt are the same or distinct is the stuff of a multitude of writings that, with assorted twists and turns, runs regularly through the contemporary literature of anthropology, psychology, psychoanalysis, literary analysis, and philosophy. Driven by what sometimes seems to be a typological imperative, writers in these disparate fields vary widely in defining the grounds on which one might distinguish between them – if one decides that they are indeed distinct from one another.

For most contemporary writers both guilt and shame are pathologies and the typologies illuminate their distinct evils. Freud, for example, identified

[25] See Hunter (1994: 116) for a discussion of the role of gossip as a social restraint. She quotes Campbell: "Gossip and its outcome, ridicule, are in a certain manner the external sanctions which support the internal sanctions of individual action, self-regard and the sense of shame."
[26] The common fifth-century meaning of *dikê* as punishment or trial (cf. *Euthyphro*, 2a) would not fit into Protagoras' story as something to be distributed to all.
[27] In the early 1950s, Piers could conclude after a brief survey of the psychoanalytic literature on shame and guilt at the time by noting: "We realize then that most previous authors consider shame a comparatively insignificant emotion" (1953: 11).
[28] By 2002, prominent psychologists working on shame and guilt could write that there is "a rich and varied theoretical literature pertaining to these emotions" (Tangney and Dearing 2002: 2). In 1995, Tangney had written more tentatively that there had been a "resurgence" of an interest in shame, but that the literature still failed to see a distinction between guilt and shame in the psychology literature (1995: 1132).

guilt with self-reproach based on the internalization of values, while shame was based on disapproval from outside and particularly associated with self-exposure.[29] This distinction came to play in the anthropological writing about shame and guilt cultures[30] that worked its way into Dodds' writing. Some writers (à la Dodds and contra Williams) see shame as perceived as the more primitive emotion, with guilt as the "more moral and adaptive emotion" (Tangney 1995: 1133). Tangney, writing from the perspective of the discipline of psychology and building on the work of Helen Block Lewis (1971), bases her claims on the studies of subjects' definitions of their own experiences of shame and guilt. Tangney then argues, in contrast to the outlook drawn from the Greek meaning of *aidôs*, that guilt is "other-oriented" whereas shame "involves a marked self-focus" (1995: 1137). In Tangney's most recent work, shame is "an extremely painful and ugly feeling that has a negative impact on interpersonal behavior" while "[g]uilt-prone individuals appear better able to empathize with others and to accept responsibility" (2002: 3). Other psychologists say guilt arises from the transgression of prohibitions, shame from the failure to reach one's own goals (Piers 1953: 11). Helen Merrell Lynd, in her landmark study *On Shame and the Search for Identity* (1958), argues along similar lines: "[S]hame may be said to go deeper than guilt; it is worse to be inferior and isolated than to be wrong, to be outcast in one's own eyes than to be condemned by society" (1958: 207). Lynd's study goes on to offer an elaborate table setting a "guilt axis" against a "shame axis"; on the guilt side, for example, lies "concerned with each separate discrete act"; on the shame side lies "Concerned with the over-all self" (1958: 208–9). And Nussbaum in her volume *Upheavals of Thought* calls guilt a "dignified emotion" (2001: 216) and "potentially creative" (218), in contrast to the "primitive shame" on which she focuses earlier, a shame that comes from a childish sense of dependence on others (216).[31]

Some see guilt as a legal (human or divine) concept (Taylor 1985: 85), or the "violation of internalized moral codes . . . wholly independent of others' knowledge of the violation" (Karp 1998: 279–80), and as a "response to *transgression*" (Miller 1985). For Piers guilt is "the painful internal tension generated whenever the emotionally highly charged barrier erected by the superego is being touched or transgressed" (1953: 16). For Singer it is aroused "by impulses to transgress the internalized prohibitions of

---

[29] According to Lynd (1958: 21). Lynd (1958: 262n21c) reviews the mid-twentieth-century literature that incorporated Freud's basic distinction.

[30] See most significantly Ruth Benedict's study of Japan in *The Chrysanthemum and the Sword* (1946).

[31] In a more recent volume, Nussbaum (2004: chap. 4) discusses shame in considerable detail, but again it becomes an emotion from which one escapes with maturity. She does, however, allow that shame can be "constructive," noting that the "person who is utterly shame-free is not a good friend, lover, or citizen" (216).

punishing parents" (1953: 70); shame leaves aside the conflict between ego and superego and instead "arises out of a tension between the ego and the ego ideal" (Piers 1953: 23) and is aroused by "a failure to live up to the internalized ideals of loving parents" (Singer 1953: 2, 70). For the psychoanalyst Leon Wurmser, shame entails one's sense of the lack of power, a failure to reach one's *"image of the ideal self,"* whereas guilt is not responsive to an image of the self but to a "complex system of *ideal actions*...and of condemned actions" (1981: 74). Wurmser maintains a distinction between shame and guilt, but his analysis of shame conforms to Williams' in that he does not need the external observer in order for shame to come into play. For both Williams and Wurmser, shame is intrapsychic, but for most writers shame relates us to the world of observation, to the world of the gaze. The permutations marking the differences and similarity between these emotions go on and on with little consistency across studies.[32]

One may well wonder along with Williams about the apparently pressing need among so many commentators to distinguish so precisely shame from guilt, but as Williams points out the concern may well come from a Kantian focus on a morality where the heteronomy of shame – the dependence on others – does not sit well with the (perhaps mythical) liberal democratic image of the autonomy of the ethical and democratic individual, the one who votes independently and expresses her own views openly in deliberative settings. Shame undercuts the independence so valued in the modern liberal world. For my purposes, the distinction between these two so-called moral emotions is important insofar as we attend to the dependence of the emotion on the social context, both in terms of how we know what is shameful (through the opinions of others, the beautiful things discovered long ago) and the sense of shame that surfaces as the result of being the object of observation by others. As a social emotion, shame inhibits actions, keeps private what is private, and enables political life. It is the inhibiting – and enabling – qualities that concern me, for by inhibiting, shame restrains our freedom of action and speech, but without shame we would live as those men described by Protagoras, having the technical crafts, but using those crafts only to take advantage of and kill one another.[33] Shame in contrast to most of the understandings of guilt is an emotion consistent with the communal life of the individual. It plays this role only to the degree that we have learned from others in our education about what is shameful; but

---

[32] See Cairns (1993: 14–26) for a far more extensive summary of the discussions of guilt and shame, especially among psychoanalysts and psychologists than is given here. Also Konstan (2003) for a succinct summary identifying some other themes that surface in this comparison between the two emotions.

[33] See Burnyeat's helpful discussion of shame as "the semivirtue of the learner" in the context of Aristotle's *Nicomachean Ethics* for another perspective on the positive side of this emotion (1980: 78).

even more important, it functions only insofar as we ourselves are observed by others. Both the shared understanding of what brings shame and the necessary attention to the gaze of others make shame a fundamentally social passion, Zeus' gift, offered to all humans so that cities could be founded and men might develop the capacity to live with one another peaceably. Without *aidôs*, though, *dikê*, the sense of what ought to be derived from the customs and the traditions of the community, is not enough for the founding and preservation of cities. The city needs the gaze of the other.

4. THE GAZE, THE TRUTH, AND THE "OTHER"

Oedipus has brought to light the horrible truth about his birth and now he has blinded himself: "Why is it necessary for me to see, for whom seeing there is nothing sweet to see?" (1334–5). He pleads with the chorus to cast him into the sea, where he never "will be seen again" (1413). When Creon appears on stage, he says to Oedipus: "But if you are not ashamed (*kataischunesth'*) before the offspring of mortals, nevertheless show respect for/shame before (*aideisth'*) the all nourishing light of the ruler Helios, to show such a pollution thus uncovered (*akalupton*)... but as quickly as possible go into the house" (1424–9). The dreadful deeds must be hidden. The shameless Candaules wanted to uncover that which was beautiful, the naked body of his wife. Creon's appeal to shame is for the sake of hiding the ugly, the vile, the impious. In both cases, though, shame is connected with sight, the eyes, observation, and what is to be seen or hidden. Shame requires an observer – or many observers – and our own awareness of those observers. Candaules' wife feels shame not when she removes her clothes, but when she realizes that Gyges has seen her. In the jargon of today, "the gaze" permeates our understanding of shame.

Psychologists tell us that shame is often associated with the desire to hide, specifically to remove oneself from the gaze of others.[34] Whereas guilt – as in the language of the courtroom where individuals may be found "guilty" – often entails punishment or the expectation of punishment, shame inhibits actions not because one anticipates punishment, but because one fears being seen. It is thus, as Scheff has called it, "*the* social emotion, arising as it does out of the monitoring of one's own actions by viewing one's self from the

---

[34] Tangney (1991) writes of shame as an overwhelming feeling of being small and worthless and powerless and marked by a desire to hide and escape from any interpersonal interaction. Niedenthal, Tangney, and Gavanski (1994: 586–7) write as well: "Shame is an overwhelming feeling characterized by a sense of being 'small' and worthless in the eyes of both the self and others. With this feeling of shame comes a desire to hide or escape from the situation." In later work Tangney and her coauthors, however, report on their investigations using self-reported stories that showed that shame was experienced more often than guilt was when people were alone (Tangney et al. 1996). "Shame was just as likely to be experienced when alone" (1996: 1157; also 1264).

standpoint of others" (1988: 398; also 2000). What seeks covering by shame is more than just a deed, but one's whole self. Oedipus wishes his whole body to be cast into the sea, not only to have his deeds hidden.[35]

The authors who note that the emotion of shame expresses itself in the desire to hide often trace this aspect of shame linguistically back to the Indo-European root *skam*, a variant of **kem*, which means to cover, veil, or hide. According to Wurmser: "The prefix s (s^kam) adds the reflexive meaning – 'to cover oneself'" (1981: 29).[36] Charles Darwin exploring the universal biological foundations of the emotions in his work *The Expression of the Emotions in Men and Animals* picks up this possibility when he writes: "Under a keen sense of shame there is a strong desire for concealment" and adds a footnote to this point: "Mr. Wedgwood says...that the word shame 'may well originate in the idea of shade or concealment, and may be illustrated by the Low German scheme, shade'" ([1872] 1955: 320). While considering the source of the physiological expression of shame, namely the blush (of which more in a moment), Darwin points to the centrality of the observer and the centrality of being observed to the emotion of shame. He identifies other physical responses besides the blush that accompany the human animal when overcome by shame, noting most especially the avoidance of eye contact: "An ashamed person can hardly endure to meet the gaze of those present, so that he almost invariably casts down his eyes or looks askant" ([1872] 1955: 320–1). To look at another is to see another seeing oneself, to see oneself as the object of the gaze. Avoiding eye contact is one way to become "invisible," to refuse to acknowledge the gaze of another. In Sylvan Tomkins' language: "The shame response is an act which reduces facial communication... By dropping his eyes, his eyelids, his head, and sometimes the whole upper part of his body, the individual calls a halt to looking at another person...and to the other person's looking at him" (1995: 134). Tomkins in strikingly clinical language calls shame more starkly "a response of facial communication reduction" (1995: 136).

Oedipus does more than look "askant" or drop his head; he gouges out his eyes. Others reflecting on shame describe it as a desire to "sink into the ground" (Heller 1985: 5) or to become invisible. In Lynd's language: "Experiences of shame appear to embody the root meaning of the word – to uncover, to expose, to wound. They are experiences of exposure, exposure of peculiarly sensitive, intimate, vulnerable aspects of the self" (1958: 27).

---

[35] In an effort to distinguish shame from guilt along this axis, see the title of the article by Niedenthal et al. " 'If Only I Weren't' Versus 'If Only I Hadn't': Distinguishing Shame and Guilt in Counterfactual Thinking." And the review essay by Kilborne (1995) with the title "Trust that Cannot Go Naked: Shame in Many Forms." Cairns writing about both guilt and shame comments: "The notion of the 'other' or the audience is common to both, both are associated with the eyes and visibility, they share the characteristic of blushing" (1993: 14–15).

[36] See also Kilborne (1995: 278); Seidler (2000: 2).

In Wurmser's "teleological" reading, shame's "aim is disappearance . . . most simply in the form of hiding: most radically, in the form of dissolution (suicide)" (1981: 84). Fear of exposure assumes an audience that observes, a Gyges hidden in the bedroom. Shame makes us want to escape that audience, but more importantly it points to our awareness of that audience, that there are indeed those who gaze at us, that we do not live as isolated independent creatures, free from Tomkins' "facial communication."

While Darwin and his contemporary followers may find in shame and its physical manifestations a universality, which actions and what parts of our person are to be hidden will vary across time and space. For Gyges and his future wife it is the body of a woman who is not one's wife that must be hidden. In *Republic*, Book 5, when Socrates' proposal that men and women practice gymnastics naked together provokes laughter, Socrates remarks that long ago for the Greeks (just as to many barbarians "now") it seemed shameful (*aischra* is used here) and laughable to see men naked (432c). In the writings of contemporary psychoanalysts and psychologists what is to be hidden often is not only a body, but more specifically one's own vulnerabilities, weaknesses, and inadequacies. Those vulnerabilities and inadequacies, though, will be defined by time and place and shame again displays its dependence on the social context in which one lives. A Hector shamed by fears of being perceived as "womanish" could find praise in the contemporary language of the "sensitive man."

To reveal or uncover the vulnerabilities of another before an audience of others is to cause that individual shame. Among the Greeks, to do this specifically was considered an act of *hubris* that was itself often subject to punishment.[37] For the Athenians the hubristic act, intentionally revealing another individual's weaknesses and thus causing shame, was politically destabilizing, establishing hierarchies of better and worse, and arousing hostilities among the citizen body composed of equals. Athens even had a *graphê hubreos*, a law prohibiting acting hubristically toward another citizen. Sometimes the law was interpreted simply as using physical violence against another, but it also, at least according to Fisher, referred to the humiliation of another by revealing his weaknesses, thus causing him shame (Fisher 1992). Reference to this law surface in the frequent allusions in Plato's dialogues to the hubristic Socrates. Socrates, as the hubristic inquisitor ironically and shamelessly mocking his own incapacities and ignorance, exposes the weaknesses of others to an audience – be that audience Socrates alone or a group of others who are listening in on the interrogation.

Alcibiades the arrogant and proud man, disdainful of the traditions of the Athenians, nevertheless describes in Plato's *Symposium* his own reaction to

---

[37] Fisher (1992) argues against the old view of *hubris* that saw it as an offense against the gods and urges a reevaluation of the term in its social and especially moral and psychological rather than theological context.

the hubristic Socrates, the only man who can make him feel ashamed, who makes him aware of his own weaknesses: "I run away from him and flee . . . and often I think it would be sweet if he were no longer among men" (216bc).[38] Alcibiades' response to Socrates' ability to make him see his own inadequacies is the desire to cover himself and escape from Socrates' sight, to hide from him. Yet, in our very desire to hide and escape the gaze lies the recognition that there are others observing – and judging. That is why Alcibiades wishes Socrates would vanish: then, he would no longer have to see himself reflected in Socrates' sight.

The gaze of others publicizes our frailties and vulnerabilities and the uncovering of our frailties, what is most private, most distinctly our own, elicits the vivid physiological expression of shame, the blush, a response that in turn increases our vulnerability to observation. While Mark Twain may humorously have said "Man is the only creature who has the ability to blush, or the need," for Darwin the blush in its uniqueness to the human species reveals our capacity to understand what it means to be seen by another. While monkeys, Darwin writes, may redden from passion, only humans blush. As Darwin explains, the blush is distinctive among bodily responses to the emotions because it relies so heavily on the intellect. Writes Darwin: "We can cause laughing by tickling the skin . . . trembling from fear of pain, and so forth, but we cannot cause a blush . . . by any physical means . . . It is the mind which must be affected" ([1872] 1955: 309–10). It is the mind that acknowledges or imagines ourselves as seen by others. No monkey can achieve that sensibility. "It is not the simple act of reflecting on our own appearances," Darwin continues, "but the thinking what others think of us which excites a blush" (325). The irony is, of course, that the blush, calling attention to one's face, reveals our desire to hide. As Lynd writes about the blush: "Blushing manifests the exposure, the unexpectedness, the involuntary nature of shame. One's feeling is involuntarily exposed openly in one's face; one is uncovered. With blushing comes the impulse to 'cover one's face,' 'bury one's face,' 'sink into the ground' " (1958: 33).

I have already discussed Thrasymachus' blush in the Introduction to the book, but Platonic characters affected by the hubristic Socrates blush on other occasions, for example, in the *Protagoras* and the *Lysis*; in each case the blush calls attention to the interlocutor's vulnerability. In the *Protagoras*, when Socrates inquires of the young Hippocrates why he is so eager to study with the visiting Sophist and asks: "Who will you become after you go to Protagoras?," Hippocrates blushes (*eruthriasas*, 312a). In this case, it is only Socrates who observes, but Plato as the author of the dialogue ensures that his Socrates can see this blush. As Plato has Socrates report, although the conversation started in the dark of early morning, "now a

---

[38] See the regular references to Socrates' *hubris* in Alcibiades' speech (215b, 219c, 221e).

bit of dawn appeared" (312a). While the art of rhetoric to be learned at the feet of the Sophists may give Hippocrates political power in the city, Hippocrates, subject to the Socratic "gaze," knows well that such ambitions reveal his weaknesses before a man who tells the young and old alike that they must attend to their souls more than anything else, be it their bodies and money (*Apology*, 30a), or their reputations among the many (*Crito*, 47a; *Gorgias*, 522d). In the *Lysis*, Socrates asks the young Hippothales who is the "beauty" in the gymnasium, that is, the boy who has provoked the most sexual interest. Hippothales responds by blushing. Socrates' next comment reveals why Hippothales blushes and prompts an even greater blush from the young man. For Socrates tells Hippothales that he has been given by the gods the skill of recognizing a lover and a beloved (204bc). Hippothales' vulnerability – his subjection to eros – is the object of Socrates' gaze and that of those around him. The shame and the blush it evokes is not in this case for a deed that is ugly, nor even because Hippothales submits to love, but because Socrates and the others around him have discovered and are remarking on his vulnerability to the power of desire, on his weakness and incompletion, on his needs. The "need-less," independent Socrates, regularly and proudly affirming his own ignorance whenever he has the opportunity, caring naught for the gaze of others, would never blush.

When Hippothales blushes or when Hippocrates blushes, they do so because they are unable to conceal their vulnerabilities from the eyes of others, because they are unable to hide from view a truth about themselves that they would prefer that Socrates and others not know. Socrates, impervious to the gaze of others, walking barefoot and wearing a ragged cloak, complete and invulnerable himself, has nothing to hide from others. The blush may be a signal of the failure at efforts at concealment – or perhaps we can in some circumstances say at lying. The blush – and even the effort to cover the blush by hiding one's face – makes the observer aware that the one gazed upon, like Hippothales, is eager to hide something; the blush may alert the observer to an unrevealed truth or, as in Hippocrates' case, a revelation about himself that points to a vulnerability he had not recognized before, but suddenly cannot hide before Socrates. The desire to hide from another, to sink into the ground, to deny that one is the object of observation by glancing aside, all reveal a desire not to acknowledge a truth about oneself. The emotion of shame entails the desire to cover the truth. The blush, though, is an impediment to that desire to hide and instead becomes the incentive for the observer to uncover the truth that lies behind the blush. Is nature pushing us to truth seeking?

We are back to the word *alêtheia*, truth as the process of revealing and uncovering what lies hidden or forgotten. The covering longed for by the one who feels shame opposes the truth. As the social creatures of Protagoras' story we need *aidôs*, respect before others, to live communally, but that respect also hides who we truly are, what we really desire, what we would do if we were left completely free and uninhibited by the gaze of others. Shame protects us as both observer and as observed from both the ugly and the beautiful, from both who we are and what we can do. Oedipus, out of shame, wants to be cast into the sea or, as Creon urges, needs to be sent into the house, so that he may be removed from the sight of men. The vile and the ugly out of *aidôs* before the sun god Helios must be hidden. And yet the Sophoclean play exposes – most shamelessly – the impious acts of Oedipus. Sophocles through the action of the play brings these hideous deeds out into public view, exposing them to all the citizens of Athens. Sophocles' other plays do the same with other characters, other deeds. It is only this uncovering by the playwright – undaunted by any sense of shame that would force him to hide what is vile about ourselves and our passions – that enables us to know truly who we are, what we are capable of, and what is our relationship to the divine.

The shameless Candaules wanted to uncover the beautiful, to show Gyges a beauty he had not seen before, but the shame of the barbarians kept that true beauty hidden. Without the dramatic presentations of Sophocles, the truly ugly – but also the beauty of a Sophoclean divine order – would remain hidden. Without his revealing dramas we would know less about ourselves, the fates, the gods. It is the philosophers' stripping away that which we desire to hide from the gaze of others that brings on shame and it is the playwrights' casting aside the shame that would inhibit their uncovering of the nature of our existence who can reveal *hê alêtheia*, that which is true.[39] It is in this sense that shame opposes Socratic philosophy, for instance, as the activity dedicated to the pursuit of truth. The social emotion that Protagoras had said is Zeus' gift, enabling men to found cities and escape from the chaos of their natural condition, opposes the philosophic endeavor of uncovering. The boundaries that shame imposes between a public world open to the gaze of all and a private realm of personal vulnerabilities cloud our vision.

5. SHAME AND THE LIBERAL INDIVIDUAL

The blush, as the response to shame, reveals our unsuccessful wish to hide, but in the very process of seeking to hide ourselves, it also reveals our dependence on the opinions of others and thus our lives as a member of the social network. The covering that is an act against the philosophic endeavor of uncovering at the same time reveals our existence as social beings, living in the vision of others. To feel shame is to live in the minds of others,[40] to

---

[39] From a contemporary perspective, see the controversy surrounding Jean Elshtain's appeal to shame and veiling as hiding the truth about oneself from others (Locke 1999: 34).

[40] Those who understand shame as dependent only on an imaginary other, remove from shame its inherent social role.

understand the self not as an autonomous and independent individual. The emotion of shame that according to Protagoras' myth lies at the beginning of cities contrasts with the premises underlying the theoretical model of the liberal individual, the autonomous self so familiar in our contemporary world. This is the individual capable of choices who acts freely, emancipated from the controlling, and perhaps castigating, glances of others. Shame sits awkwardly in the liberal tradition as Williams points out so effectively, but it also settles well within the political and philosophical traditions that reject the possibility of "the unencumbered" self[41] and comprehend the individual only within the context of the consciousness of others. We can identify many exponents of such a vision, but for the moment let Sartre in *Being and Nothingness* in his own discussion of shame be our spokesman.[42] Shame is, according to him, "the *recognition* of the fact that I am indeed that object which the Other is looking at and judging." In acknowledging oneself as an object, he continues: "I can be ashamed only as my freedom escapes me in order to be a *given* object... Beyond any knowledge which I can have, I am this self which another knows" ([1943] 1984: 350). For Sartre, "the Other is the indispensable mediator between myself and me. I am ashamed of myself *as I appear* to the Other... Shame is by nature *recognition*" ([1943] 1984: 302). Only as a creature observed and aware of that observation can I become aware of myself.

Shame so dependent on the gaze of the other becomes a fulcrum that divides the individual as independent and isolated from the individual understood as enmeshed in a context of others. The question underlying this book is: does democracy (like philosophy), à la Protagoras and his favorable interpreters, require shame, the contextual individual, or is democracy built on a transcendence of shame, on uncovering practices that resist shame and the history that defines what is shameful? Or to put it another way: is democracy grounded on the communitarian individual who experiences shame in a historical context or on the liberal individual who is free from both history and shame? The autonomous individual at the heart of so much democratic theory[43] does not welcome the emotion of shame that subjects him or her to the controlling gaze of another. The individual enmeshed in social relations, controlled by emotions, responding to those relations and expressing *aidôs* for the past and before one's fellow citizens stands in opposition to the rational creature, unencumbered by emotions, making choices on his or her own,

---

[41] Sandel (1982) has introduced the language of the "unencumbered self" into our contemporary discourse. Of course, the image of such an unencumbered individual is a caricature of the liberal individual. Nevertheless, the language offers a powerful model that helps us see alternative political stances in their starkest terms.

[42] One could, of course, consider the vast literature that currently builds on theories of recognition deriving initially from Hegel's discussion of the master and slave ([1807] 1967: 229–40).

[43] I use the language of Farrar (1988) here.

underlying the liberal democratic model.[44] Freedom of speech as a democratic practice is a practice of openness, of a refusal to hide one's thoughts because of a shame that would bring humiliation or disapproval in the eyes of others. Respect and reverence before the judgments of others, in contrast, limit the freedom and uncovering capacities of speech and opportunities for individual choice.

Rochelle Gurstein argues in her book *The Repeal of Reticence* (1996) that the history of American culture is in part the story of the transcendence of shame, the uncovering of what had been covered before, whether it be through scientific studies of sex or the media's invasion of the private lives of leaders. That process of overcoming, of denying shame its due, she contends, is connected with democratization, its eroding of the distinction between public and private so that all becomes public and nothing is hidden. There are then no boundaries to limit what can be seen or behind which we can hide and escape the judgmental gaze of others. The elimination of shame reduces all to the same level. In Gurstein's reading of this erosion, shame becomes an aristocratic weapon that maintains hierarchy or (more positively stated) a resource with which to reaffirm boundaries.[45] If we think back to the Aristophanic stage, Old Comedy displayed a powerful expression of freedom of speech. Nothing restrained what could be portrayed on stage.[46] There we find the uninhibited representation of what is normally hidden (the leather phallus and reddened female genitals). There we see men who are no different from animals and gods who are no different from men. There all is equally open. This is the thoroughly democratic theatrical endeavor born during Athens' life as a democracy.[47] No reverence and no boundaries inhibit the playwright or the actors.

---

[44] An irony would appear here in John Stuart Mill's arguments for the open ballot. See Chapter 10 of his *Considerations on Representative Government* ([1862] 1998).

[45] For another defense of shame in the world of contemporary discourse see Jean Elshtain (1995). Elshtain portrays herself standing out on a limb by commending shame in contemporary democracies: "Shame – or its felt experience as it surrounds our body's functions, passions, and desires – requires veils of civility that conceal some activities and aspects of ourselves even as we boldly and routinely display and reveal others when we take part in public activities for all to see" (1995: 55). In Elshtain's case, though, the argument for shame with its "few defenders" is not with a view to the cohesiveness that sets us in the social context of the mutual gaze and reverence, but rather with a view to worries about the publicization of what is private and thus the "politics of displacement" whereby politics instead of being a communal activity becomes the flaunting of an unconcealed self. This allows, she argues, for an individualism run riot in the public sphere.

[46] I note some possible qualifications to this in Chapter 6 when I discuss comedy and especially Aristophanes' play *Thesmophoriazusae*.

[47] This is hardly to suggest that Aristophanes himself was in favor of the democratic regime at Athens. His comedies are filled with critiques of it, but the performance of comedy entails the equalizing and the publicity characteristic of democracy.

With the rise of liberalism – whether we see it as a seventeenth-century phenomenon in Locke's *Letter on Toleration* or a nineteenth-century one with John Stuart Mill's *On Liberty* – the realm of privacy is no longer a world hidden away from public scrutiny like the private parts from which the term *aidôs* originates. Rather, it gains its own dignity, becoming the site within which one practices individual freedom – a freedom from the intrusion and judgmental gaze of others. In Locke's *Letter* this is a freedom explicitly from the magistrate's intrusion into one's spiritual life, into the life of one's soul. In Mill's essay it is the freedom from the control of a society as a whole over one's opinions, expressions of those opinions, self-regarding actions. The liberal world allowing for this space of privacy, grounded on the autonomous individual choosing his or her own life plan, has little truck with the world of shame where when uncovered we try to hide from the controlling gaze of others. The model of the autonomous liberal individual leaves no space for *aidôs*.

Part of what makes Pericles' Funeral Oration as reported by Thucydides seem so modern to many[48] is Pericles' claim that in Athens "we live as citizens freely both towards that which is shared and in seeing the daily activities of each other. We do not have any anger towards our neighbor if he does anything according to his own pleasure, nor do we look at him with the sort of looks that might be painful even if they are not punishments in themselves" (2.37.2). At this point in his speech Pericles takes pride in this regime that he calls a *dêmocratia*, where the citizens are free from the judgmental gaze of others as they engage in their private lives. Though fearing and thus obedient to the laws, Pericles' Athenians live freely, both publicly and privately.[49] Protagoras in his myth sees the polity as dependent on the gaze and the respect for what it is that others respect. Democratization as the shedding of shame, in Protagoras' view, threatens the cohesion provided by the contextual framing of shame. The glory of democratic Athens for Pericles, in contrast, is precisely the shamelessness that allows others to live free from those castigating glances of their neighbors. Does shame have any place in the democracy of antiquity or the liberal democracies of today? Is shame a source of cohesion cast aside by liberalism only at its peril, as Gurstein for one suggests – or is it an oppressive force that enslaves us to a history of the "beautiful things discovered long ago" as Herodotus' Gyges had phrased it? Is it a restraint on our freedom, or is it the key to making us capable of social life? Do we turn to Protagoras or to Pericles?

---

[48] See Turner (1981: 187) who remarks on the display of the Funeral Oration on placards during World War I in Britain; also Kagan (1991: 141, 271).

[49] This description of the Athenians as minding their own business when it comes to the lives they choose to live will be modified just a few lines later in 2.40.2 when the one who chooses *not* to engage in public affairs is judged, according to Pericles, to be "useless (*achreion*)."

Subjected to the controlling gaze of others, one loses one's independence. Controlled instead by the opinions and values of others, the liberal individual melds into the social world. Heller, for instance, who had argued that shame and culture are "coeval" also remarks that "the internalization of shame *legitimates* the system of domination. The more shame is internalized, the less brutal force is needed in order to integrate a social structure" (1985: 40).[50] Hobbes, the prince of the isolated individual with rights and no shame in his natural condition, includes shame among his list of the passions in Chapter 6 of *Leviathan*, describing it in language that is similar to that of our contemporary analysts: "*Grief* for the discovery of some defect of ability is SHAME, or the passion that discovereth itself in BLUSHING, and consisteth in the apprehension of something dishonorable." But he goes on to note: "and in young men is a sign of the love of good reputation and commendable; in old men it is a sign of the same, but because it comes too late, not commendable" ([1651] 1994: 32). Why is shame among young men commendable for this author who otherwise sees in the aristocratic concern with honor such a threat to political stability? Shame plays a socializing role. It is the mechanism by which the young learn from the community. It is the spring that teaches the social virtues captured so vividly by the laws of nature Hobbes lists in Chapter 15 of *Leviathan*. The authorizing, independent individual at the foundation of the leviathan must be transformed – once he enters civil society – into an individual subjected to the castigating glances of others. The transition from the state of nature to civil society is from the isolated individual to contextual citizen, from the shameless to the shame ridden. The old men who feel shame clearly have not learned in their youth the principles of social life and insofar as they remained shameless in their earlier years they were threats to social order.[51]

---

[50] Heller herself does not bring into her discussion of shame the language of Foucault here; others do, for example, Fernie who writes of shame as a "Foucaldian resource of power used especially for the repression of women" (2002: 74).

[51] Contemporary criminal justice studies that explore shame as a mechanism of punishment capture Hobbes' point as well. They see shame as "a means of making citizens actively responsible," as "a route to freely chosen compliance," and most especially the "re-integration" of the criminal into the community (Braithwaite 1989: 10). The claimed efficacy of shame is based on the contention that "low crime societies are societies where people do not mind their own business" (1989: 8). While Braithwaite's book articulates a hopeful plan that sees crime controlled through shame, others are skeptical of the potential of such social control in the liberal world of isolated individuals. Writes one such critic: "What may work in a highly interdependent communitarian society like Japan seems hopelessly idealistic here" (Karp 1998: 290) and more vividly, "what is unique about shame is that it is indicative of a bond between the offender and other members of the community. Where there is no bond, there is no shame . . . Effective shame depends on the stake a person has in the community. If a person cares nothing about the disapproval of others, shame is a useless tool" (Karp 1998: 287–8) and the society returns to the harsher forms of punishment that assume the responsible autonomous agent. See also the reservations of Garvey (1998).

The liberal world of rights and protections came into being to shield a realm of privacy where individuals could make their own choices. In such a world the evocation of shame is a violation of that privacy, forcing us to live not for ourselves in our private worlds, but to live in the eyes of others. And yet the nagging Protagorean gift of Zeus keeps intruding and forcing us to question whether the social life of the city can survive the casting aside of shame, whether even in the liberal society of individuals there is the circular shaming of those who do not accept the priority of individuality and the escape from shame.[52] Zeus had said that those who did not share in *aidôs* were to be cast out of the city as diseases. Is shame – that which hides the truth and that which limits individual choice – the disease? Or is shame – that which affirms our lives as social creatures existing only insofar as others perceive us – the cure?

6. PLATO'S GYGES

Let me now return to Gyges, but this time to the Gyges of the *Republic*. In this version, Gyges does not kill the king and marry the queen to found his dynasty because he had violated the beautiful things discovered long ago when he saw the queen naked. Rather, he ascends to power and satisfies his desires because he finds deep in a chasm, on the finger of a dead giant, a ring that enables him to become invisible, that is, impervious to the gaze of others. With this magical power, he kills the king and seduces the queen. In other words, his invisibility grants him freedom from the gaze of others, freedom from *aidôs*, the inhibitions that the fear of the judgmental looks by others would place on him. He will not have to look askant or sink into the ground. He will not blush. Free from observation, thus free from shame and from potential punishments, why should this ancestor of Gyges, Glaucon asks in the *Republic*, be just? Why should he not kill the king, marry the queen, leave a kingdom for his children, and satisfy whatever desires he may have? The challenge for Socrates from this point on in the *Republic* is to show that absent shame, punishment and the gaze of others, it is still in one's interest to be just. The just, the argument of the *Republic* goes, are happy irrespective of the gaze of any others.

Glaucon presents for Socrates two men – one perfectly just, the other perfectly unjust. The unjust man, though, appears just; the just man appears unjust. Which one is happier? Their true natures cannot be observed, viewed

---

For recent reactions to the place of shaming punishments in liberal society, see Nussbaum (2004: 227–50). We see the battle between shame and the autonomous individual surfacing in such debates as these.

[52] For a discussion of honor and, by implication, its obverse shame in democratic societies, see the chapter in Tocqueville's *Democracy in America* ([1835–40] 2000) entitled "On Honor in the United States and in Democratic Societies" (II.3.18; 589–99).

by others. Their souls are both free from the inhibiting emotion of shame, but it is the unjust man who appears just who lives as god (*isotheos*) among men in the freedom to do whatever he may desire (360c).[53] Socrates commends his interlocutor. "With what strength you purify as though they were statues each one of the two for their judgment!" (361d). Glaucon has cleaned his statues so well that the metal forms of the just and unjust men glisten and blind observers to what is within. With the eyes we gaze upon only the polished exterior. Socrates in his response to the challenge of Glaucon must show that appearances – and thus shame – are irrelevant, that the just individual does live free from the gaze of others, that his or her happiness comes from the quality of the soul, not from the respect of those around one, not from living through others. The soul that Socrates explores in the *Republic* is an apolitical, asocial soul, an ordered soul governed by individual reason and the pursuit of what is beyond sight. It is a soul not in need of the gifts of Zeus brought to mankind by Hermes. As I shall argue in my reading of the *Apology* in Chapter 5, Socrates transforms the meaning of shame – removing it from its social context, from the realm of the gaze, from the realm of the blush. In Plato's dialogues, Socrates turns his interlocutors away from the *aidôs* of Protagoras to the soul, the part of the self that remains indifferent both to the gaze of others and to the beautiful things uncovered by those who lived long ago. However, he without *aidôs*, Zeus had declared, is a disease for the city. For this Socrates will be executed.

---

[53] As noted in Chapter 2 (page 39) Aristotle often uses the phrase "to do whatever one wishes" for his description of the democratic life.

PART III

PARRHÊSIA

The Practice of Free Speech in Ancient Athens

4

The Practice of *Parrhêsia*

For George Grote, the nineteenth-century Philosophical Radical and close associate of John Stuart Mill, "[t]h eleven chapters of Thucydides" that comprise Pericles' Funeral Oration are "among the most memorable relics of antiquity" ([1851–6] 1900: 6.142); in particular, Grote's *History of Greece* highlights those passages that pay tribute to "an unrestrained play of fancy and diversity of private pursuit" (6.148). Sounding very much like the friend of Mill that he was, Grote explains: "[T]he stress which he [Pericles] lays upon the liberty of thought and action at Athens, not merely from excessive restraint of law, but also from practical intolerance between man and man, and tyranny of the majority over individual dissenters in taste and pursuit, deserves notice" because "all its germs of productive genius, so rare everywhere, found in such an atmosphere the maximum of encouragement" (6.149).

The liberties of the ancients have had their defenders and their attackers – as well as those who have questioned whether those liberties really existed.[1] Indeed, Grote (most likely in response to Benjamin Constant's essay on "The Liberty of the Ancients Compared with that of the Moderns" from 1819) justifies the "peculiar attention" he devotes to the passage in the Funeral Oration on the "rich and varied fund of human impulse" in Athens "because it serves to correct an assertion, often too indiscriminately made, respecting antiquity as contrasted with modern societies – an assertion that the ancient societies sacrificed the individual to the state, and that only in modern times has individual agency been left free to the proper extent" (148).[2] How free

---

[1] For an extensive history up to the present, see the list of references in footnote 6 in the Introduction.

[2] For a full discussion of how George Grote's and John Stuart Mill's participation in the debates concerning the freedoms of the ancients served a way of addressing contemporary political issues see Urbinati (2002).

the Athenians actually were or even what freedom may have meant to the
ancient Athenians, the subject of much debate then, now, and in between,
is well beyond the scope of this chapter and book.[3] Rather, the goal here
is to explore briefly how one particular freedom that the Athenians identified closely with their democratic regime – the freedom to speak "frankly,"
parrhêsia – functioned within the Athenian polity and posed for them questions about the nature of their democratic regime. Most important for my
purposes are the theoretical challenges that the opportunity to speak without inhibition raised for the life of a political community. After a survey of
the practice, I turn in the next chapter to the trial of Socrates. In the trial
of Socrates, we see the full explosion of the tensions that parrhêsia generated for the life of a community that prided itself on its commitment to that
practice. In the next and final section of the book, I look at a selection of dramatic works from the Attic stage, Thucydides' History and Plato's dialogue
the Protagoras in order to highlight the effort by these works to explore the
source and consequences of those tensions.

Parrhêsia has most frequently been translated as "free speech" or
"freedom of speech," but recently a number of scholars express greater sat-
isfaction with the term "frank speech" (Foucault 2001: 12; Monoson 2000:
52–3; Henderson 1998; Momigliano 1973–4: 260).[4] Nehamas (1998: 164)
and Foucault (2001: 12) traces the root of parrhêsia to "saying everything."[5]
The phrase "free speech" or "freedom of speech" as a translation of parrhêsia
ties the word too strongly to the passive language of rights rather than the
active expression of one's true beliefs.[6] Instead, the language of parrhêsia
indicates the profound differences between a conception of freedom of speech
grounded on a notion of "rights," of individuals protected from the intrusion
of governmental forces, from the social world of castigating glances, and the
Athenian world where the rights of the individual as realms of protection
and of privacy simply do not function.[7] As Moses Finley writes of Athens in
Democracy: Ancient and Modern (no doubt with a fair bit of exaggeration),
there were "no theoretical limits to the power of the state, no activity . . . in
which the state could not legitimately intervene provided the decision was

---

[3] Some resources for this debate are noted in the previous footnotes, but the most important and
thorough work in this area is that of Raaflaub (1983; 2004); he offers extensive references.

[4] Momigliano writes of parrhêsia as "frequently being used to mean either the virtue of frankness or the vice of loquacity" (1973–4: 260).

[5] The term, according to Momigliano, first appears in Euripides' Hippolytus, which was performed in 428 BCE (1973–4: 259). I quote the specific passage in Chapter 6, but see the more
extensive discussion in Foucault (2001: 30–1).

[6] Mulgan (1984: 12) writes: "There are terms for special freedoms, such as parresia, freedom of
speech, but they have no etymological connection with freedom." See, however, Democritus
Fragment 226.1, which suggests that parrhêsia is inherent in eleutheria: oikêion eleutheriês
parrhêsia (Diels and Kranz 1961).

[7] Cf., however, Miller (1995). Also Ober on what he calls "quasi-rights" (2000).

taken properly... Freedom meant the rule of law and participation in the decision making process, not the possession of inalienable rights" (1988: 116).[8] Or, to cite Mulgan: "There is indeed very little surviving evidence of theorizing about the advantages of a tolerant regime such as that of Athens, very little can be seen as a defense of individual liberty from collective control, apart from Pericles' funeral speech. In Pericles' speech, nevertheless, the tolerance of Athens is justified not in terms of anything due to individuals, but because it has benefited the city as a whole" (1984: 13). Virginia Hunter, so interested in the role of gossip in Athens, questions the reliability of Pericles' self-praise in that oration: "It appears then that at all levels Athenians were encouraged to pry and to probe, to know what their neighbors were doing and had done. Little effort was required to obtain such information for most Athenians lived in small, face to face communities, where they were on intimate terms with their demesmen" (1994: 117). *Parrhêsia* as free speech or speaking all is not a "right" in our terms; rather, it captures both the egalitarianism of the regime that rejected the hierarchy implicit in the treatment of Thersites[9] and the expectation that speech reveals the truth as one sees it, that speech opens and uncovers. It is this revealing speech that the democratic citizen of Athens, engaged equally with other citizens in the deliberative Assembly and the public life of the city, expresses.

Through the prism of *parrhêsia* we can see one of many significant contrasts between the political life of democratic Athens and the contemporary expectations of political actors enmeshed in a world of representation. In a representative system with concerns about reelection hovering over representation, not to mention the uncertain principles underlying the concept and practice of representation weighing heavily on the legislator, speech is not one's own nor is it necessarily revelatory of one's own views; if one speaks what one sees as truth and expresses one's own mind openly, we may call such a person principled or, perhaps, brusque or offensive or unrepresentative of her district or perhaps even a fool. The democratic regime of Athens, in contrast, depended on the participation of its citizens speaking their own minds[10] – not on attempting to incorporate the views

---

[8] Earlier expressions of this view, hardly as sympathetic generally as Finley's, are apparent in Constant's essay and in Fustel de Coulanges ([1870] 1956).

[9] The egalitarianism, of course, did not include women or slaves. Ajax's (in)famous remark that silence is becoming for a woman is emblematic here, though the playwright Sophocles who has Ajax speak this adage in his madness (*Ajax*, 293) and Aristotle quoting this phrase spoken by a madman (*Politics*, 1260a30) may be exploring some of the ambiguous implications of such limits on the speech even of women. On the other hand, as Momigliano points out, there is no Latin equivalent of *parrhêsia*. In Rome, "the general attitude...seems to have been that only persons in authority had a right to speak freely" (1973–4: 261).

[10] I will discuss qualifications to this point in my consideration of the Mytilenian Debate in Chapter 7, Section 2, and ask about the degree to which such speaking of one's own mind was indeed possible in democratic Athens for the good politician.

of others in one's own speech nor on the shading of one's convictions with the art of rhetoric. Such shading violated the principles of *parrhêsia* and revealed a self-interest that opposed the welfare of the city as a whole. It was the Sophists who used speech to hide through the art of rhetoric. *Parrhêsia* was a practice of opening and revealing one's true beliefs, not hiding them or abandoning them. In a political world grounded on representation such as we find in the modern world, we could say that in legislative bodies speech should in fact *not* be free. Rather, it should be bound by the commitment to the district or to the groups from which the representative arrives at the deliberative setting. The introduction of representation into a democratic regime profoundly transforms the place and significance of *parrhêsia*.

By allowing the anachronistic language of rights to surface in a consideration of the ancient pattern of *parrhêsia*, one loses two important aspects of this practice: 1) the daring and courageous quality of the practice; those who spoke openly in Athens may have been at risk of legal action if they spoke on behalf of proposals contrary to the established laws and if they questioned the fundamental principles of their system of government;[11] and 2) the unveiling aspects of the practice that entailed the exposure of one's true thoughts, the resistance to hiding what is true because of deference to a hierarchical social and political world or a concern with how one appears before the gaze of others, that is, shame.[12] Diogenes the Cynic, the most shameless of all characters from the ancient corpus, who boldly performed "the things of Demeter and Aphrodite" in the open, in public, responded when he was asked what is the most beautiful thing among human beings, "*Parrhêsia*" (Diogenes Laertius 6.69).[13]

Parrhêsia in this sense of a certain shamelessness emphasizes the equality of the democratic system where speech is not limited by obsequiousness, but rather entails the effort to uncover the truth on the part of each citizen.

[11] Monoson (2000) in her book deals extensively with this point as do Foucault's lectures on *parrhêsia* (1983 and 2001). However, see the discussion in Chapter 2 concerning the status of the *graphê paranomôn*, the law prohibiting the introduction of decrees that would violate the *patrios nomos* and the uncertainty about whether or when such a law might have been applied. Foucault also points beyond the legal consequences to the personal implications of the practice, which I do not discuss here. I am grateful to Monoson for providing me originally with a manuscript copy of Foucault's lectures well before they were published when I was first beginning work on this project.

[12] Williams, without mentioning the ancient practice, captures the essence of *parrhêsia* when he writes: "Truthfulness implies a respect for the truth . . . you do the best you can to acquire true beliefs, and what you say reveals what you believe" (2002: 11). Williams is discussing this within the context of the Academy's diminished appreciation of truth, truthfulness, accuracy, and sincerity, but the issues he raises extend well beyond the ivy walls and reflect the continuing relevance of the ancient interest in *parrhêsia* as saying what one believes to be true.

[13] See, for instance, the remarks by Long quoted in Chapter 3, note 19.

Parrhêsia is, we can say, the democratic practice of shamelessness.[14] It is on this latter aspect that I shall focus. As an unveiling practice, free/frank speech, the "saying all," is the opposite of shame as discussed in the previous chapter. Shame hides and covers while *parrhêsia* opens and reveals. Conflicts and tensions arise because, of course, a democratic polity – any polity – needs both.

In Aeschylus' *Persian Women* from 472 BCE, the Messenger arrives from Greece at the Persian court and reports to Queen Atossa that some "Fury – some malignant power" (353) brought down the Persian fleet and with it precipitated the retreat of King Xerxes from Greece. The chorus of Persian elders who remained at home comprehends the personal losses that accompany this defeat: "The new made brides turn from their silken beds/ Of youth and pleasure and soft luxury... bewailing/ Their young lords" (540–5). But, beyond the death of youths, they see as well the death of their regime:

> From east to west the Asian race
> No more will own our Persian sway,
> Nor on the king's compulsion pay
> Tribute, nor bow to earth their face...
>
> ——
>
> Now fear no more shall bridle speech;
> Uncurbed, the common tongue shall prate
> Of freedom; for the yoke of State
> Lies broken on the bloody beach.
> (584–94)[15]

The Greek of this ode has the tongue of mortals in fetters, *en phulakais* (592). The overthrow of Persian tyranny then is marked by the unfettering of the tongue. Despotism restrains while the free city of Athens releases speech; it is the free city of the unfettered tongue that resists, with forces way outnumbered, the men of the Persian army whose tongues speak neither of truth nor of freedom. The pride of the Athenians in their practice of *parrhêsia* issues boldly from the lips of Aeschylus' Persian chorus. The glory of Athens lies in this freedom.[16]

The Aristotelian *Constitution of Athens* written some time in the fourth century tells the following story about the sixth-century tyrant Peisistratus:

When Peisistratus was on such a trip, they say that there happened the incident concerning the farmer in Hymettus who was farming the area which was later called the country-side without a tax. Peisistratus saw someone working very hard digging

---

[14] Foucault (2001: 17–19) limits *parrhêsia* to criticism and thus sees it primarily in its hierarchical setting. I wish to discuss it in both the hierarchical and unveiling settings.

[15] I use the translation by Vellacott (1961: 139).

[16] More than a century later Isocrates in the *Panathenaicus* will use a similar image, this time, though, connecting it directly with the word *parrhêsia*, which by this time made it into a verbal form: "It has come upon me to speak freely (*parrhêsiazethai*), and I have unbound my lips (*leluka to stoma*)" (12.96).

rocks. On account of his surprise, he ordered his servant to ask what the man was growing on the land. The man said: 'Whatever evils and pains there are, and of these evils and pains it is necessary to give Peisistratus a tenth of them.' The man said this not knowing to whom he spoke, but Peisistratus was pleased by his free speech (*dia tên parrhêsian*) and by his love of work and made him free from all taxes. (16.6)

This lowly farmer digging out the rocks from his fields, unaware of the exalted identity of who it was who engaged him in conversation, spoke without respect (*aidôs*) for his ruler. No deference to hierarchy inhibited him from revealing the misery he suffered as the result of Peisistratus' policies. He spoke truly (as he saw it) about the land and about the tyrant of Athens. For this honesty in speech, the admirable Athenian tyrant, in the tale recorded by Aristotle, rewarded the farmer. The story in the *Constitution of Athens* recounts an event that supposedly took place almost two centuries before the composition of the work and praises the tyrantlike Peisistratus for welcoming the fearless and open criticism of his policies.

Given the temporal distance between Peisistratus' rule in the mid-sixth century and the writing of the *Constitution of Athens*, this story tells us very little about the actions of Athens' tyrant, but a great deal about what will elicit praise in the mid-fourth century: the appreciation of honest speech, of *parrhêsia*. The language of the plays of the fifth century, the speeches of the fourth century, even the philosophic dialogues of Plato, all identify *parrhêsia* as a distinctive practice treasured by democratic Athens. Socrates, for example, in conversation with the prickly Callicles in the *Gorgias* urges him to take advantage of the *parrhêsia* that belongs to him as an Athenian and that is lacking for the foreigners who have spoken earlier in the dialogue (487b). The enjoyment of *parrhêsia* is a mark of citizenship separating out those who stand outside the citizen body. For Aeschines in his speech *Against Ctesiphon* the preservation of the regime is the same as preserving *parrhêsia*: "Let no one of you forget this, but let each one know that when he goes into a court as a juror in a suit concerning a *graphê paranomôn*, on that day, he will cast his vote concerning his own *parrhêsia*" (3.6). Beyond the literary evidence, physical remains attest to the pride the Athenians felt about the practice of *parrhêsia*: a fifth-century inscription records that the Athenian Assembly voted to name one of the state ships *Parrhêsia* (IG II2 1624.81).[17]

More recent authors writing about ancient Athens often glorify this practice, filling their description of the Athenian assemblies with grandiose and romantic visions of the life fostered by the democratic regime in Athens. Grote, whose hagiography of Athenian democracy was cited at the beginning of this chapter, remarked in essays as he prepared for writing his extensive history that every Athenian citizen could become "accustomed to hear the functionaries of government freely censured and overhauled: every man

---

[17] Cited in Henderson (1998: 406n16) and Hansen (1996: 92, 101n19).

when he felt himself wronged, stood a good chance of being able to create general sympathy for redress. Thus revenge... was discouraged since the dialogic encounter in the assembly effectively sobered personal animosities" (Demetriou 1999: 114). In similarly exalted language, we hear Grote extolling the Athenians of Cleisthenes' era when citizens were "trained to the duty of both speakers and hearers, and each man, while he felt that he exercised his share of influence on the decision, identified his own safety and happiness with the vote of the majority, and became familiarized with the notion of a sovereign authority which he neither could nor ought to resist. This is an idea new to the Athenian bosom; and with it came feelings sanctifying free speech and equal law – words which no Athenian citizen ever afterwards heard unmoved" ([1851–6] 1900: 4.139). Momigliano writing more than a century after Grote reaffirms: "The writers of the fifth century still emphasize the value of *aidôs*, insofar as speech is concerned. But in the same century a new notion spread, the notion that freedom of speech is a positive, or at least a remarkable achievement" (1973–4: 259). We find similar enthusiasm more recently in the words of Jeffrey Henderson: "For the mass of citizens who listened, judged, and voted, *parrhêsia* fostered a critical attitude and a sense of intellectual autonomy, and so became the frontline defense against flattery, bullying, corruption, deception, or incompetence on the part of the speakers" (1998: 256–7). Or for Josiah Ober "it was not only the *principle* of freedom of speech (as a defense of negative freedoms) but also the constant and positive *exercise* of free speech (in deliberations about the common good) by persons with diverse ideas that was essential for the flourishing of the democracy" (2001: 177). For some this *parrhêsia* in the Athenian Assembly and in the courts is even the seed bed of dialectic and thus the source of the Greek philosophical tradition (Berti 1978).[18]

When, at least according to a number of speeches of the orators from the fourth century, the practice of *parrhêsia* as the expression of what one considers true deteriorated into deceptive oratory and flattering demagoguery, its demise evokes lamentation and a romantic longing for the good old days of honest speech – just as we find in the more contemporary reflections on this ancient practice. Aeschines in his speech *Against Timarchus* captures this dismay when he compares the object of his accusations to the speakers of the previous century:

And so moderate were those speakers from the past, Pericles and Themistocles and Aristeides, that speaking while holding one's hand outside the cloak, as we now do as a matter of habit, we all do nowadays as a matter of course, they thought to be daring and held themselves back from doing it themselves. I think I can point out a truly great sign of this. I know well that everyone has sailed to Salamis and has

---

[18] For a similar claim about the origins of philosophy see Grote ([1851–6] 1900: 5.405–6).

witnessed the statue of Solon that stands there in the agora with Solon's hand inside his cloak. Now this, O men of Athens, is a copy of the form of Solon, which portrays the fashion of how he spoke to the *dêmos* of Athens. Consider, O men of Athens, how different Solon and those men I recalled a moment ago are from Timarchus. They were ashamed (*êischunonto*) to speak with their hands outside the cloak, but this one not long ago but yesterday, ripping off his cloak in the Assembly he moved his arms about violently like a gymnast in the pankration, his body so badly and shamefully (*aischroôs*) marked by strong drink and gross behavior that those men who were well thinking covered themselves shamed (*aischunentas*) on behalf of the city, that we used such men as our counselors.   (*Against Timarchus*, 1.25-6)

The arm outside the cloak allows for the dramatics that distract from the truth (or absence thereof) of the speech and enable demagoguery to replace the simplicity of *parrhêsia*. *Parrhêsia* opposed rather than supported the practice of a rhetoric that obscures and distorts the truth for the sake of individual benefit. The truly parrhesiastic[19] speaker eschews the art of rhetoric. Rhetoric with its goal of deception is not an expression of *parrhêsia*, but rather its perversion.[20] Demosthenes captures this point when he remarks in his *Philippic IV*: "This is the truth spoken with all freedom (*taut' esti t'alêthê, meta pasês parrhêsias*), simply in goodwill and for what is best, not a speech using flattery for the sake of harm and deceit, making money for the one speaking and handing the affairs of the city to its enemies" (10.76).

The contrast between rhetoric and *parrhêsia* is a familiar trope throughout the speeches of the fourth-century orators. Rhetoric according to their own rhetorical offerings hinders the practice of *parrhêsia* and undermines the role of free speech as an activity of truth seeking within the democratic regime.[21] Not surprisingly, the orators of the fourth century fill their own speeches with the interrelationship between *parrhêsia* and the democratic regime, extolling the opportunities for frank speech that the regime offers and lamenting the misuse of the practice by their sophistically skilled contemporaries. "Democracies," as Demosthenes says in his *Funeral Speech*, "have many other beautiful and just things to which those who think rightly ought to hold fast, and especially *parrhêsia* from which it is impossible that

---

[19] I introduce this neologism and its cognate "parrhesiast" with apologies, but with the hope that it captures the distinctly Athenian implications of the term in order to keep in mind the open expression of what one believes to be true. Foucault (2001) uses "*parrhesiastes*."

[20] Hesk writing explicitly on *Deception and Democracy in Classical Athens* remarks on the Athenian ideology of truth telling with reference to the contrast established between "non-hoplitic trickery" (i.e., the Spartans) and "hoplitic openness" (2000: 64). See passim, but especially Chapter 4.

[21] A scholar such as Connor (1971) is far more positive about the benefits brought to Athenian politics by the "new politicians" of the fifth century, who practiced the art of rhetoric taught by the Sophists, than are the Greek orators of the fourth century. For a more favorable spin on the contribution of the practices of the Sophists see also Grote [[1851-6] 1900: 8.352-99) and Yunis (1996).

the truth not be safe and sound, that the truth not be made clear" (60.26).
Or Isocrates in *To Nicocles* writing of what it is that monarchs lack moves
beyond the political realm to the private lives as well and remarks on those
things that foster a valuable education: "Also, there is *parrhêsia* and the
opportunity to openly point out to one another, both friends and enemies,
the faults (*hamartiais*) of each another" (2.3).[22] No one will speak openly to
a king about his faults and thus he loses the resources for self-improvement.
The original appeal to *parrhêsia*, then, rides on the uncovering qualities of the
practice, not on the corruption of the practice brought in with the Sophist's
education in a rhetoric designed to hide the truth.[23]

Others have presented full accounts of what we currently know about
parrhêsia as manifest in the political life of the city of democratic Athens.[24]
I will not repeat their work, but only briefly review here the central aspects
of that practice relevant for my argument. The tradition of *parrhêsia* was,
of course, most particularly relevant for the life of a city where the Assembly was the primary venue for political decisions. As Demosthenes says at
the beginning of his speech on behalf of liberty for the Rhodians: "I think
it is necessary, O men of Athens, that when debating about such issues to
give *parrhêsia* to each one of those deliberating" (15.1). At the beginning
of every session of the Athenian Assembly a herald would stand before the
several thousand citizens gathered on the Pnyx. In a loud voice he would
ask, "Who wishes to speak?" opening the floor to every citizen to address
the assembled population. The *Boulê* or Council would have determined the
agenda for the Assembly and they would speak first on the issues concerning
whatever measure was being proposed; the actual proposer of the particular measure under consideration would also have the opportunity to speak
early in the deliberations, but once they had spoken, the herald opened the
discussion to all. Aeschines in his speech *Against Timarchus* explains the procedures of the Assembly that brought *parrhêsia* into practice there: "When
the purifying sacrifice has gone around and the herald has recited the traditional (*patrious*) prayers, he bids the presiding officers to announce what
is to be next in order concerning the sacred affairs of the fatherland and the
heralds and ambassadors and the holy matters. After these things the herald
asks: 'Who of those who are above fifty years of age wishes to speak?' When
all these have spoken, he then bids any of the other Athenians who so wishes
to speak, those to whom it is permitted" (1.23).

[22] See also *To Nicocles*, 2.28.
[23] Monoson (2000: 60) writes about Demosthenes: "When on several occasions, Demosthenes
identifies his efforts to criticize a common Athenian viewpoint with the ideal of speaking
with *parrhêsia*, he explicitly contrasts his speech with flattering, deceitful, or self-promoting
oratory." She supports this claim with references to the *Fourth Philippic* 76, *Third Olynthic*
3; *First Philippic* 51; *On the Chersonese* 32; and *Third Philippic* 3–4.
[24] Raaflaub (2004: 221–5); Foucault (2001); Monoson (1994; 2000: chap. 2); Wallace (1996);
Momigliano (1973–4).

Socrates in Plato's *Protagoras* describes as well the openness of the Assembly. In that dialogue Socrates pushes his interlocutor who has claimed to teach the political craft to explain what precisely this political craft is and how it can be taught so that it creates good citizens. In order to clarify the question, Socrates describes the Assembly as a place where "when it is necessary to deliberate on something concerning the governance of the city (*poleôs dioikêseôs*)," anyone "carpenter, bronze worker, shoemaker, merchant, shop-owner, rich, poor, noble, lowly born" can stand up and participate in the deliberations (319cd).[25] The Assembly, as Socrates explains here – and as his interlocutors certainly know – allows all citizens, irrespective of social and economic status, to speak. This opportunity for all to speak is sometimes referred to as *isêgoria* and often, but not always, closely tied with *parrhêsia*. Henderson, for example, distinguishes between *isêgoria* as the practice that gave all citizens an equal opportunity to speak in the Assembly once the herald had asked, "Who wishes to speak?" and *parrhêsia*, which was the opportunity of every citizen not only to speak but "to voice frank criticism" (1998: 255). Raaflaub focuses on *isêgoria* as the older expression that captured the notion "not so much that a citizen, without being oppressed by a tyrant could express his opinion freely – that is, express it all – but that his opinion had the same weight as that of all other citizens who enjoyed full citizen rights" (2004: 222). In contrast, *parrhêsia*, according to Raaflaub, came in during the period of polarization around the Peloponnesian War when not only equality to have one's opinions heard, but also the freedom to speak critically and openly was defended (2004: 224–5). For Momigliano likewise: "*Isêgoria* implied equality of freedom of speech, but did not necessarily imply the right to say everything. On the other hand, *parrhêsia* looks like a word invented by a vigorous many for whom democratic life meant freedom from traditional inhibitions of speech" (1973–4: 260).[26] The terms *isêgoria* and *parrhêsia* clearly slide into one another, but it is *parrhêsia* that has more import for my interests as the term that captures the willingness to exhume the truth without concern about whom the truth may offend, though *isêgoria* captures the equality of opportunity to practice *parrhêsia*.

That there was the opportunity to speak did not necessarily mean that the attendees at the Assembly were required to listen. Socrates, in what may well be an ironic portrait of the activities in the Assembly, continues in his

---

[25] Farrar (1988: 79) comments with reference to this passage: "The Athenians, he asserts, recognize the existence of expertise with regard to 'technical' matters, but with respect to political questions they practice what amounts to free speech" (319b–d).

[26] See also Foucault (2001: 72) and J. D. Lewis (1971: 129) who notes that in Xenophon's *Cyropaideia* (1.3.10) *isêgoria* moves out of the political realm to mean a "lack of restraint in expressing opinions at social gatherings, a lack brought on by consumption of alcohol."

challenge to Protagoras to remark that while those in attendance may be happy to listen to the expert in the case of building a house or ship, should someone they think is not a craftsman (*dêmiougon*) attempt to offer advice to the Assembly, no matter how "beautiful or wealthy or well-born" he may be, they laugh at him and create a ruckus and drag him from his place (319c). We hear of such a scene from Xenophon who reports that poor young Glaucon who was trying to become a leader of the people (*dêmêgorein*) and was eager to become a leader in the city was most laughable (*katagelaston onta*) and consequently dragged off the *bêma*, the speaking platform (*Memorabilia*, 3.6.1).[27]

Aeschines, in contrast, again in his *Against Timarchus*, offers us a finely detailed sense of the decorum expected of those who spoke in the Assembly by quoting a law that supposedly governed the procedures in the Assembly: "If any one of the speakers speaks in the council or among the *dêmos* not about what has been brought before the Assembly or about each topic separately or twice about the same matter on the same day, or if he speaks abusively or speaks evilly (*kakôs*), or interrupts or in the midst of the discussions speaks on anything that is not before the Assembly... or takes hold of one who is in charge of the Assembly, then when the Assembly or the Council concludes, the ones in charge can write that person down as subject to a fine of not more than 50 drachma for each such injustice" (*adikêma*, 1.35). Beyond expectations of decorum, whether they were followed or not, there were also (and more significantly) restrictions on who among the citizens could enjoy *parrhêsia* in the Assembly. These were limitations according to law that were supposed to focus on the moral character of the citizen. First, of course, one had to be a citizen, but even a citizen could be disqualified if he (the pronoun is intentional) had been convicted of beating his parents[28] or of not supporting them or if he was a male prostitute[29] or if he still was a debtor or if his father owed money.[30] To Androtion, whom Demosthenes accuses of having proposed a decree in the Assembly even though he had been found guilty of prostitution, Demosthenes says, "being the sort of person that [Androtion] is," he must either show that he was innocent or accept the punishment for having spoken and having made proposals where and

[27] Roisman offers a range of other examples of such behavior (2004: 264–8).

[28] Aeschines, *Against Timarchus*, 1.28.

[29] E.g., Demosthenes, *Against Androtion*, 22.30; Aeschines, *Against Timarchus*, 1.3.14 (where *parrhêsia* is used). At 1.20 Aeschines notes that such a man is not allowed to speak his mind (*gnômên eipatô*) in the Boulê nor among the people (*dêmôi*) even if he is the most skilled in speech. Also 1.28 (*dêmêgorein*) and passim. As Wallace notes: "The Athenians did not make it illegal to be a male prostitute; indeed, they collected a part of the prostitute's profits by means of a tax. However, they restricted the rights of such men to govern the state" (1994: 128).

[30] Demosthenes, *Against Androtion*, 22.33 and *Against Arsitogeiton*, 26.1.

when he was not allowed to do so (22.29).[31] As Demosthenes says in his second speech *Against Aristogeiton*, the laws clearly forbid men who are lawbreakers – such as those who owe money to the state – from speaking. The reason is that they will cause harm to that which is shared, that which is common (*ta koina*, 26.2). Or Aeschines asks of those who have beaten their parents and failed to support them, how, if they have brought harm to those whom they should treat as gods, will they not also bring harm to what is common in the city (*ta koina tês poleôs*, *Against Timarchus*, 1.30)?

Freedom of speech is enshrined not for the benefit or freedom of the individual; it exists in the vision of these orators for the sake of the city. The one whose actions and character demonstrate a supposed incapacity to add to the welfare of the common (*ta koina*) can make no claim to the practice of *parrhêsia*. As discussed in Chapter 1, *parrhêsia* at Athens does not allow for the individual self-expression or autonomy so important in contemporary discourse. It rests on serving a regime that depends on the open expression of its citizens' views. The one who is marked as a male prostitute would not speak, it was thought, to the welfare of the whole,[32] nor would a "shield thrower," nor would one who owed money, nor one who beat his parents and causes harm in his own home.

Aeschines emphatically affirms that it was the concern with the moral character of citizens that lay behind these limitations placed on the exercise of *parrhêsia* and he supports this contention by remarking that when the originator of the law (supposedly Solon) considered who should and should not speak before the Assembly, he ensured that the opportunity to speak was open to all citizens, irrespective of wealth or background: "He does not deny the benefit of going to the platform (*bêma*) if someone was not the son of ancestors who served as generals, nor if he practiced a craft in order to earn his necessary nourishment; those he especially welcomes, and for this reason he frequently asks who wishes to address the Assembly" (1.27). And Aeschines adds shortly after: "He thought that the speech that came from a noble and good man, even if it was spoken badly and simply, was useful to those who were listening. But from a boisterous man and one who had used his own body most foolishly, and had shamefully spent his family's wealth, such a one even if he spoke eloquently, he thought, would not benefit the hearers" (1.31). While *parrhêsia* becomes in Aeschines' vision a mechanism of equality, its denial was not only a way to ensure the safety of the city but served also as a punishment for those who had defied the moral standards of the community, for those who lacked any sense of shame. That the loss

---

[31] Hunter writes of men who maltreated their wives, did not perform their military duty or threw away their swords, or were prostitutes: "If one of these spoke in the assembly, anyone might challenge him there, calling upon him to undergo a scrutiny" (1994: 104).

[32] See Winkler's discussion of just this point in his treatment of Aeschines' *Against Timarchus* (1990: 56–7). Also Dover (1989: 109) and Halperin (1990: 94–9).

of *parrhêsia* could serve as a form of punishment suggests again the value citizens placed on it. Nevertheless, despite references in a variety of texts from the fourth century to such punishments, we should also be careful to note that there is only one specific case referenced in the ancient corpus to the so-called *dokimasia tôn rhêtorôn* (scrutiny of the speakers) and that is Aeschines' speech against Timarchus from around 345 BCE (Hansen 1974: 24).[33]

It appears from a reading of the speeches of the fourth-century orators that by the fourth century the Assembly no longer practiced the decorum of the earlier periods of Athenian history that Aeschines perhaps imagined and had so praised in his *Against Timarchus*. His *Against Ctesiphon* offers another story of *parrhêsia*, no doubt one again tinged with the all too familiar tendency to romanticize the behavior of his forefathers. Nevertheless, listen to his speech:

I would wish, O men of Athens, that the council of the Five Hundred and the Assemblies were correctly governed by those who are in charge of them, and that the laws which Solon legislated concerning the seemly behavior of the speakers were in force, so that it would be possible that first those of the citizens who are the oldest, as the laws affirm, would come modestly to the platform without the clamor and disorder. And from their experience to advise the city what is best for it. Then the ones wishing [to speak] of the other citizens according to age and in turn would uncover their thought on each issue. Thus, it seems to me, the city would be ruled in the best fashion and there would be the fewest court cases. But now all those which we previously agreed worked well have been dissolved... The speech of those who are the best and the most moderate of those in the city has been silenced.

(*Against Ctesiphon*, 3.2–4)[34]

In contrast to this romanticism about the practice of *parrhêsia* as the mark of the egalitarian regime of the Athenians, the practice enjoyed by citizens but not foreigners, by the virtuous but not the vile, concerns about the practice itself surface in the literature of antiquity as well. In Plato's *Protagoras* where Socrates offers his portrait of the Assembly in the passage quoted previously, we may certainly sense some ambiguity and irony when Socrates describes the Assembly as the place where all – carpenter and bronze-worker, shoemaker, and merchant – can speak freely.[35] With the fifth-century author appropriately dubbed the "Old Oligarch," there is no ambiguity. In his little pamphlet with its peculiar sharp twist of critical sarcasm, the "Old Oligarch" praises the Athenians for being so successful at maintaining the political power of the "bad"/poor rather than allowing

---

[33] It is from this speech that I have drawn most of my evidence about the practice in Athens – as indeed have most of those writing on *parrhêsia* in Athens.

[34] See also Aeschines, *Against Timarchus*, 1.21–2.

[35] Contrast the portrait of the assemblies offered by Socrates in the *Republic* (492b–c; 493a–d).

the "good"/rich to rule. He notes in particular: "Someone might say that they ought not to allow everyone to speak in turn and serve on the council, but only those who are most skilled and the best men (*tous dexiôtatous kai andras aristous*). But they, in this matter, also deliberate in the best fashion allowing even those who are the lowliest sorts (*tous ponêrous*) to speak. For if those who are best were to speak and deliberate, for they themselves it would be good, but it would not be good for the men of the people. But now whoever wishes stands up and even if this is a lowly person, he discovers and pursues what is good for himself" (6). The pamphlet of the "Old Oligarch" is an ideological piece, but more serious issues exploring the implications of *parrhêsia* surface elsewhere in the literature of the ancient Athenians. Foucault (2001) has pointed out that *parrhêsia* as truth telling in the Assembly travels significantly from that venue to the agora to the gymnasia and to the homes where Socrates engages in dialogue with young and old, citizens and foreigners. And this movement from public life to private life has multiple consequences that point to the multihued texture of the practice.

Book 8 of the *Republic*, in particular, helps alert us to the problematic nature of this venerated practice as it shifts to varied social venues. There, Socrates describes the democratic regime of free men, full of freedom (*eleutherias*) and, as he explicitly says, *parrhêsia*,[36] where each person has license (*exousia*) to do whatever he may wish (557b). Behind this freedom, as pleasant and beautiful as it may be in Socrates' sketch, lies an undercurrent of worry as Socrates' democratic regime marches directly toward tyranny. When Socrates remarks on the "freedom of the multitude, where slaves and not slaves and women and men enjoy freedom and *isonomia*" (563b), Adeimantus interjects with the quote from Aeschylus that I have cited before: "Shall we not according to Aeschylus 'say whatever comes into our mouths'" (563c). Of course, saying whatever comes into our mouths without fear of punishment opens the door not only for the expression of the truth of one's own beliefs, but also for blasphemous speech against the gods, for speech that not only unveils what is true, but speech that can harm others and the city as a whole.

This freedom of speech – a hallmark of the Athenian democracy, enshrined in the name of a ship of the state, separating citizen from foreigner – becomes

---

[36] Foucault reads the use of *parrhêsia* here as "pejorative": "This pejorative sense occurs in Plato, for example, as a characterization of the bad democratic constitution where everyone has the right to address his fellow citizens and to tell them anything – even the most stupid and dangerous things for the city" (2001: 13). I do not see *parrhêsia* as pejorative in the *Republic* passage since the democracy that it characterizes is the only regime that incorporates within it the "greatest number of paradigms of regimes and types of people" (561e) and thus would be a regime in which a Socrates could flourish. Foucault also sees Plato as concerned about the chaotic diversity that emerges from *parrhêsia* (2001: 84–5). I rather see a Socrates who welcomes the diversity that allows for a philosopher such as himself.

an ambiguous freedom.[37] In Socrates' portrait, the freedom of democracy means the loss of the capacity to understand limits and boundaries, distinctions between necessary and unnecessary desires, which lets the regime fall violently into tyranny.[38] As the orators of the fourth century suggest, Athens of the fourth century likewise lost the capacity to distinguish between a noble *parrhêsia* that revealed truthfulness and an ignoble rhetoric that covered and distorted truth. The shading of the boundaries between a freedom to be treasured and a freedom to be feared tarnished the pride of Athenian democracy in the fourth century. In *On the Peace* Isocrates remarks: "I know that it is an uphill battle to oppose your opinions and that although this is a democracy (*dêmokratias*) there is no *parrhêsia* except among those who are most without prudence (*aphronestatois*) and who care nothing about you" (8.14). In the *Areopagitica*, he continues this theme, criticizing the decline in contemporary morals by recalling the virtues of the earlier regime when democracy at Athens first appeared. Then, it was a gentle regime before "lawlessness (*paranomian*) was confused with freedom (*eleutherian*) and before *parrhêsian* was confused with equality with in the law (*isonomian*) and the license (*exousian*) to do all things with happiness (*eudaimonian*)" (7.20). The treasured freedom of speech in this work from around 355 BCE no longer is treasured, but is a practice contributing to the lawlessness of the city drunk on its own excesses. That potential tarnishing of the practice was, however, acknowledged considerably earlier as the playwrights, especially Aristophanes and Euripides, explored the darker side of the passion for this freedom to express what one truly believes, to live as the parrhesiast.

In the comedies of Aristophanes and the tragedies of Euripides we find this undercurrent of the potential harm that may come from the freedom for all to speak frankly. The dramatic works expose the latent dangers of free speech, just as Socrates' free democracy foreshadows the precipitous slide into tyranny from the unbounded freedom of the democratic regime and the democratic man. For Aristophanes and Euripides free speech is not simply an egalitarian expression of opinions as ecclesiasts openly debate public policy with a view to the welfare of that which is shared, *ta koina*. It can instead be an exclusionary practice perpetuating inequalities and it can uncover truths that give rise to tragedy. The shamelessness of *parrhêsia* can be destructive of the political community as well as creative and necessary for the philosophic life. The trial of Socrates lets us see these concerns put into practice.

---

[37] Roisman also sees the ambivalent role of *parrhêsia*, but he does so noting the way in which "the power of speech . . . could problematize the power hierarchy in the city with the *dêmos* at its head" (2004: 261).

[38] I develop this argument in Saxonhouse (1998).

5

The Trial of Socrates

In the archonship of Laches (400/399) Anytus, Meletus, and Lycos brought a public indictment against Socrates. It read:

Swearing an oath Meletus the son of Meletus of Pitthos brought a public action against Socrates the son of Sophroniscus of Alopeke; he said Socrates was guilty of not believing in the gods that the city believed in, and that he brought into the city other new divinities. Further, he is guilty of corrupting the young. The punishment is death. (Diogenes Laertius 2.40)[1]

Meletus as the main accuser was liable to a fine of 1,000 drachma if fewer than one fifth of the jurors found Socrates guilty. Thus began the trial of Socrates. It ended when the jurors voted 280 to 221 for a guilty verdict and when they followed with a vote for the penalty of death. Meletus did not have to pay any fine.

1. WHY WAS SOCRATES EXECUTED?

The trial of Socrates has served for many generations as a symbol of the violation of freedom of expression, the case that sets the individual committed to the "examined life" against a city that can find in this examination impiety and the corruption of the young. It is the incident that speaks to all who fear oppression for the expression of one's beliefs and thoughts. As J. S. Mill writes in *On Liberty*:

Mankind can hardly be too often reminded that there was once a man named Socrates, between whom and the legal authorities and public opinion of his time there took place a memorable collision. Born in an age and country abounding in

---

[1] Xenophon describes the *graphê* (indictment) against Socrates as "something of this sort (*toiade*): Socrates is unjust (*adikei*), not believing in (*nomizôn*) the gods in whom the polis believes (*nomizei*), and brings in other new *daimonia*. He is unjust and also corrupts (*diaphtheiron*)" (*Apology of Socrates Before the Jurors*, 10).

individual greatness, this man has been handed down to us by those who best knew both him and the age as the most virtuous man in it... This acknowledged master of all the eminent thinkers who have since lived – whose fame, still growing after more than two thousand years, all but outweighs the whole remainder of the names which make his native city illustrious – was put to death by his countrymen, after a judicial conviction, for impiety and immorality... Of these charges the tribunal, there is every ground for believing, honestly found him guilty, and condemned the man who probably of all then born had deserved best of mankind, to be put to death as a criminal.   ([1851] 1978: 23)

Over and over, other writers refer to Socrates as a "martyr for free speech."[2] The irony of Socrates' case, though, comes from the fact that he was sentenced to death, made this martyr to free speech by a democratic regime identified with freedom and, as we have seen, most especially with the freedom of speech. This was the regime whose citizens voted to name a publicly financed ship *Parrhêsia*. How can we reconcile the democratic freedoms of Athens with the execution of the man who dared to speak freely about his own ignorance, virtue, and the pursuit of excellence? A common response to Socrates' execution is bewilderment that the democratic regime at Athens could actually carry out the trial and impose the death sentence. "How could a jury in Greece's greatest democracy have put to death Greece's greatest philosopher?" asks Connor (1991: 49). Brickhouse and Smith begin their detailed analysis of Socrates' trial with the question: "Why did the jurors – members of the world's first democracy – find him guilty?" (2002: 1). Underlying the question is the assumption that because Athens was a democracy, the citizen jurors should not have found him, practicing *parrhêsia* according to their customs, guilty.

For others, though, the wonder and glory of Athens is that it took so long to bring Socrates to trial. Only in a democracy, it is claimed, could he have survived. Grote writing specifically about the trial comments:

When we reflect upon this great body of antipathy, so terrible from number and from constituent items, we shall wonder only that Sokrates could have gone on so long standing in the market-place to aggravate it, and that the indictment of Meletus could have been so long postponed... The truth is, that as history presents to us only one man who ever devoted his life to prosecute this duty of an elenchic,

---

[2] The language is from Berti (1978), but similarly dramatic exclamations can be found throughout the literature. Martin Luther King, Jr. in his "Letter from Birmingham City Jail" wrote: "To a degree academic freedom is a reality today because Socrates practiced civil disobedience" ([1963] 1986: 294). He is repeating exactly what he wrote two years earlier in an address on "Love, Law and Civil Disobedience" ([1961] 1986: 50); and Villa quotes (2001: 14) Arendt's essay "Philosophy and Politics" from 1954 where she says "The gulf between philosophy and politics opened historically with the trial and condemnation of Socrates" as well as Euben (1990: 204). See also Bollinger and Stone (2002: ix). For a sweep of Socrates' place as a martyr for free speech (or not) see the engaging chapter on Socrates in Lane (2001).

or cross-examining missionary, so there was but one city, in the ancient world at least, wherein he would have been allowed to prosecute it for twenty-five years with safety and impunity; and that city was Athens... It was th[e] established lib- erality of democratical sentiment at Athens which so long protected the noble eccentricity of Sokrates from being disturbed by the numerous enemies which he provoked.   ([1851–6] 1900: 8.466–7)

Further on, Grote reiterates his defense of Athens: "It is certain that there was at Athens both a keener intellectual stimulus, and greater freedom as well of thought as of speech, than in any other city of Greece. The long toleration of Sokrates is one example of this general fact, while his trial proves little, and his execution nothing, against it" ([1851–6] 1900: 8.467).

Many writers follow Grote's lead and avoid the quandary posed by Socrates' execution by using Socrates' case in order to illustrate the openness (not the intolerance) of Athenian democracy toward speech. These authors affirm the view of Athens as fundamentally tolerant, with Socrates' trial, "the decision to prosecute an old man for saying and doing what he had been say- ing and doing for so many years," as an aberration, perhaps brought about by "the wounds of recent history" (Parker 1996: 147).[3] The "recent history" to which Parker here refers is the violent tyranny of the Thirty set in place by the victorious Spartans after the Peloponnesian War. In 399 when Socrates was brought to trial, the democracy had only recently been reestablished and Socrates' association with members of the Thirty suggested to some his polit- ical connections with the enemies of democracy. This reading of Socrates' trial comes in part from Aeschines' *Against Timarchus* where he chides the Athenians: "You, Athenians, killed Socrates the Sophist because he appeared to have taught Critias" (1.173); Critias was one of the Thirty Tyrants, as was Charmides, unnamed by Aeschines, but also one of Socrates' associates who became a member of the Thirty.

In this version of Socrates' trial, it is not an issue of freedom of speech or the violation of *parrhêsia*, but the insecurities of the newly resurrected democracy that allow an anxious Athens to bring to trial a Socrates who appears less than loyal to the stumbling regime. To exacerbate the situation Socrates' exhortations to asceticism – not caring about money or good food – could even be attributed by some to a desire to emulate the Spartan way of life, just at a time when anti-Spartan feeling would have been at its height.[4] Or in another of Grote's readings, the aberration in the tolerant Athens may not have been bound up in political events at all, but have been the result of paternal jealousy, fathers who were disturbed by the pleasure their sons

---

[3] Roberts (1994: 250) quotes a book entitled *Democracy in Europe* from 1850 in which the author marvels that Socrates was "able to ply his pesky trade as long as he did" and concludes that "there was far more toleration in Pagan Athens, than in Christian Spain."

[4] For this argument see Strauss (1993: 201) and Connor (1991: 54–5).

seemed to find in conversing with Socrates.[5] Such explanations ignore the culture of *parrhêsia* and look to other conditions of the social life in Athens to explain what seems to so many to be inexplicable.[6]

The inclination to safeguard Athens' reputation is strong: Wallace, for example, admits that "an element of popular prejudice" certainly existed, but "nothing happened to Sokrates until he was seventy years old" (1994: 142–3). Defending the freedom that pervaded the Athenian polity, Wallace adds that the astronomer Damon was not ostracized for his religious views and that "year after year the Athenians, including the lower classes, paid to hear various characters in Euripides utter the grossest blasphemy [and]... for more than forty years he [Plato] was allowed to say what he wanted, unharmed, behind the walls of his Academy" (1994: 143). Scholars who suggest that Athens was less tolerant than some might wish with regard to unconventional speech may refer to Anaxagoras' supposed trial for saying the moon was just a large stone and to the decree proposed around 432 BCE by Diopeithes against blasphemy for those who do not acknowledge the divine or "who teach about things in the air" (Plutarch, *Nicias*, 23.2; *Pericles*, 32.1). But whether Anaxagoras was ever charged on the basis of Diopeithes' decree and even whether the law was ever enforced against anyone at all remains unclear. Diogenes Laertius records Protagoras' (in)famous statement: "Concerning the gods, I am not able to know either that they are or that they are not. For many things prevent knowing this, both the absence of any clarity about it and the shortness of human life" (9.51–2). Diogenes then continues: "On account of this beginning of his written work, he was thrown out by the Athenians, and they burnt his works in the agora, after the books were collected by the herald from each person who had them among their possessions" (9.52). And yet, the evidence from the far more contemporary Plato in his dialogue with Protagoras as Socrates' interlocutor suggests that when Protagoras visited Athens shortly before the Peloponnesian War, far from having his books burned in the marketplace, his arrival was heralded and met with much enthusiasm by a fair number of the Athenians.[7] The concerns were not about his blasphemies, but about the sort of education in the art of politics that he offered to the young.

---

[5] See citations in Strauss (1993: 199, 350n37). Strauss himself discusses this theory of "paternal jealousy" with appropriate modesty. "No analysis of the trial places father-son relations at center stage, and I am not about to do so here. I would argue, however, that the continuing debate in Athens about fathers and sons is an important undercurrent, a secondary motif, in the hammering out of Socrates' fate" (1993: 199).

[6] Munn (2002: 290) at one point in his analysis of the trial avoids the theoretical issues of a democracy trying Socrates by suggesting that the trial was the result of a personal vendetta with Meletus, disagreeing with Grote who had identified Anytus as the mastermind behind the trial. This ignores the Athenians in the jury who went along with the accusations – all the way to decreeing death.

[7] Chapter 8 discusses Protagoras' visit as represented by Plato.

Wallace, for one, maintains: "I believe that the Athenians only got exercised about intellectual speculation when this activity was conducted in public and affected the polis. The proof of this is most obviously furnished by Plato. Plato's philosophy was fundamentally antidemocratic and also probably impious by normal Athenian standards" (1994: 143). Echoing Pericles' oration, Wallace concludes: "The Athenians punished those who were judged to have harmed the polis, its public enemies, but they left the private citizens alone" (146). Hansen in his turn almost tries to excuse Socrates' execution by noting that the trial is "the only attested case of an Athenian having been put on trial for what he thought or said" (1995: 20–1). He then apologizes for the Athenians: "The condemnation and execution of Socrates demonstrates that the Athenians did not always live up to their own ideals; but that those ideals were not just empty words is apparent both from the presumption that the trial of Sokrates was unique in Athenian history and from the fact that Sokrates . . . lived to be seventy" (21).

There are others who are not so generous with Athens or so ready to defend her, who continue to find it difficult to understand how a democracy so devoted to *parrhêsia* could have snuffed out the life of one dedicated to that very practice by so unreservedly questioning all those around him. Perhaps the most famous recent expression of this bewilderment at democracy's execution of Socrates comes from I. F. Stone. This legendary spokesperson for freedom of speech in America had been appalled (or as he says "horrified" and "torment[ed]") that Athenian democracy – that great realm of supposed political freedom – executed someone who had spoken freely (1988: xi). His torment over the issue led him to begin the study of ancient Greek when he was well into his seventies. The hemlock and Athenian democracy seemed so antithetical to Stone that the only way for him to reconcile the execution of Socrates with Athenian democracy after all his investigations was not to find Athens guilty, but to explain the trial by Socrates' inveterate hostility to democracy. According to Stone's theory, Socrates was too proud and dismissive of democracy to point out to Athens that it failed to live up to its principles by condemning him. If only, Stone protested, Socrates had been willing to recognize democracy's advantages, he could have avoided the fatal hemlock. Socrates was just not sufficiently democratic to enjoy the benefits of free speech that democracies espouse.

Vlastos similarly lays some of the blame on Socrates' "aggressiveness," not so much in his dismissiveness of democracy as in his religious zeal: "If Socrates had been content to pursue his philosophizing in private conversations with fellow seekers after truth, he need have had no fear that his unorthodox religious views would have gotten him into trouble with the law. Since he wrote no books, the opinions he debated with his friends would not have made him vulnerable to prosecution. What did, was the aggressiveness of the public mission" (1991: 297).[8] In similar language, Hansen comes back to the issue. He "sums up": "Sokrates was sentenced for not sharing the ordinary Athenian's views about the gods." Yet, he continues, Socrates was "not put on trial for having these views, but rather for having propagated them to his followers every day, year in, year out" (1995: 26). As Hansen phrases it: "Sokrates was not charged with being an atheist, but with being a missionary" (1995: 26). As an atheist who recruited others to his (dis)beliefs, Socrates threatened the very welfare of the city according to this view.[9] Further, Hansen notes: "What was dangerous about Sokrates was not the views he had about democracy, but his propagation of such views to anyone who cared to attend his daily discussions in the Agora" (1995: 21). Hansen is eager to defend the Athenians' commitment to freedom of speech and freedom of conscience and thus suggests that Socrates just went too far: "Sokrates might have avoided the trial if he had been more cautious, and he might have incurred a milder punishment if he had been more modest" (1995: 30).

Munn in his trenchant analysis goes beyond an initial suggestion that the trial was the result of a personal vendetta on the part of Meletus to the broader issue of Socrates' contempt for the sovereignty of the assembled public, but again the blame falls on Socrates, not the democracy: it was Socrates' arrogance, Munn asserts, that set his personal *daemon* above the collective wisdom of the city and that brought to Socrates democracy's condemnation (2000: 286–7). Munn concludes that we can find many reasons for the trial and execution, but he himself finds Socrates guilty of clinging to principles that still refused to acknowledge "the sovereignty of the people" (2000: 291).[10] In similar fashion, Stone had cited Socrates' pride and arrogance vis-à-vis the *dêmos*. Such discussions turn away from interpreting democracy as a realm of freedoms understood in the language of rights toward democracy as a set of institutions that allowed for popular rule – even if that rule might abridge the freedom to criticize it.[11]

According to the interpretations of the trial such as those offered by Munn, Stone, and Vlastos, Socrates himself brings on the hemlock by his

---

[8] Villa recently has followed Vlastos' lead in arguing for a Socrates perceived as aggressive in his stance, not so much with regard to his impiety, but with regard to his hostility to the people. He was, as Villa argues, a *misodemos*, "an enemy of the people" (2001: 3).

[9] See Lysias, *Against Nicomachus* (30: 18–20) for a sense of the hostility to those who might interfere with the performance of the ancestral rites.

[10] Munn's language here resonates anachronistically especially of Rousseau. Hansen without using the language of "sovereignty of the people" does suggest that in addition to Socrates' beliefs about the gods there was "his critical view of the Athenian democratic institutions" (1995: 19).

[11] On the laws against sedition in the United States see Curtis (2000). See the extended discussion in Chapter 1.

own arrogant dismissal of the freedoms offered by the democratic regime
more than by the impiety for which he was tried. For them, Socrates –
though he practices *parrhêsia* – is the antidemocratic man who trivializes the
sovereignty of the people and scorns the laws by which they as a community live. These interpretations emphasize democracy as the sovereign people
deliberating about a common future and decreeing the laws by which they
govern themselves. They understand democracy as popular sovereignty, not
as the absence of restraint, the freedoms of Book 8 of the *Republic* where the
institutions of democracy are absent and Socrates focuses on the psychological and (what we would today call) the cultural aspects of democracy. These
two different conceptions of democracy clash harshly in efforts to understand the trial of Socrates. I. F. Stone focused on democracy as a regime
of freedom where the execution of Socrates is an aberration. Munn, ever
attentive to issues of popular sovereignty, sees the execution almost as consistent with the principles of democratic governance where the decisions of
the people are the laws. For us, these varied readings of the execution suggest
the complexity of setting Socrates' trial within the multilayered language of
democracy. That language when beholden to conceptions of a sovereign
people may well deny the freedom of speech that we nevertheless so closely
associate with democratic practice.[12]

The theories that emphasize Socrates' impiety in their turn must struggle
with the problem of what exactly impiety is. What would an ancient Athenian
mean by piety? Is it to practice the cults or to believe in the gods? The
Greek *nomizein* that is used in the indictment against Socrates gives us little
guidance here and scholars have gone both ways and in between as well
(Connor 1991: 50n10, 53, 55; Parker 1996: 151). Socrates' presumed impiety,
though, touches on the core problem of *parrhêsia* and democracy. Could a
society grounded on devotion to the peculiar gods of Athens, irrespective
of the democratic organization of its political life with its assemblies and
public festivals, endure a shameless Socrates who questioned divine things
just as he questioned human things? Could it endure one who appeared
uninhibited by any reverence for a hierarchy that set the gods above men,
or at least the gods of one's own city above the gods of other cities? After
all, Plato begins the *Republic* with Socrates showing little reverence for the
gods of his own city when he praises the new god of the Thracians more
than the gods of Athens (327a). And then there was Socrates' reaction when
Chaerephon went to Delphi to ask the god Apollo who was the wisest man;
as Socrates tells this story in Plato's *Apology*, the oracle answered that no
one was wiser than Socrates.[13] Socrates' response when told of the oracle's

---

[12] One need only think of the chapter on civil religion in Rousseau's *Social Contract* here, but
see also Rabban's remarkable book (1997) and Curtis (2000).

[13] Xenophon's report of the oracle's response to Socrates is markedly different: "When
Chaerephon once asked at Delphi about me with many people present, the oracle responded

answer is to contest the words of the god, to question and perhaps prove the god wrong. Ultimately, he fails in this endeavor and describes himself by the end of the speech as carrying out the tasks to which he has been assigned by the god and the oracle to perform, but only after his interrogation of the politicians, the poets, and the artisans as part of his effort to show the fallibility of a reliance on the oracle and thereby the gods as the source of knowledge. Socrates reacts to the speech of the god with the same level of critical inquiry – or the effort to uncover – that he devotes to human things.

Can the culture of democracy endure the blasphemy that may accompany the freedom of daring speech practiced in the deliberative Assembly and the fantasy world of the comic stage? Can it endure the citizen who so brashly challenges the wisdom of the gods? Can it suffer the one who inspires what Dana Villa calls "a corrosive intellectual honesty" (2001: 20) in his fellow citizens? Part of the difficulty that those assessing why Socrates was executed bring upon themselves comes from the contemporary attachment between freedom of speech and freedom of religion. The First Amendment of the U.S. Constitution covers both: "Congress shall make no law respecting an establishment of religion, or prohibiting the free exercise thereof; or abridging the freedom of speech."[14] For the writers of the First Amendment, freedom of religion could easily be incorporated into the same amendment as freedom of speech or vice versa. Neither freedom would harm, but only help, in ensuring the perfection of the regime dedicated to individual freedom from governmental interference.[15] Such a view, though, depended on the notion that public order did not come from a pious devotion to the gods of the city. As Jefferson had written: "It does me no harm for my neighbor to say that there are no gods or twenty gods; it neither picks my pocket nor breaks my leg."[16]

While this view holds well for the early liberals who saw a conformity of religious beliefs as unnecessary in a political world that separated public and private, for the Athenians freedom of speech could not be uttered in the

---

that there was no one among humans who was freer (*eleutheriôteron*) nor more just (*dikaioteron*) nor more moderate (*sôphronesteron*)" (*The Apology of Socrates Before the Jurors*, 14). There is nothing here about Socrates' wisdom that might provoke the Socratic questioning of the god's own wisdom.

[14] The First Amendment, of course, continues, "or of the press; or the right of the people peaceably to assemble, and to petition the Government for a redress of grievances," but these are obviously not applicable to a discussion of the direct democracy of Athens two millennia before the invention of the printing press.

[15] See Chapter 1, pages 18–19, for a brief review of how these freedoms joined to become one amendment (apparently without much discussion) and the political theory behind this modern liberal perspective in contrast to the Athenian perspective.

[16] I am indebted to Lorraine Pangle for pointing out to me the relevance of this quotation in this context.

same breath as a totally alien notion of freedom of religion.[17] The former is *parrhêsia*, the latter *anaidôs*, the lack of respect for what demanded reverence. The former refers in part to an Athens where the herald in the Assembly asks: "Who wishes to speak?," but he does so only after the prayers to gods of the city have been said, after the city affirms its piety and respect for the gods. *Parrhêsia* led to debates in the Assembly critical to deliberations about what the city would do and what laws it might pass for itself. It did not lead to the questioning of the divine. That was not, as the Athenians understood it, part of *parrhêsia*. As Richard Mulgan reminds us, "Whatever view we take of the reasons for the trial of Socrates...no one, least of all Socrates himself, questioned the legitimacy of the charge itself. It was taken for granted that a citizen could be convicted of corrupting the young and believing in strange gods" (1984: 15).

While the Assembly and the law courts provided the institutional setting for the daring frankness associated with *parrhêsia*, the difficulty emerged as to where the boundaries of frankness might have been set when one looks outside the political institutions and the comic stage. As noted previously, in Book 8 of the *Republic*, Socrates describing the freedom and license (*eleutheria* and *exousia*) of the democratic regime "full of *parrhêsia*" (557b) finds Adeimantus saying: "Won't we...with Aeschylus, say 'whatever just came to our lips'?" (563b). Adeimantus reminds the audience at Cephalus' house (as well as contemporary readers) that whatever comes to one's lips may just as easily lead to blasphemy as to praise of the gods. Blasphemy is certainly one of the freedoms enjoyed by the inhabitants of the schematic and unreal democracy Socrates describes in the *Republic*; they see no distinction between speaking about themselves and about the gods, or seeing themselves as both human and divine. They thus transform the gentle regime of democratic freedom first described in the *Republic* into the unbounded force of the tyrannical regime where the tyrant rules drunkenly over both humans and gods (573c). Blasphemy and tyranny emerge directly from the egalitarianism, the license to say whatever comes to one's lips and the unwillingness to make distinctions between good and bad speech that pervade the democracy Socrates describes in Book 8.[18]

As he sketches the democratic regime, Socrates follows Adeimantus' suggestion in Book 8 about life in such a polity, saying whatever comes to his

---

[17] See the excellent discussion of John Stuart Mill's interpretation of Socrates' execution in Biagini (1996: 35–6). As Biagini shows, Mill understood how the pre-Christian ancients might understand the criticism of religious practices and beliefs as "other-regarding" and thus not protected from the intervention of governmental authority in the way that self-regarding actions such as contemporary religious beliefs would be.

[18] We hear echoes of this concern (though without the issue of blasphemy, but rather of hate speech), for example, in Bollinger (1986: 247) who worries that the free speech principle in American jurisprudence "could become a method of inculcating a kind of toleration that turns naturally into passivity and uncritical obedience."

lips and offering a vision of the horses and asses of a democracy who do not step aside for whomever – citizen or not – these animals might meet on the road. The extension of this picture of democracy is to imagine humans not stepping aside for the gods, not showing *aidôs*, respect or reverence, for that which is divine, rebuffing any hierarchical model that might set them into a subordinate relation to the divine. If the animals of the democracy do not show *aidôs* for the human form, why should humans display *aidôs* for the gods? In a regime of such equality without *aidôs*, where there is no deference to hierarchy between men and animals or between gods and men (or by extension between animals and gods), blasphemy as such is meaningless and the outrageousness of Aristophanes' comedies immediately comes to mind. The freedom to speak whatever comes from one's lips belongs in a democratic regime (and on the comic stage) that has banished *aidôs*. The democratic regime lacking *aidôs* – unlike the Callipolis with its hierarchical structure ensured by the noble lie that Socrates and his interlocutors founded earlier in the *Republic*, unlike the Athens described in the *Laws* where *aidôs* is the despotic master subsuming all to a slavery before the laws (698b) – is a regime in which Socrates himself could survive. The multihued democracy described in Book 8 has room, as Socrates imagines it, for all sorts of souls: "On account of its license," Socrates says, "it has every species of regime" (557d).[19] It is also a regime in which the condemned man does not drink the hemlock, but "stays in the middle of things…and wanders as if a hero" (558a). But, this multihued democracy is emphatically not a description of the democratic regime at Athens in which Socrates lived and practiced his inquiries, the regime in which he is executed.[20] *Aidôs* had not deserted Athens.

As Socrates continues to develop his portrait of the "gentleness" of this imaginary democratic regime that takes the concepts of equality and freedom to their extremes, he asks: "Is not the gentleness towards certain of the condemned charming? Or have you not yet seen in such a regime those men for whom there has been the vote of death or exile, nevertheless still remaining and carrying on right in the middle of things with no one paying much attention or seeing him stalking the land like a hero?" (558a). Athens, for sure, does not allow those sentenced to death to continue to "stalk the land as a hero." Only if Athens had been able to dispense fully with *aidôs*, as does Socrates' democracy of the *Republic*, only if Athens could have allowed the condemned to live within the city, could it be the fully free and parrhesiastic city it imagined itself to be. Only then would it have matched Socrates' imaginative description of democracy as a city without *aidôs*. Protagoras in his myth had said that the one without *aidôs* should be killed as a disease in the

---

[19] See also Strauss (1964: 131) for the openness of democracy to the philosopher.
[20] See the discussion of the relation between Athens and the description of democracy in the *Republic* in Chapter 2, page 48 and the reference in note 26; also Saxonhouse (1994).

city. The Athenians have taken Zeus' injunction (as reported by Protagoras, of course), and not Socrates' democratic theory, to heart.

The story of Socrates' execution that appears in Socrates' speech as presented by Plato in the *Apology of Socrates* is that of a man who exercises the democratic virtue of *parrhêsia* to its fullest, but not in the deliberative body of the Assembly. Rather, shedding *aidôs* like the Lydian women of whom Gyges spoke, he exercises it everywhere, whether he is in the private or public spaces of Athens. What may be the most famous and often cited line from Socrates (or at least from the *Apology*) – "the unexamined life is not worth living" – appeals to a life dedicated to uncovering, to searching for a truth that lies behind veils of customs, behind the public and private facades, behind the hierarchies established only by traditions. For Socrates the examiner nothing is too sacred to remain covered by a deference to or reverence for what is. Like the democratic man active in the Assembly, Socrates judges that he must reveal and examine all wherever he is as a condition of his legitimate participation in the life of the city. In much the same way as for the comic poet who presents all on stage, for Socrates nothing is too sacred to escape thrusting it forward for observation and examination. When Socrates affirms that the unexamined life is not worth living, his speech recalls Polyneices' speech from Euripides' *Phoenician Women*, which I will discuss in detail below.[21] Polyneices, unable to speak freely, lacking *parrhêsia* while living as an exile, finds this life of a slave intolerable. Both Polyneices and Socrates demand the freedom to uncover their thoughts to those with power, to speak without deference for the hierarchies in force and tell those in power that they act or think foolishly. To live otherwise is for Polyneices to be a slave, for Socrates to be less than human.

In the *Apology*, Socrates practices *parrhêsia*, his freedom of speech, as he dismisses any hierarchical structure that would place him in a subordinate and obsequious position before the jury of democratic citizens, that would make him like Polyneices a slave in a foreign land. Displaying no *aidôs* for those who are about to judge him,[22] honoring his own *daemon* rather than subjecting himself to the power of the assembled people, he rebukes the Athenians for failing to follow their own ancient constitution when they tried the generals for impiety in abandoning the corpses at the battle of Arginusae. He takes the focus away from himself and turns the gaze on them. He becomes their critic and chastiser, the one who speaks to them honestly about their faults, without awe. He is the parrhesiastic democrat, not their suppliant.

Rather than read Socrates' trial either as an indictment of Athens for being less tolerant than it claimed to be or (in Grote's terms) as praise for

---

[21] Chapter 6, pages 140–1.
[22] See Brann (1978) for the significance of the varied forms of address that Socrates uses in the *Apology* for the jurors.

an Athens that allowed Socrates to live for so long saying what he did or (in I. F. Stone's terms) as Socrates' own fault, my goal is to explore what the trial says about the principles upon which democracy is built and the place of *parrhêsia* (and more generally philosophic exploration) in it. This, of necessity, takes us back to *aidôs* and *anaidôs*, shame and shamelessness. *Parrhêsia* in its capacity of revealing denies the division between public and private, what is shared and what is hidden; one's innermost thoughts are revealed and opened in the practice of free speech. There is no realm of privacy before the Socratic practice of *parrhêsia* and there is no esteem for hierarchy – divine or human. But, as I asked above with regard to issues of piety and impiety, can political communities sustain such universal unveilings as occur in the completely free democracy of, for example, Book 8 of the *Republic*? Or does the community need the Athenian Stranger's *aidôs*, which establishes the mastery of the laws rather than the people, that provides the friendship based on that *aidôs* necessary to defeat the Persians in 489 (*Laws*, 699c)? The same challenge faces the individuals in Euripides' tragedies or Aristophanes' comedies on whom I shall focus in Chapter 6. Can all be probed and revealed without the destruction of the political community? Does nothing need to remain unspoken? Socrates in the *Apology* seems to answer no; all must be opened and the *Apology* becomes the uncovering and opening up of Socrates himself before the Athenians and of Athens herself under the scrutiny of Socrates' probing inquiries.

Alexander Meiklejohn[23] writes with the sort of hyperbole that so often attends the trial of Socrates: "It may well be argued that if the *Apology* had not been written – by Plato or someone else – the First Amendment would not have been written. The relation here is of trunk and branch" (1948: 20). He and I. F. Stone along with many others misrepresent the case of Socrates' trial when they write about the trial as an issue of free speech in our language. Meiklejohn's "trunk" suggests that the experience of Socrates' trial and execution melds seamlessly into the issues of free speech as part of the free democracies we address today. Clearly, this cannot be correct. The practice as the uncovering of one's self and one's true beliefs is far removed from the protected articulation of any form of expression or any words – believed or not to be true. We must read Socrates' trial in the context of ancient Athens, not in the language of today's debates about the extent to which free speech is to be tolerated or is to be extended. The trial, as I see it, is not one that raises questions of religious toleration or a right to free speech or even a democracy being true to itself, but rather points to the tension between the willingness to openly speak "the truth," a term repeated over and over in Socrates' speech, and the respect for what is old and traditionally binds cities together in a Protagorean fashion.

---

[23] See Chapter 1, pages 25–9.

Plato's contemporary Xenophon also writes an *Apology of Socrates*, but his report of Socrates' speech at his trial is very different from Plato's. He focuses on showing that Socrates thought death to be more choiceworthy than life (1). In Xenophon's version of the speech, Socrates describes himself as being free and the oracle describes him as "most free" (16) because he is not a slave to his appetites nor dependent on others for pay or gifts. He lives without suffering from a sense of lack and thus is not dependent on others to satisfy the desires of his body; his pleasures reside in his soul (18). This reading of Socrates' life condenses freedom into a relation that Socrates has with his own self. For Plato's Socrates, the questioning and the unveiling aspects in which he engages intrude upon the political world of the city. The unexamined life that he refuses to live can at times be foundational for the city, especially the unexamined life of the pious man. The process of unveiling explores the divinity of what is uncovered. I propose to read Plato's version of the *Apology* as a tale of *parrhêsia* leading to the shameless uncovering that culminates in Socrates' famous phrase concerning the unexamined life. The speech is a document that investigates how this shameless exercise of free speech challenges the Athenian audience, which enjoys *parrhêsia* in their public realm, but that also demands *aidôs* for themselves, that is, the Athenians to whom Socrates speaks so boldly ignore the contradictions between the two as they try to incorporate both into their political regime. The discussion that follows is to set Socrates' *Apology* as written by Plato into the context of the practice of *parrhêsia*, truth and shame, and not to see it – in Meiklejohn's language – as a precursor to the American Constitution.

2. PLATO'S *APOLOGY*: THE UNVEILING OF SOCRATES AND THE TRANSFORMATION OF SHAME[24]

When Candaules' wife took off her clothes before Gyges in the bedroom of her husband, she cast off (as Gyges had predicted) her *aidôs*, her shame. No longer revering the "beautiful things" discovered by the Lydians long ago, she could now plot the murder of her husband the king and with her new-found sense of independence choose her own husband. Previously (so far as we know), she had lived by the lessons of shame that governed the Lydians, lessons that said that one should not look on that which is not one's own, that women should not shed their clothes before men other than their

---

[24] Here, I ignore entirely the belabored debates about the historicity of Plato's *Apology*, whether these are Socrates' words or not, and read it instead as a text intended to speak to the place of *parrhêsia* in our public and private lives. There are, of course, a multitude of ways to interpret this intriguing speech and I make no claim that this is the definitive reading, only that I have found in the speech resources to help one reflect on the relationship between freedom of speech and the embodiment of philosophy in the person of Socrates.

husbands. Gyges (with the encouragement of Candaules) violated that law when he entered his king's bedroom. In Herodotus' tale, both Gyges and his queen have cast aside *aidôs*, and in the fairytale ending to their story they live happily ever after.

Plato's story of Socrates' trial has many of the same elements, the shedding of shame prescribed by "the beautiful things" discovered by the Athenians long ago and the willingness to look – shamelessly – beyond what is one's own. Socrates' speech of unveiling *parrhêsia* first rejects the *aidôs* that cements the social structure of the city and then redefines shame, destroying it as an emotion that entailed revering one's fellow citizens, following their traditions, and accepting their hierarchies. Instead, shame under Socrates' refashioning becomes an emotion that takes one beyond his or her particular customs and traditions to the universal principles governing the cityless soul. In the *Apology*, Socrates casts off the clothes with which others have dressed him; he stands naked in the courtroom before the gaze of others, before the 501 jurors, before the large number of interested Athenians who have come to observe – and before the innumerable readers of the *Apology* who have been captivated and continue to be captivated by his speech over the millennia. Socrates reveals himself without deference to what the men of his city or the jurors who sit in judgment expect of him.[25] Some see this lack of respect for his fellow citizens, using the modern language of the "sovereign" people, as antidemocratic, as offensive to the institutions of democratic Athens; I see it as an expression of his democratic freedom to practice *parrhêsia*, speech without deference.

The *Apology* is a speech of democratic *parrhêsia*, the frank uncovering of oneself. As such, it is as well an effort to reinvent the sources of shame, of nonlegal restraints on one's actions, of what might cause an individual to hide his or her true self from the gaze of another.[26] To accomplish this, Socrates must fight against the "beautiful things from long ago" that tell his fellow citizens what needs to be hidden, what is worthy of evoking shame, the inhibiting emotion. Like the image of the democratic regime that practices a sort of amnesia presented in Chapter 2, Socrates must show an independence from ancient hierarchies, from the past. He must break shame away from what has been. His restructuring of shame away from the gaze of others and from the traditions of one's society takes *aidôs* out of Protagoras' model where it served as the glue for civil society, as the "civilizing" emotion. In Socrates' handling, this new shame born of the *parrhêsia* he practices at his trial threatens the unity and stability of the sleeping polity that fails to practice the *parrhêsia* it claims to revere.

---

[25] Alcibiades warns in the *Symposium* that no one can know Socrates (216c–d), but the *Apology* is the speech in which Socrates grandly displays himself before the Athenians.

[26] Goodhill (1998) from a different perspective points to the place of the "gaze" in the democratic culture of Athens.

Socrates begins his *Apology* affirming the power of speech to cover and
uncover, to hide or reveal the truth.[27] Socrates' accusers have with their
speeches hidden rather than uncovered the truth; Socrates' task is to pull
away the curtains that have concealed the truth. The recurrent language of
the introductory passages of the *Apology* (and, indeed, of much that follows)
is that of truth. His accusers, Socrates tells us, have almost made him forget
(*epelathomên*, 17a) himself, or lose the truth about who he is. They have
covered him with the veils woven by their persuasive speech. But, he informs
his vast audience, his accusers have not freely spoken true words. They have,
in fact, lied (*epseusanto*, 17a). Clever speakers, according to the definition
Socrates offers, must speak what is true (17b), but his accusers have said
nothing that is true; forms of the phrase *t'alêthê* are repeated and then related
once again in this passage. "From me," Socrates tells his audience, "you will
hear the entire truth (*pasan tên alêtheian*)" (17b).[28] "By Zeus," he asserts,
he will not garnish his speech with beautiful words (*ou kekalliepêmenous*,
17b) that are untrue. He will use the every day speech of the agora without the fancy flourishes and deceptive cosmetics (*kekosmêmenous*, 17c) that
embellish the lying speech of his accusers. No covering powders will hide or
enhance the appearance of his own words. Unadorned will be his presentation, and unadorned will he stand before the jurors.

Socrates warns his listeners that the lies of his accusers will soon be apparent. They have described him as skillful in speech (*deinos legein*), but as soon
as he speaks, Socrates claims, they will be proved wrong. They should, he
insists, worry about the shame that will come to them once the "deed" of his
speech reveals their lies, for they have spoken most shamelessly (*anaischunto-
taton*, 17b), not fearing that their lies would be revealed. The shame with
which Socrates threatens his accusers at this point is a shame that cares about
the gaze of others, that acknowledges another looking on and seeing one's
vulnerabilities, the shame that causes the blush when one is caught violating
accepted customs, in this case of speaking truthfully in the courtroom.[29] It is
this sense of shame that is likely to inhibit his accusers, he believes, because
they do not seriously care about the education of the young or about piety as
they claim; they, like their fellow citizens, however, do care about how they
appear before others. It is the same shame that brings on Thrasymachus'
blush when he gets caught in the tangle of Socrates' questions. They all fear
exposing their weaknesses to the gaze of others. Socrates' reinvention of

---

[27] Hesk has a very valuable discussion of the role of deception in the ideology of Athenian
democracy and "the collective impulse of the Athenian polis towards honesty" (2000: 41)
where "the notion of 'deceiving the demos' was specifically prohibited by law" (2000: 163).

[28] As Villa (2001), Nehamas (1998), and others have suggested, the "truth" that Socrates
reveals here is certainly not a doctrine nor an objective good, but a way of life, a practice of
living.

[29] Again, see Hesk (2000) on deception in general.

shame in this speech will free it from just this judgmental gaze and reverence that Protagoras had so praised as the grounding of political life. Socrates' speech in which he presents himself "naked" before those sitting in judgment of him arouses for him no shame, no desire to hide himself with all his "faults" behind veils of fabrications and falsehoods, or to pretty himself up with assorted beautifying cosmetics.

By the end of the introductory passage, Socrates shifts attention from the "truth" that he will speak and the untruths his accusers have spoken to justice, or just things (*ta dikaia*); while to speak the truth is the virtue of the speaker, justice is the virtue of the judge he tells the jurors (18a). And yet for him, justice and truth blend. Appealing to the jurors' commitment to justice, he repeats over and over the failure of his accusers – both past and current – to speak the truth about what he says, about what he does, about who he is (*alêthê*, 18b [twice]; 20b). In order to be just, the jurors must hear the unembellished truth from the man accused. Justice in this sense requires the unveiling practice of *parrhêsia* since only through the practice of *parrhêsia* can the truth be uncovered.

Addressing the old slanders that have circulated about him, Socrates tells the famous story of Chaerephon's journey to the oracle at Delphi, prefacing this section of his speech by remarking to the jury: "Know well, that I will speak the entire truth to you" (*eu . . . iste; panan humin tên alêtheian erô*, 20d). This truth, he tells them, will expose his peculiarly human (as opposed to civic or even manly) wisdom (*anthrôpinê sophia*); this is, of course, the wisdom that he knows that he does not know. Socrates does not hide his ignorance. Rather, he happily (even boastfully) exposes it. Others – the politicians, the poets, the artisans – all pretend to know when they do not. They hide their ignorance, ashamed of the inadequacies that belie their facades of self-assurance. When Socrates uncovers their ignorance to them through his persistent interrogations, they are shamed by their ignorance and eager to hide their own inadequacies.[30] Prior to telling the jurors, the Athenians, and the readers of Plato's dialogue about his encounter with the poets, Socrates remarks: "I am ashamed to tell you . . . the truth" (*aischunomoai humin eipein . . . t'alêthê*, 22b). Nevertheless, he continues; it must be told irrespective of whose inadequacies are uncovered. Shame does not nestle a "civilized" Socrates within the confines of the city through respect for those whom others respect. The truth he has discovered about the poets and the others, that he is ashamed to speak (yet speaks), reveals their vulnerability. No better than inspired seers, the poets knew not of what they sang and

---

[30] Eisenstadt (2001) addresses the issue of shame in the *Apology*, but mostly as the source of Anytus' and the Athenians' hatred for and anger at Socrates. There are several problems with this essay, one being that she says that Socrates used *aidôs* thirteen times in the text, while each example is *aischunê*. But she is correct in noting that "awakening of shame" is the precursor to philosophy.

lacked the wisdom they claimed. The story is the same for the men of politics and the artisans whom he questioned, leaving them all exposed before
the gaze of others – and angered at Socrates for revealing the vulnerabilities
that shame them before their fellow citizens.

Thus Socrates, appropriating Herculean language, describes for the jury
his wanderings and his "labors" (22a). They explain the hatred of him
(*apêchthonomên*, 21d, 21e [twice]) from those whom he questioned. Affirming yet again that he speaks the truth (22a), he explains that the reputation of wisdom correlated well with its absence. Socrates complains that his
accusers – at least the "first ones," as he calls them – with their lies (*pseudê*,
18a) slandered him with stock phrases of teaching about things above and
things below the earth as if they were accusing Anaxagoras or some other
man of science. This is not the truth that Socrates teaches. The truth he
teaches points to a new way of life that begins by admitting ignorance and
attends to the unseen soul. "I think they would not be willing to speak the
truth (*ta . . . alêthê*)," he says of the men of Athens in general, "because it is
clear that they, knowing nothing, are pretending (*prospoioumenoi*) to know"
(23d). They are shamed by their ignorance. Socrates is not shamed by his.

Socrates' agenda in this questioning of these fellow citizens that brings
on this shame, he tells us, is to prove the god of the oracle wrong, to discover someone wiser than himself whom he will parade before the god to
show the god his own ignorance. All – humans as well as the gods – are
subject to the exercise of Socratic *parrhêsia*; no fetters of deference restrain
his tongue whether he speaks to men or to gods. Socrates reads the Delphic
oracle reported by Chaerephon as intended to indicate the insignificance of
human knowledge with himself serving as an example (*paradeigma*, 23b)
of the worthlessness of what it is men can know. Unlike the poets and the
artisans and the politicians he questioned, Socrates lacks any shame about
his own ignorance; indeed, he exults in it and proudly proclaims what other
men cover, that his wisdom "in truth" (*têi alêtheia*, 23b) is worth nothing.
So influenced has he been by this realization, he tells his judges, that he, sacrificing all leisure, continues to labor questioning others and showing them
that they are not wise. As a result of his efforts to show the insignificance
of human knowledge, he lives in ten thousandfold poverty. Thus, he flaunts
before all not only his ignorance, but his poverty as well, apparent failings
that most others would wish to hide.

Today we marvel at the brashness of these words: Socrates is a man of
integrity, a man of truth, a man who scorns what others value. But we must
read his words in context and especially in the context of the trial taking
place in democratic Athens.[31] This is a man who says to his jurors that he
is not controlled by the same shame that guides their actions, who does

---

[31] See especially Brann's article on the *Apology* where she illustrates how "offensive" the speech
is to the Athenian jury (1978).

not share in the *aidôs* of Protagoras' myth. What they might try to cover –
their ignorance, their poverty, their lack of leisure, their disregard for their
family, their inability to speak elegantly – Socrates presents openly, frankly,
even boastfully. Indeed, he celebrates his own insufficiencies in his speech
before the jurors. He mocks what causes them shame. Worse still, Socrates
teaches his technique of uncovering the inadequacies of others to the young
men who follow him around (*hoi neoi moi epakolouthountes*, 23c); the
young seeing the shamelessness of Socrates become shameless themselves
in their own efforts at shaming others. Socrates is educating/corrupting the
young not so much by introducing new gods into the city, but by teaching
the shamelessness that questions the reverence due to the "beautiful things
discovered long ago," due to the values of the city, to the hierarchy of age,
and to the gods. When shame serves as the glue of a community, the educator
in shamelessness such as Socrates dissolves the glue.[32]

Socrates concludes his response to the old "slanders" with which the
jurors have been inundated by reminding them and the larger audience
("O Athenian men," 24a) that he has spoken true things (*t'alêthê*) for them,
neither hiding (*apokrupsamenos*) nor speaking with reserve (*huposteila-
menos*), all the while recognizing that his refusal to hold back in what he
says leads to his being hated (*apêchthanomai*, 24a). He now turns from the
old slanders to the new ones and begins his apology in response to Meletus,
an easy target. Though Socrates suggests that he will investigate each aspect
of the charge against him, this becomes instead an investigation of Meletus
who, Socrates shows, does not speak freely, saying what he truly thinks.
Socrates accuses his accuser of joking (*charientizetai*, 24c) about matters
that are serious and pretending (*prospoioumenos* again, 24c; cf. 23d) to be
serious when he is not. Meletus' true self, or true agenda, is hidden behind
these pretenses and Socrates' task is to uncover it. Thus, the questioning of
Meletus by Socrates begins and we see that though Meletus claims to know
who corrupts the young, he does not know who makes them better.

Socrates pounces on what he considers Meletus' outrageous claim that all
the Athenians except Socrates make the youth of Athens better as evidence
that Meletus has not spoken truthfully, that though he claims to care about
the young, he does not. And thus Socrates calls down shame on Meletus
(*ouk aischron soi dokei einai*, 24d), for claiming to be what he is not (a man
concerned with improving the youth of the city), for pretending and for lying
about himself. Socrates continues that Meletus is not only lying about who
he is and what his interests are, but in his claim that Socrates intentionally
harms the young he is making a false statement (*pseudêi*, 25e). He insists
that Meletus must know that to make one worse willingly causes harm to
oneself. Therefore, he must know that no one harms another willingly. Since

---

[32] Villa uses similar language when he describes this as the "dissolvent nature of Socratic
rationality" (2001: 3, also 21).

Meletus must know this, Socrates concludes that he must be lying when he says Socrates willingly harms others.

Turning to the second part of the accusation – that Socrates does not believe in the gods, but also introduces new gods into the city – Socrates again tries to point out that Meletus in his arrogance and intemperance is joking (*charientizomenou* again, 27a) and playing games (*paizontos*). Meletus, again not practicing *parrhêsia*, does not say what he truly believes. Thus, we find him speaking against himself (*kai enanti' emautôi legontos*, 27a) as Socrates develops his argument. Putting words into Meletus' mouth, Socrates asks, as if he were Meletus, whether "the wise Socrates and the other hearers" will realize that he is deceiving them (*exapatêsô*, 27a). Socrates, here in the courtroom, reiterates once again that he at least will not deceive for he will speak in his accustomed fashion (*en tôi eiôthoti tropôi*, 27b). As at the beginning of the speech, Socrates makes clear, no cosmetics will color his apology; he reveals his true self by speaking daringly before the court of the Athenians belittling and mocking his accusers. It remains his accusers relying on an inbred hostility to Socrates and on the slanders they have heard about him rather than on what is true (*alêthês* yet again, 28a) who violate the practice of free speech in their deceptions as they bring Socrates to trial.

After Socrates has interrogated Meletus and challenged him to show how someone who believes in *daemons* could not believe in the gods from whom they are born, he turns to the example of the demigod Achilles – "a sort of bastard born from a nymph" (*nothoi tines . . . ek numphôn*, 27d) – as a model for his own response to the slanders that will, he predicts, condemn him. Socrates, seventy years old, stooped with a pug nose and bulging eyes, makes a rather peculiar analogy between himself and the great Homeric hero. He begins this particular section of the speech by introducing an imaginary interlocutor, "someone (*tis*)," who would say to him: "Are you not ashamed (*aischunêi*) to have spent your life doing what now puts you in danger of dying?" (28b). To this hypothetical questioner Socrates responds with the unlikely analogy of Achilles who chose to avenge the death of Patroclus rather than continue to live, who chose to kill the killer of his friend rather than to spend a quiet life back in Phthia.

The reference to Achilles draws on a character like himself, Socrates suggests, someone who saw no shame in choosing death over living the "bad life (*kakos ôn*)" (28d), welcoming death rather than failing to fulfill the demands of justice. In Achilles' case, though, the willingness to face death comes from a desire to avenge a friend's death by killing his enemy. More significantly for our purposes, in Socrates' version of Achilles' story, which ignores the theme of vengeance, he faces death, fearing that he will be the object of laughter (*katagelastos*, 28d) if he sits by the ships of the Achaeans not repaying the harm that has been done to him by Hector. Socrates' analogizing himself to Achilles makes sense only in that both he and Achilles do not fear death as they each stand firm in their commitments, scorning what others praise, namely, the preservation of life. Achilles does this, though, to cause harm to an enemy through a justice that demands vengeance, Socrates through a justice that entails benefits for his fellow citizens, serving as the gift sent by the god to the city (31a).[33]

Socrates appropriates for himself the military metaphor that comes from Achilles' pursuit of just things, assimilating his own peculiar philosophic way of life to that of the military hero – or, shall we say, appropriating for the philosopher the stature of the heroic warrior. He presents himself as one stationed where he is either by himself (*tis heauton taxêi*) or by a ruler (*archontos tachthêi*, 28d), and then adds that as such a one he remains firm, attending to nothing else before shame (*pro tou aischrou*, 28d). In the course of the few lines developing this analogy with Achilles, the concept of shame suddenly has been transformed by Socrates. The hypothetical interlocutor who inquired whether Socrates should not be ashamed had asked his hypothetical question assuming that the preservation of life is what men care about, what motivates most men. If one does not value the chance to continue living, then the threat of death on the battlefield or from the penalties meted out by the city will have little impact. To scorn death and to express no fear of it as Socrates does so persistently throughout the *Apology* (and Achilles does throughout the latter books of the *Iliad*) is to scorn the passion on which the city builds its penal code. Both Achilles and Socrates stand in this sense outside the city. In the *Iliad* the gods must come down to the plain of Troy in order to reintegrate Achilles into the world of the living by bringing to his tent the aged Priam. In Socrates' case we must move on to the *Crito* for this reintegration. There it is the dream of the goddess who tells him that on the third day he will return to Phthia (again connecting Socrates to Achilles with this reference to Achilles' homeland) that prefaces that reintegration (*Crito*, 44ab). For both heroes – the demigod and the seventy-year-old, bug-eyed, snub-nosed philosopher – it is reverence for the gods, not for the hierarchies or traditions of their fellow citizens, that centers them in the community.

Achilles, in his own passion to avenge the death of his friend, acts as an individual independent of the community with which he traveled to Troy.[34] Achilles may have first appeared in the *Iliad* controlled by the traditional standards of glory and renown that motivated the Achaean warriors (*Iliad*, 12, 310–21), his anger sparked by the lesser prizes he receives for his magnificent deeds on the battlefield. But he grows beyond the conventional

---

[33] West (1979: 155) explicates the differences between Socrates' version of the Homeric story and the story that appears in Homer's *Iliad*. West offers an elaborate discussion of this analogy, but like me is disturbed by the awkwardness of it given the profound differences between Achilles and Socrates and their respective situations. Euben (1990: 216–26) also offers an extensive analysis of this troubling section of the *Apology*. See also Weiss (1998: 8–9).

[34] For the development of this reading of the *Iliad* see Redfield (1975) and the discussion in Chapter 3, section 3, note 20.

understanding of shame so dependent on honors and appearance and turns instead to a shame no longer governed by the community's sense of what ought to be.[35] The death of his friend arouses no shame, but rather the anger that leads to vengeance. In his pursuit of vengeance he acts without concern for the gaze of those around him. This independence, more than their common willingness to face death in the end, unites Socrates and Achilles. They identify for themselves the source of shame. It lies not in the judgmental eyes of their fellow citizens, but in their own private judgments of how justice is to be served – by avenging the death of one's friend or by refusing to hide behind deceptive speech. Socrates, the one who will persuade Polemarchus that justice cannot be Achilles' harming of one's "enemies," takes from Achilles so bent on killing Hector not his understanding of justice, but rather the willingness to identify for himself what he judges as shameful, what he judges is necessary to die for, irrespective of the judgments of those who gaze upon them either in admiration or contempt.

Socrates uses Achilles on his path to taking the shameful out of the social and political context in which Protagoras' Zeus had placed it. The experience of shame is no longer to show awe before those individuals with whom one lives as fellow citizens, but now rather to obey those who are "better, both gods and men" (29b), be they citizens or gods of the city or not. The hierarchy that underlies Socrates' reassessment of shame no longer entails awe before what and who had been declared "beautiful" over the years, but before whoever "stations" him where it is best (*beltiston*, 28d). This is the truth (*têi alêtheia*, 28d) he tells us. And it is a truth he followed whether fighting at Potidaia or Amphipolis or Delium – or in the city of Athens where he was stationed by the god (*tou de theou tattontos*, 28e) and "commanded to live philosophizing" (*philosophounta me dein zên*, 28e). To scorn the god by disobeying him and not philosophizing, that truly (*hôs alêthôs*, 29a) would have been unjust. Socrates identifies for himself before whom he will show awe – and it is the god, his own *daemon*, not even the oracle of Apollo nor the city of men to whom he shows this respect.

In a speech filled with imaginary interlocutors who question Socrates as he questions others, Socrates next envisions a hypothetical offer that the Athenians could make to him: they could say to him that they would release him, but in return they would demand that he no longer spend his life living as he has been and most especially that he stop philosophizing, with pain of death if he would do otherwise (29c).[36] Here is where those like Munn

---

[35] The brief but extremely influential article by Adam Parry (1956) is critical for an understanding of Achilles' motivations.

[36] The irony here as many have noted already is that in making this hypothetical proposal, the Athenians would deny Socrates *parrhêsia*, the opportunity to say what he truly believes. We must, of course, remember that this is Socrates putting these words into the speech of some hypothetical Athenians, not the Athenians themselves speaking.

find support for the claim that Socrates offends the Athenian notion of the sovereignty of the people.[37] Socrates hypothetically responds to the Athenian men (*ô andres Athênaioi*, 29d) with their hypothetical offer: though he says he embraces and loves them (*aspsazomai men kai philô*), he will continue to obey the god, not them, though they have all spoken to him (29d). And to rub in this arrogant dismissal of the authority over him of the men of Athens who might make him this offer, he confirms that so long as he breathes and is able, he will not cease philosophizing and pointing out to them that they themselves should be ashamed (*aischunêi*) that they care as they do for wealth and honor and reputation, but not for wisdom nor truth (*alêtheias*), nor that their souls (unseen by others) be as good as possible (29de).

The shameful is no longer a social emotion that depends on how others perceive you, the emotion I explored in Chapter 3, which was called by some the "civilizing" emotion. Socrates is removing the gift that Protagoras said Zeus gave to humans so that they could live in cities together. Socrates does not live in the eyes of his fellow citizens, and he urges that they too escape the gaze of others. His life and the speech he presents to his judges are not limited by their expectations. He replaces shame before them with shame before the gods and before himself. His life of philosophizing is the life of the democratic parrhesiast, "saying what he is accustomed to saying" (29d) without deference to the jurors who sit in judgment of him or the fellow citizens who have come to hear his speech in the courtroom.

Socrates, the skillful speaker (*deinos legein*, 17b) that he claims not to be, accomplishes with his defense a startling inversion. From an apologia for himself before the courtroom, he creates instead an apologia for Athens; from Socrates as the one who has to defend himself against the charges brought by the old slanders and new accusers his speech turns into an indictment brought by Socrates against the Athenians. Socrates now accuses the Athenians of potentially harming themselves by killing him. Thus, he finds himself making an apology on their behalf (*apologeisthai . . . huper humôn*, 30d) rather than on his own. The world has been turned upside down; accuser is accused, the proud is the one who should feel shame, the free are enslaved, and from all these inversions, Socrates, the one who had been on trial, emerges as the unlikely hero of the story, the one who will "save" Athens by his "shameless" speech.

Socrates began this section of the *Apology* analogizing himself to Achilles, the great hero of the *Iliad*. He concludes it by happily analogizing himself to

---

[37] Socrates' refusal to try the ten generals from Arginusae as a group suggests a difficulty with Munn's claim here; Socrates explains that although the people wanted to do this "shouting and bidding him" (32b) he refused because this was done *paranomôs* and *para tous nomous* (32b), against the laws. Socrates sets up a distinction here between constitutionalism and popular sovereignty and comes down in favor of the "constitution." On this general theme in ancient Greece see Ostwald (1986) and Chapter 2.

a gadfly; he goes from a demigod to an annoying insect, from great heroic warrior to a bug. The Homeric heroes with whom he associated himself at first may be born from the immortal goddess and the mortal father, but Socrates himself as gadfly is the gift of the gods sent to awaken the "great and noble (*gennaiôi*) horse" that is Athens (30e). The "noble," the well-born is, in Socrates' portrait of his city, beholden to the lowly insect. Hierarchy falls; *aidôs* disappears. The horse is subject to the insect and all is well. It is almost as if Socrates were saying that the well-born, fair-haired Agamemnon, ruler over so many forces, should listen to the twisted, scraggly Thersites.

When Socrates says to all Athenians and not only to those who sit in the jurors' seats: "Do not be angered at me speaking true things" (*legonti t'alêthê*, 31e), he admonishes the Athenians using their own principles of *parrhêsia*. They, however, in their anger at him for practicing *parrhêsia*, by allowing him to be indicted, have themselves abandoned the practices of democracy, which had brought them so much pride, the opening of speech to the Thersites among them, to those who spoke what they believed. It is this openness on which this regime of democratic deliberation was built. "Not any one among humans will be saved neither by you nor by any other multitude if he nobly (*gnêsiôs*) opposes and prevents the many unjust things which are contrary to the laws from happening in the city," Socrates warns (31e). The tongue without fetters of which the Persian Chorus had sung in Aeschylus' play is lost in the Athens that Socrates now portrays in his speech. The city that paid for a ship with the name *Parrhêsia*, he tells his jurors, in fact, does not allow for the unfettered speech of its citizens.

Instead, the city has forced him to take this political practice that also lies at the heart of his own philosophic life, remove it from the political world, and bring it into the gymnasia and the homes of the wealthy like Cephalus, Callicles, and Callias where he engages in dialogue with the young. Socrates takes the public practice of *parrhêsia* beyond the assembly, beyond the law courts, beyond the comic stage, and ignores the boundaries of public and private. *Parrhêsia* goes from the democratic practice that threatened the regime, to the philosophic practice of the world Socrates inhabits. Yet, though he claims to act within the private realm, not the public world of Assemblies and law courts (*idiôteuein alla mê dêmoiseuein*, 32a, cf. 31c and 36c), Socrates disingenuously ignores the inevitable blending of public and private. Speaking truth in the private sphere as if he were a father or a brother to the young of the city, he brings the private world very much into the public sphere. The *parrhêsia* he practices in private becomes public as he urges his interlocutors not to care about what they had previously cared for (36c). In private, he unveils the public lies on which the citizens of Athens, attached to their past traditions and their ancient heroes, depend.

Socrates concludes the first and longest part of his speech before the jury by reaffirming that he stands outside the accustomed patterns of behavior in the courtroom, though he acknowledges that this will anger even more the jurors who are about to vote on his innocence or guilt. Others standing before them, he tells them, would bring to the courtroom their families, proffering many tears in an effort to stir the pity of the jurors. Again developing a hypothetical interlocutor, this time a juror who has become angered at Socrates for refusing to engage in these tactics so familiar to the courtroom, Socrates responds to this imaginary person with a quotation from Homer to show that he does have a family; he, neither a stick nor a stone, was born of parents and has himself fathered three sons, but he will not ask them to come forth to arouse the sympathies of the jury. Unlike the jurors and unlike others who have stood accused before the city, he cares only for what is noble, what is virtuous. And in this way, he claims (most arrogantly we can say) that he acts for the sake of the reputation of the city. The man who before has shed all concern with reputation here wraps the city in reputation, worried about how it will appear to strangers rather than to itself (35b). The city, he suggests, cannot judge itself; it will stand judged by those outside it, outside its own customs. Those from the outside, gazing at the citizens of Athens, will cast scorn on them for killing "the wise man" (38c). Socrates here tries to move the Athenians to this universal perch that takes them beyond their own laws to a truth that is revealed when those local standards are torn away. In the *Apology*, Socrates strips himself naked before the Athenians. Likewise, he tries to make Athens visible to herself as he strips the city of Athens before her own judges, revealing the truth of her own injustices (39b).

The transparency of Socrates reverberates throughout the speech. "I make myself visible" (*phanoumai*, 33a), he affirms. Responding to one who hypothetically might say that he has learned something in private from Socrates that is not what others hear, Socrates remarks: "He does not speak the truth" (*ouk alêthê legei*, 33b). No barrier hides any parts of Socrates while allowing other parts to reveal themselves. There is no secret Socrates. Socrates, in fact, is the open, democratic man who without acknowledging boundaries sees all as equal, interrogating rich and poor alike (33b). The *parrhêsia* he practices is not exclusive as is the Athenian *parrhêsia* we will see in the plays of Euripides, a *parrhêsia* that only citizens of the democracy enjoy. Socrates speaks to all across the ages, to young and old (33b) and asks for responses. Socrates is the fully democratic man who makes *parrhêsia* truly equal and truly revealing. He is the complete democrat, as opposed to the democratic city that does not and perhaps cannot sustain an unvarnished commitment to the principles of equality and the abstraction from the past that underlies the regime.

In the second part of the *Apology*, Socrates insists that should he accept the proposed punishment of exile, the young, wherever he is, "will listen to me speaking, just as they do here [in Athens]" (37d). Is this simply a version of the delight we experience when we see others appear foolish, the phenomenon we today call *schadenfreude*? Or is it (more likely) that the pursuit of truth, though we are never told what that truth is, itself gives pleasure, that the young are responding – whether in Athens or in Thebes – to a universal longing, an erotic desire to remove pretenses in pursuit of an uncovered truth? The examined life, Socrates proposes, is what arouses all of us, if only we were not shaped and molded to fit into the political communities that require our reverence toward and shame before the city's truths, the beautiful things discovered long ago. The passion for the examined life, for uncovering ourselves and others, is a universal passion, Socrates suggests, a human emotion stronger for him than the emotion of shame. The language of truth (*t' alêtheia*) floods the *Apology*. "I have spoken the truth," Socrates reiterates again and again (e.g., 33c and 34b).[38] And over and over he repeats, Meletus is the one who lies and repels those who are drawn to the beauty of truth. Socrates dismisses throughout the emotion of shame that our modern psychologists analyze as the passion that evokes the blush and makes us wary of the gaze of others, desirous of sinking into the ground when our faults are revealed.

The Athenian judges reject the universal stance that Socrates recommends to them of looking at the city from the outside and acknowledging the city's faults. The Protagorean model remains, bound by the importance of shame and the gaze within the community; they vote to execute the man who shamelessly practices *parrhêsia* before them.[39] In the final portion of his speech after this vote has been taken, Socrates reflects on why the jurors have chosen to condemn and then to execute him. They may think it is because of a lack of arguments/words (*aporiai . . . logôn*, 38d, twice); but no, it was, he says, "a lack of daring and shamelessness (*anaischuntias*) and an unwillingness to say what would be most pleasant for you to hear . . . of the sort that you are accustomed to hear from others" (38de). He has completely inverted the language of the Athenian democracy. "Daring" is not to speak frankly; it is to pander to the jurors. "Shamelessness" is not to exist freed from the castigating glances of one's fellow citizens; it is to remain controlled by their gaze. Athenian democracy in this version has not allowed for *parrhêsia*; it has shown itself bound by Protagorean shame. It is Socrates, not the city, who in the *Apology* incorporates within himself the principles the city falsely claims for itself. In so doing, he also incorporates its tensions, the insistence on

---

[38] According to the *Thesaurus Graecae Linguae* there are 36 appearances of the root *alêth-* in the relatively brief *Apology*.

[39] Ober (1998: 262) points out how Isocrates at the age of 82 in 354/3 assimilates himself to the Socrates from the *Apology*: "Isocrates, like Socrates, presented himself as a persecuted intellectual, ill understood by his fellow citizens, who failed to grasp the great good that he in fact accomplished for the polis. By assimilating himself to Socrates, Isocrates situated himself at the cutting edge of the critical enterprise: the point at which the individual citizen pushed the prototypical Athenian political virtue of frank speech (*parrhêsia*, 10, 43–4, 179) to, and probably beyond, the limit."

self-revelation along with the dangers that willing self-revelation constitutes for the existence of the community.

When Socrates transforms the meaning of shame, taking it from its concern with what is observed by others and making it independent of both history and the gaze of others, he allows for the full expression of *parrhêsia*, of frank and open speech. The freedom from the past is democratic, but the indifference to others and the past that this new meaning of shame entails undercuts the community, which draws the democratic citizens to attend the Assembly and engage with others in self-rule. Momigliano wrote in his essay about freedom of speech in antiquity: "Freedom of speech turns out to be an Athenian fifth century idea. In earlier times the notion of liberty (*eleutheria*) did not include freedom of speech: indeed, another important notion of Greek archaic ethics, *aidôs* ("modesty") implied that silence and reticence were characteristic of the good man" (1973–4: 258–9). Socrates enjoyed and practiced this new freedom, but he ignored the "silence and reticence" that the Athenians may still have associated with the "good man." The drive to uncover the shameless truth set him in tension with the city that still depended on shame and tradition, irrespective of the founding moment of democratic amnesia.[40]

Socrates in his role as gadfly, Socrates in the pursuit of "the true" or "true things" must practice *parrhêsia* to uncover, unveil, and like Thersites he must ignore hierarchical relations (such as the defendant before the jurors, the lone citizen before the collective body of the *dêmos*) that restrain speech. This is the life and the agenda of the philosopher. But, the Athenians do not accept the reasoning behind Socrates' daring free speech. The articulation of what one believes to be true does not always persuade or lead others to what is true. *Parrhêsia* may be a cultural icon of the democratic experience in Athens, capturing the fundamental principles of freedom from history and rejection of a hierarchical order to society, but the unveiling

---

[40] Castoriadis (1991: 113) writes similarly about the ancient condition and brings those concerns to the contemporary world: "law materializes in the discourse of the people, freely talking to each other in the *agora* about politics and about everything they care about before deliberating in the *ecclesia*. To understand the tremendous historical change involved, one only has to contrast this with the typical 'Asiatic' situation." He continues: "This is equivalent to the creation of the possibility – and actuality – of free speech, free thinking, free examination and questioning without restraint. It establishes *logos* as circulation of speech and thought within the community. It accompanies the two basic traits of the citizen ... *isegoria*, the right for all equally to speak their minds, and *parrhêsia*, the commitment for all to really speak their minds concerning public affairs ... What are the people actually doing with these rights? The decisive traits in this respect are courage, responsibility, and shame (*aidôs, aischune*). Lacking these, the 'public space' becomes just an open space for advertising, mystification, and pornography – as is, increasingly, the case today. Against such developments, legal provisions are of no avail, or produce evils worse than the ones they pretend to cure. Only education (*paideia*) of citizens as citizens can give valuable, substantive content to the 'public space.'"

it entails may challenge reflexively the conditions that gave rise to it or, as we will see in the next chapter, it may cause harm – comically as in Aristophanes' *Thesmophoriazusae*, tragically as in the *Phoenician Women*. Such issues give rise to the flirtations with speech that is not necessarily frank, which may be shrouded in forms of deception, and looks to principles that go beyond the goal of uncovering the truth that so dominates the *Apology*.

I have offered a reading of the *Apology* that does not highlight the ironic aspects of the speech.[41] It is a reading focused on the insistence on uncovering; yet, without question, irony marks important points in the language used to draw out the truth, for example, the truth of Meletus' ignorance or the foolishness of the likely punishment expected from the Athenians. Irony, for sure, is in play when Socrates compares himself to the gadfly as well or proposes a punishment that suggests the Athenians treat him as if he were a victorious Olympian athlete. While *parrhêsia* dominates the speech with Socrates' refusal to show the *aidôs* expected of a man defending himself before the city and its laws, the ironic elements uncover the very limits of what *parrhêsia* can accomplish, the ways in which this democratic practice cannot on its own lead the listeners to the truth or the new Socratic understanding of shame. Socratic irony will surface significantly in the discussion of the *Protagoras* in Chapter 8, which will serve as the culmination to the discussion that follows in the next and final section of this book. There through attention to selected texts from the ancient corpus I address the limits of *parrhêsia* as a political and social practice in a democracy.

---

[41] This is not to suggest that irony is absent from the *Apology*, but I consider this speech with Vlastos' admonition to approach Socrates' words with the acknowledgment that "in almost everything we say we put a burden of interpretation on our hearer" (1991: 44). Given the recent interest in rhetoric in ancient Athens, it is surprising that so little attention is given to the *Apology* by scholars interested in this practice. See, for example, Hesk (2000) and Yunis (1996). Vlastos' work remains the most thorough investigation of irony in Socratic speech generally, but see also the extension of that principle in Grant's (1997) exploration of the role of hypocrisy in political life.

PART IV

THE LIMITS OF FREE SPEECH

6

Truth and Tragedy

Today we consider it a matter of decency not to wish to see everything naked, or to be present at everything and "know" everything. "Is it true that God is present everywhere?" a little girl asked her mother; "I think that's indecent" – a hint for philosophers! One should have more respect for the bashfulness with which nature has hidden behind riddles and iridescent uncertainties. Perhaps truth is a woman who has reasons for not letting us see her reasons.

(Nietzsche, *The Gay Science* [V.2.20])[1]

Greek tragedy and comedy, though often set in Thebes or Mycene or in the case of comedy in such places as Cloudcuckoobury, were part of the civic festivals of Athenian democracy and served as venues in which the playwrights might encourage reflection on, among much else, the political life of the city. While Aeschylus' Persian Chorus sing of the unfettered tongue in the free city of Athens, other plays from the remaining corpus of Attic plays also pay tribute in speech to this peculiar freedom enjoyed by the Athenians. But, the appearance of this practice within the dramatic action does not always earn the unqualified praise we find in Aeschylus' *Persian Women*. The playwrights, especially Euripides, also suggest how this democratic practice has become exclusionary in Athens, freeing some and yet silencing others, and they portray as well the destructive effects of the openness and revelatory power of this practice for members of the community. We begin in this chapter to explore the ambiguities of this practice of *parrhêsia*, which so marked the Athenians' experience of their democracy.[2]

---

[1] I am grateful to Tracy Strong for alerting me to this passage. The translation is from his translation of the passage in Kofman (1988).

[2] Halliwell in his extensive study of what can and cannot be expressed in Athenian comedy remarks in a similar vein: "In a society which is pervasively sensitive in matters of honor, shame, and reputation, the harmful potential of frank speech, particularly in public life, may lead to a recognition of a need for constraints on freedom of the spoken word" (1991: 48).

Aristophanes' *Thesmophoriazusae* and Euripides' *Phoenician Women* will serve as the primary texts for a consideration of the dramatic artists' hesitations about some of the consequences of speaking freely in the public spaces of the city.[3]

We might note first, though, that it is, of course, on the comic stage itself that one finds the fullest expression of the freedom to speak frankly. The Old Comedy of Aristophanes, with its bawdy language, vivid and indeed colorful representation of private parts on stage, and blasphemous jokes about the gods, not to mention contemporary political characters, expresses the openness of speech in antiquity – the freedom to speak without fetters, without *aidôs*, the freedom to mock the traditional hierarchies and refuse deference to one's superiors, be they gods or political leaders. Old Comedy, with its thorough-going shamelessness, arriving in Athens only in 486, well after the democratic regime had been established, was "a product of democratic patronage" (Halliwell 1991: 66).[4] Tragedy, a much older art form, had its roots in the aristocratic, hierarchical past of pre-Cleisthenic times.

Nothing, it seems, was too private to be hidden from the gaze of the audience of comedy – not the genitals (or representations of thereof), the digestive functions, the pretenses of political leaders, or the foibles and vanities of the gods themselves. All these parade shamelessly on Aristophanes' stage. Halliwell even calls comedy "a kind of ritualized shamelessness" (2002: 123 and passim).[5] Though there may have been laws dating from Solon's time restricting the use of specific names in comedy, Radin (1927) for example argues that, given inflation, the amount of the fine (which may have been large when the law was passed) was sufficiently meager to make it foolish to prosecute.[6] More serious with regard to restrictions on the language of comedies were the *aporrhêta*, that which must not be spoken. Included in this category was calling someone a shieldthrower or a patricide or matricide or ridiculing acting generals or magistrates (Henderson 1998: 264).

I will be interested in this chapter with why it may be harmful beyond the offense it may have for the reputations of specific citizens.

3 Obviously, there are many other texts that could serve as well for an exploration of this topic. I think especially of Euripides' *Orestes*, which investigates seriously the resistance to speaking what is shameful and has a section in which the demagogue speaks with "unlearned free speech (*amathei parrhêsiai*)" (905). See especially Foucault for an extended discussion of the *Orestes* (2001: 57–73).

4 See also Halliwell (1991: 66n69) for a series of citations that support his claims of a "link between comedy and democracy."

5 For a full discussion of the exposure allowed on the comic stage see Halliwell (1991).

6 Hansen (1995: 21n96) argues that the decree with regard to names was passed in 440/39, but abrogated in 437/6 and notes that there is no evidence that a trial on this law ever took place. See also Halliwell (1991: 70).

Though such constraints seem to have been in effect during the latter half of the fifth century when Aristophanes' comedies were produced, the comedies are nevertheless remarkable for their "liberty to transgress the bounds of common inhibitions in speech" (Halliwell 1991: 67) and their willingness to open all to the gaze of the audience.[7] For my purposes, though, the dramatic content that explores the difficulties posed by the revelatory powers of unveiling speech – on the stage or off – rather than the dramaturgical shamelessness deserves explication.

1. *PARRHÊSIA*: INCLUSION/EXCLUSION

In Euripides' *Hippolytus*, the queen Phaedra, wracked by the fear that the discovery of her lust for her husband's son would bring shame on her family, plans to commit suicide. Only by killing herself, she concludes, may her husband, son, and "the children to whom I gave birth live flourishing, as men free to speak frankly/freely (*eleutheroi parrhêsiai*) in the famous city of the Athenians" (420–3). In Euripides' *Ion*, the young Ion, a temple boy of Apollo at Delphi who had been abandoned at birth and uncertain of his parentage, is told that his father is Xouthus, husband to the queen of Athens; yet, before returning to Athens with Xouthus, who despite his marriage to the Athenian queen remains a foreigner in Athens, Ion searches for his mother and prays that she turn out to be an Athenian. If she is an Athenian, then, according to the citizenship laws of Athens (anachronistically applied), he too would be an Athenian and there would be "from my mother for me *parrhêsia.*" He worries about this because the stranger in Athens "dwells with the mouth as slave (*stoma doulon*) and does not have *parrhêsia*" (672–5). The *Ion* in general is a play about inclusion and exclusion, purity and racism.[8] *Parrhêsia* may be a treasure for those who are included as members of the community, but it also marks the difference between the slave and the freeman, the insider and the outsider.

---

[7] According to Henderson (1998: 259–69), although the practice of free speech may have enabled any one to criticize the powerful, it was a practice not frequently enjoyed. Thus, "by frankly criticizing the powerful, the comic hero(ine) did what *isêgoria* and *parrhêsia* ideally allowed but could not fully provide for" (269). As with so much about the ancient world, it is difficult to assess how much the ideals expressed in the literary remains made it into actual practice. See also Halliwell (1991) for an exhaustive study of what may have been and what may not have been allowed on the comic stage.

[8] I go into more detail about the theme of exclusion and inclusion in the *Ion* in Saxonhouse (1986a). Foucault (1983: 12) calls the *Ion* "the parrhesiastic play," "the decisive Greek parrhesiastic play" where the god Apollo plays the silencing or covering role in contrast to Ion and his mother who play the "parrhesiastic roles" (1983: 25). See also the analysis of the play in Foucault (2001: 36–57).

Euripides' version of the *Suppliant Women* often surfaces as one of the few literary texts in which we can find passages that explicitly defend Athenian democracy and the political culture that goes with it (lines 353–456).[9] These passages occur in an exchange between Theseus, the leader in Athens, and an Argive messenger. Theseus defends Athens' regime against the messenger's hostile question: "How would the people (*dêmos*), not keeping words straight, be able correctly to set straight the city? . . . Whenever a worthless man, a nothing previously, by his tongue receives honor from the people, this is sickness for the better sort of men" (417–25). In a powerful response, Theseus affirms: "When the laws are written down, the man who is weak and the man who is wealthy have equal justice (*tên dikên isên*). It is possible for those who are weaker to speak the same things to the one who is fortunate . . . This is freedom: Who has counsel concerning what is best for the city wishes to bring it to the attention of all (*es meson*). And the one speaking will be famous, and the one not wishing to speak remains silent. What is more equal (*isaiteron*) for the city than this?" (433–41). Before the skeptical foreign messenger, Theseus extols the life of a people living in a free polis (*eleuthera polis*, 405) where the people (*dêmos*) rule in turn (406) and where written laws ensure that the strong and the weak enjoy equal justice, all equally participating in the deliberative life of the city.

The vision Theseus offers of his own city is noble. And yet, after his lengthy speech, Theseus speaks sharply to the foreign messenger about his "excessive speech (*perissa phônôn*)" (459). Excluded from the city of free men, the messenger insofar as he is a foreigner does not enjoy the *parrhêsia* of the citizens of Athens. As in the *Ion* and the *Hippolytus*, *parrhêsia* is exclusionary, marking those who are within and those who are outside. The circle that excluded Thersites from participating freely with the Achaean generals as they deliberated about whether to return to Greece has grown – but perhaps not all that far. The praise of Athens that Euripides puts into the speech of his characters is shaded throughout his plays by a sensitivity to exclusions that can be embodied in the practices of freedom.

This point is especially notable because of an unexpected twist that Euripides introduces into his version of the *Suppliant Women*. Though Theseus silences the windy talk of the messenger, he nevertheless grants speech to members of the community most frequently denied the opportunity to speak freely: women. When Theseus' mother Aethra asks if she may speak for Theseus' and the city's welfare, Theseus responds in a surprising fashion for those of us raised on the sorry stories of Greek misogyny: "Many wise things come from the female race" (294). When Aethra at first hesitates to speak openly, Theseus reacts: "You have spoken shamefully (*aischron*), hiding (*kruptein*) words that are useful for friends" (296). Aethra replies: "I will

---

[9] See for example Roberts (1994: 38–9).

not then be quiet (*siôpôs'*) and then blame myself that I remained silent in a cowardly fashion (*kakôs*). And I will not keep quiet fearing that the words women speak well are useless. Nor will fear prevent me from saying what is noble" (296–300).[10] Aethra's speech here suggests that women too can display the daring *parrhêsia* inspires.

More familiar, though, is the regular misogynist language of the inhabitants of Greek tragedy. There is the maddened Ajax in Sophocles' play. To his wife Tecmessa, as she questions what he is doing heading out of his tent when the entire Greek army sleeps, he responds (as she herself reports it in a long speech to the Chorus): "Woman, silence brings beauty to women" (293). It is Tecmessa, of course, who speaks sense to a man about to slaughter the cattle he imagines to be the Greek generals who had denied him the arms of Achilles. Her question, had she not been silenced, would have forced the crazed Ajax to reflect on the mad and impassioned adventure in which he is about to engage. Similarly, in Aeschylus' *Seven Against Thebes*, Eteocles, about to kill his own brother in mutual slaughter, expresses horror and disgust at the sounds of the women who are calling on the gods to save the city. *Thremmata*, vile things, he calls them and demands that they be silent (181). His own madness leading to the reciprocal fratricide fails to yield before the stark wisdom of the women. They, rightly fearing the dangers posed for themselves and the city at large by an invading army, call on divine help; Eteocles ready for the impiety of fratricide ignores the gods. So firm (and wrong) in his sense of control, Eteocles has no capacity to listen to or understand the expression of fear by the females about the crimes on which he is about to embark.[11]

Perhaps it would be too much of an anachronistic interpretive leap to say that these playwrights question the denial of *parrhêsia* to the women who live in their midst, that they are imagining, along with John Stuart Mill so many centuries later, that the wisdom of half the human species is lost by silencing them. Yet, as playwrights, presenting their tragedies before the city as a whole, they bring into being women (or, more accurately, representations of women) who perform on the dramatic stage. They give them voices with which to speak openly – often without deference to traditional hierarchies – to those whom they encounter on the stage and to the audiences seated in the amphitheater. They take women out of the household and place them in the public realm where they can be both seen and even more significantly heard. Along with that exposure of the female and her speech on stage, the playwrights uncover the tension surrounding the silencing of the city's women who wish to speak frankly. As with the practice of *parrhêsia* in

[10] In Euripides' *Electra* Clytemnestra, in her confrontation with Electra, urges her daughter to use *parrhêsia* in explaining why she, Clytemnestra, should not have killed her husband, Electra's father (1049–56).

[11] See further Saxonhouse (1986b).

general, though, this unveiling of the speech of women is not to be understood
as necessarily arising from the playwrights' concern with the "oppression" of
the female in ancient society or the "right" of women to express themselves
frankly before others, "deserving" the same privileges as the male citizens
because of a common humanity. Rather, their speech may benefit rulers like
the *Suppliants'* Theseus who listens to those whom others (for example, Ajax
and Eteocles) would silence. By illuminating the choices and the mistakes of
others, the women's speech may expose truths that the men often do not hear:
the impiety of fratricide or the insanity of Ajax's planned revenge. Denying
parrhêsia denies in the cases of Ajax and of Eteocles access to truths that
could prevent senseless slaughter and impieties. Like Thersites in the second
book of the *Iliad*, these women are excluded from the deliberative circle; had
the traditional hierarchies been violated and had they thus been allowed to
speak freely, they might have benefited the community at large.[12]

2. ARISTOPHANES' *THESMOPHORIAZUSAE*

In Aristophanes' comedy the *Thesmophoriazusae* written in 411 or 410 BCE,
the comic poet explores – albeit in a most absurd fashion – the theoretical
challenges posed by the playwrights' own freedom to reveal and uncover
before the entire city, the dramatic *parrhêsia*, so to speak. How far can the
playwright – comic or tragic – go in opening up on stage what may most
often be covered and shielded from the intrusive eyes of others? What are the
consequences of exposing what has previously been hidden? In this particular
comedy Aristophanes reveals the power of the dramatist who controls what
is revealed and what is not by giving speech to the characters that perform
on the stage.

In the *Thesmophoriazusae*, Aristophanes has his characters enact before
the Athenians the secret festival of the women who have gathered to celebrate
the Thesmophoria. In contrast to the *Lysistrata* or the *Ecclesizusae* where the
women organize in order to affect the public life of the city, in one by ending
the war between Athens and Sparta, in the other by a total restructuring of
the city, the women of the *Thesmophoriazusae* challenge the portrayal of
"woman" as presented on the tragic stage by the male poet Euripides.

The women at the Thesmophoria, with their own leaders and heralds,
convene an Assembly in which they deliberate about how to proceed with
their decision to put Euripides on trial for writing plays that present women
as driven by excessive sexual desires, as duplicitous in all their actions, and
as overly fond of wine. The women complain that their husbands, having

---

[12] Henderson (1998: 257) points to a similar perspective in comedy as well (in *Wasps* 469–
99, 1388–414 and *Lysistrata* 507–28) and comments: "In the world of the *oikos*, a citizen
woman was ideally expected to defer to the male, but to *deny* her the right of *parrhêsia* could
be portrayed as both unreasonable and undemocratic."

attended performances of Euripides' plays and having been persuaded that the representations they see on stage are accurate portrayals of what women do when they are left alone, prevent them from satisfying their libidinous and bibulous desires, from visiting their female friends, and even from performing their household tasks effectively. For this, the women decide, Euripides deserves to die. It is Euripides' knowledge of this impending trial at the Thesmophoria that sets the action of the play in motion. At first Euripides solicits the help of the playwright and poet Agathon, a "womanish man" (136), to defend him, and when Agathon refuses, he sends his kinsman to the sacred festival to speak on his behalf. The kinsman (in some texts referred to as Mnesilochus), plucked, clean shaven, urged to speak in a "womanish voice" (267), and dressed in saffron colored robes, rings, and a hairnet goes as a woman to the Assembly being held by the women at the Thesmophoria.

Mnesilochus makes his way into the festival and the Assembly that is taking place there. This female Assembly appropriates to itself all the elements of the traditional Assembly in Athens, beginning with the curse on those who "break their oaths, who speculate on the public misfortune, who reveal what must not be spoken" (*aporrêta*, 361–3). The Assembly begins in earnest with a secretary recording the principal business of the day, namely the condemnation of Euripides. And, as in the Athenian Assembly, the (female) herald asks: "Who wishes to speak?" (379). Meanwhile, Mnesilochus prays that he will escape detection (*lathen*, 288), and remains shielded by his disguise, unrecognized for who he really is as he listens to the speeches given by the women. The First Woman rises to recite the litany of disapproved behaviors that Euripides has ascribed to women: they are adulterous, lecherous, lovers of wine, and so forth. This speaker does not question the validity of these accusations, but rather considers the consequences of presenting such character traits on stage for the whole city (especially their husbands) to see. The men, as she presents it, not questioning Euripides' representations of women, become overly suspicious of their wives, sisters, and daughters who must now devise further ruses to escape the control the men have over them.

This is a play filled with deception, so much so that any notion of truth almost disappears. Not only does Euripides dress Mnesilochus as a woman, but throughout the play various cloaks and disguises hinder the perception of the identities of various characters that float in and out in various covers. Toward the conclusion of the comedy, Mnesilochus becomes Helen, then Andromedea, and Euripides becomes Menelaus, then Perseus. Underneath all the language of veils and assorted masks lies the deeper issue of whether there is any truth to be revealed or whether the deception in which the actors on stage engage – both within the context of the plot of the play and insofar as they themselves are representations of what they are not (for example, Euripides or women) – controls who and what we can know. Is there any space for that which is without deception, without a cover, and thus for the truth? The *Thesmophoriazusae* addresses the role of the theater as deception controlling the perception of truth – or perhaps even raising the question of whether there is a truth that can be hidden or revealed or whether all rests within the poet's mastery of illusion.[13]

When Mnesilochus speaks to the women in the Assembly called by the women, (s)he proclaims that among themselves it is necessary to offer forth their speech, since there will be no "outpouring" or leaking of what they say (472). With no apparent reason, then, to hide her (his) complaints, s/he embarks on a litany of stories that tell of her illegitimate and impious sexual escapades, from stealing out of her supposed husband's bed on the first night of marriage to sexual relations on Apollo's altar. The tales s/he tells are ones that focus specifically on the way in which speech and varied ruses deceive. Mnesilochus' long speech, in the event, tries to exonerate Euripides by arguing that there are a multitude of deceptions and coverings that have hidden women's actions within the household and that Euripides was so kind as never to set on stage. It could have been much worse. We should remember, though, that Aristophanes through the voice of Mnesilochus opens up these actions and deceptions for the whole city to hear. However, Euripides by not uncovering all the possible complaints one could make about their activities, Euripides' defender argues, has protected women from still greater domination. Mnesilochus' exoneration of Euripides becomes in turn a condemnation of Aristophanes.

The women at the festival do not know how to respond to what they see as the arrogance (*perihubrizein*, 535) of this defense of the man they plan to condemn to death. At first, they fetch coals to depilate the speaker – that is, make her (him) more of a woman assuming that this will make her no longer speak ill of women as s/he had done in the speech meant to defend Euripides (538–9). Faced with such a threat, the speaker invokes the language of the male political world and the democratic political culture, namely the language of *parrhêsia*: "Are we not here female city-dwellers (*astai*)[14] for whom it is permitted to speak (*k'axon legein*) having *parrhêsia*? And because I have uttered what I thought right (just, *dikaia*) in favor of Euripides, must I be depilated in order to give justice on your behalf?" (540–3). Since the women have called an Assembly (*ecclêsiazein*, 84 and 331–51) in the same fashion as the male citizens of Athens would, all those attending, Mnesilochus indicates, should be allowed to speak openly about what they truly believe – just as they would on the Pnyx – without the fear of Odysseus' stick or, in this

---

[13] Tutschka and Saxonhouse (2002) considers the play from this perspective, especially with respect to the scenes surrounding Agathon the playwright where the question of whether there is any defined nature (*physis*) that exists independent of the creative artist surfaces. Agathon seems to have no identity, moving between the sexes and various meteorological forms. In his case, there is no hiding or revealing since there is nothing to hide or reveal.

[14] On the use of *astai* as referring to female citizens of Athens see Sealey (1990: 13).

case, hot coals applied to their pubic hair. Only through the inversions of the comic stage can there be the general portrait of women gaily practicing *parrhêsia*. Only through a befuddled character such as Mnesilochus could such an inversion find expression. The women rationalize, though, that since the speech by Mnesilochus clearly comes from a *rhêtor*, that is, one who hides rather than reveals, the one speaking it is not protected by the practice of *parrhêsia*. The women ecclesiasts capture here the confusion that Demosthenes and Aeschines express well in the next century between *parrhêsia* as the speech that defying the constraints of hierarchy daringly reveals the truth and oratory pretending to be *parrhêsia* that shields the hearer from the truth rather than revealing it.[15] Mnesilochus indeed hides who he is, but whether he speaks the truth about women is left ambiguous by the comic poet.

In fact, during the course of the comedy, Aristophanes' portrayal of the women celebrating the Thesmophoria conspicuously matches the portrayal that Euripides offers and for which the women are condemning him to death. As the comedy proceeds, Aristophanes' women tell stories of how they indeed have met with secret lovers, snuck out of their houses, smuggled in wine sacks, pretended that the children (especially the sons) of others are their own, and so forth. Euripides in his plays had unveiled the truth about the women of Athens and yet the truth, the women claim, harms them and brings about their enslavement. The frank speech of Euripides' tragic stage in the curious comic logic of this play is the cause of women's own lack of freedom. Had Euripides not revealed their character on stage so that their husbands would become suspicious of them, they would have been free to pursue delights now denied them. Punishing Euripides with death, they claim, will silence those truths and make them free. The comedy concludes when Euripides finally promises to cease traducing the women. He manages to escape punishment by the women, but only by employing a continuing series of subterfuges and illusions drawn from his own tragedies. It is not Euripides' innocence, for he is not innocent, that frees him in the end from the judgment of the women festival goers, but lies and pretenses, the fictions perpetuated by the dramatic art rather than a truth revealed by frank speech.

Aristophanes' comedy is more than just an exemplar of the openness of Athenian society that would allow blasphemies, personal attacks, and the grotesque unveiling of the ugliness of our bodies on stage. It is also a serious reflection on the problematic consequences of unveiling – of revealing the truth.[16] Such unveiling through speech, as Aristophanes suggests, has practical consequences for the lives of citizens and their women. Does *parrhêsia*, the frank presentation of the truth as one sees it in the case of the women of

---

[15] See the reference in Chapter 4, pages 91–3.
[16] For a full analysis of this as a play of deception and unveiling see Tutschka and Saxonhouse (2002).

Aristophanes' comedy, benefit the city or lead to the oppression of women who live in the city and attend the Thesmophoria as a way to affirm their own authority? The poet with great power to cover and to expose – be he Aristophanes or Euripides – can heal or poison the city. Aristophanes' play, putting on stage this secret festival of the Thesmophoria, may show that health for the city would come from the poet who knows what to cover and what to uncover. The practice of *parrhêsia* in this reading would be a practice to be controlled by the wisdom of the poets. Shameless revelation of the truth in this tale can harm and enslave as well as heal and emancipate. Aristophanes' comedy here could be read as a self-serving statement of the power of poetry. The Athenian practice of *parrhêsia* enables him (and all the dramatic artists) to play philosopher king through manipulating what is seen and unseen. Socrates' philosopher practices *parrhêsia*, as do the poets, revealing often what others may prefer to hide. The comic conclusion of Aristophanes' play, with both Euripides and Mnesilochus escaping the vengeance of the women, offers no solution as to who is to reveal and what uncoverings free or enslave. Aristophanes writes this comedy to mock Euripides and compete with him for control over what is revealed. The contest in the *Thesmophoriazusae* is between comedy and tragedy as to who owns the franchise to beneficial *parrhêsia*. The Platonic Socrates, whom we shall encounter again in Chapter 8 in this role in the *Protagoras*, becomes a participant in this contest as well.

3. EURIPIDES' *PHOENICIAN WOMEN*

A perhaps more powerful and disturbing example of the conundrum posed by the practice of free speech occurs in Euripides' own play *Phoenician Women*, a play that sets up tension between the *parrhêsia* treasured by the free man, the longing that the human being has to be able to speak the truth and not hide oneself behind obsequiousness and subordination to others, and the dilemmas into which the unveiling of a truth can lead.[17] It captures the persistent hunger for freedom of speech as a source for personal identity and the comparable need for shame and restraint in speech. The *Phoenician Women* is a strange play, described as "episodic and overstuffed" by an ancient critic (Conacher 1967: 230), included in Euripides' "melodramas" by H. D. F. Kitto and described by him as "nothing like a normal play" (1950: 372). And Francis M. Dunn complains that "characters in the play are piled one upon the other, as are the various texts that report their stories. In a similar way, the larger forces that might have given coherence to the action are multiplied in a bewildering fashion" (1996: 192). Contemporary scholars, nourished by an Aristotelian theory of tragedy, often preface their

---

[17] Foucault considers Euripides' plays in detail, especially the *Ion* and the *Orestes* in his study of *Parrhêsia* (2001: 27–74). He turns briefly to the *Phoenician Women* (28–9).

studies of this play with some initial exculpatory remarks about why one would attend to a play that is so aesthetically and thematically unsatisfying; this, despite the fact that Euripides' *Phoenician Women* and his *Orestes* were the most commonly read and quoted classical works (except for Homer) throughout antiquity (Dunn 1996: 180). An effort at a brief plot summary suggests why such excuses might be necessary.

The play builds on and revises substantially the Theban legend familiar from Aeschylus' *Seven Against Thebes* and Sophocles' *Oedipus, Antigone,* and *Oedipus at Colonus*, bringing all those plays with many peculiar twists and turns into one massive pageant. Polyneices, the son of Oedipus and Jocasta, has returned with an Argive host to claim his turn to rule over Thebes from his brother Eteocles who, too much in love with being a tyrant, has refused to yield his power. At first Jocasta (who has not committed suicide as in Sophocles' play)[18] tries to reconcile the sons. She fails, they fight, they kill one another, and Jocasta kills herself upon seeing their two bodies. Before the encounter between the two brothers, Eteocles tells Creon to rule in case he dies and informs him that he has sent Creon's son Menoeceus to bring Teiresias the seer. Teiresias arrives accompanied by Menoeceus and reveals that the city can be saved only by Menoeceus' sacrifice. Creon refuses to perform such a sacrifice and sends Menoeceus away. Menoeceus pretends to be ready to depart, but once Creon has left the stage, he prepares to kill himself for the sake of the city. Meanwhile, Antigone rushes to the corpses of the brothers, plans the burial, until Creon on earlier orders from Eteocles denies burial to Polyneices and decides it is time to expel Oedipus. Antigone defies Creon, Oedipus appears, and off father and daughter go into exile. I have not recounted all the characters and episodes in the play. And yet, within this "overstuffed" tragedy, Euripides offers a challenging exploration of the meaning and consequences of the practice of free speech, *parrhêsia*, the daring to speak what one knows is true and that we have seen as so vital a quality of the Athenian political regime.

The play begins with Jocasta's soliloquy that is followed by a scene in which the Pedagogus leads Antigone out of her maiden room (*parthenônas,* 89) to observe the invading Argive host. The Pedagogus urges Antigone to hold back briefly so that he can make sure that the way is clear lest any one of the citizens (*tis politôn*) appear and there arise for him as a slave and her as a princess (*anassêi*), that is a female, "paltry censure" (*phaulos...psogos,* 94–5). Young women and the slaves attending them, apparently, do not reveal themselves to the city. For Antigone, the movement of this play will be marked by the disclosure of herself before the city, the casting off of any shame or respect for the norms of the city and the hierarchy that has kept her along with her slave hidden within her maiden room. She moves at the

---

[18] See Loraux (1987: 15) for a discussion of how surprising this must have been.

end of the play to the emotional state where she can rise above the gender distinctions that marked her status and made her a concealed creature at the beginning of the play. At this early moment of the play, though, since no one of the city dwellers (*outis astôn*, 99) is visible and the way is clear, Antigone led by the Pedagogus secretly ascends the wall.

Antigone learns from the Pedagogus the names and stories of the Argive warriors who lead the attack on Thebes and she calls down upon them the nemesis of Zeus' thunder so that she may never have to suffer enslavement. "I would not endure being a slave" (192), she (who at this point in the play can barely appear outside her maiden room) asserts. The Pedagogus ends the instruction from the wall by sending Antigone back into her maiden room because a mob of women approaches. Women are by nature (*ephu*), according to the Pedagogus, "lovers of censure" (198). The Pedagogus concludes the scene having this to say about women in general: "There is a certain pleasure (*hêdonê*) for women not to speak what is sound (*hugeis*) about one another" (200–1). Into the mouth of a slave Euripides has put a speech condemning the free speech of women, just as Aeschylus had given such a speech to the man about to kill his brother and just as Sophocles had done with the warrior about to slaughter cattle imagining that they were the Greek generals.

The Pedagogus here may simply be expressing conventional wisdom with idiomatic phrases (Mastronarde 1994: 206; Craik 1988: 181), but playwrights who put such speeches into the mouths of slaves undermine the truths of the conventions – especially given the earlier speech of Jocasta and the role that Antigone (so protected at the beginning of the tragedy) will play by the end as she leads her father off to Athens and Colonus. Indeed, the chorus that follows the misogynist speech of the Pedagogus is comprised of the Phoenician women of the play's title who far from looking for gossip and speaking ill of other women sing in lofty phrases of travels from the Phoenician to the Cadmean land and who lament the imminent bloodshed, before they announce the arrival of Polyneices who, they claim, comes "not unjustly armed into the contest" (258–9).

In the next scene the issue of *parrhêsia* surfaces explicitly. Jocasta welcomes Polyneices and describes the life of her husband and his father, the old man bereft of his eyes longing for death (327). She then turns to the major part of her speech, expressing her concern about the foreignness of Polyneices' bride and family, an alliance that causes her great grief. Polyneices' kin did not participate in the creation of the marriage ties with a foreign family. The insularity she wants for her city underscores the insularity (and impieties) of her own family and yet, insensitive to the too narrow frame of familial relations that marks her own family, she bemoans the foreignness of his marriage alliance. It is this "foreignness" that Jocasta explores in the interrogation of her son. Polyneices expresses his anguish that his return home to the familiar halls and the gymnasium where he had been nurtured is marked by the sense of being among enemies and the fear of his own kin. He lives in a foreign city (*xenên polin*, 369), he laments, leading Jocasta to inquire (after some hesitation lest it cause Polyneices pain): "How is it to be deprived of one's fatherland? Is it a great evil (*kakon mega*)?" (388). Polyneices responds without hesitation: "*Megiston*. It is the greatest. But greater in deed (*ergôi*) than in word (*logôi*)" (389). Persistent in her inquiry, Jocasta wants to know what is so harsh for one living in exile. "The one greatest thing," Polyneices replies, "he does not have *parrhêsia*" (391). Not the distance from kin, not the absence of loved ones, but the loss of a public freedom weighs on Polyneices as the "greatest" cruelty of exile. Jocasta, his mother, not noting his callousness toward his family (and especially toward her), equates the denial of *parrhêsia* to the life of one who is not free: "You have spoken of that which belongs to a slave, not to say what one is thinking" (392). Polyneices agreeing finds the lack of *parrhêsia* the greatest evil because "one must bear the folly (*amathias*) of those who are powerful" (393). Jocasta concurs, judging it as grievous "to share in the lack of wisdom with those who are not wise (*sunasophein tois mê sophois*)" (394).

Beyond exposing the self-pitying character of Euripides' Polyneices, his and his mother's attitude toward *parrhêsia* is revealing. It is practiced only by those who are not foreigners within the city, only by those with power, not by those who are subordinate, that is, it captures the hierarchical and exclusionary relationships of the city – just as it did in the case of the *Ion*, only in that play it was with regard to Athens and not Thebes. The sense of disempowerment is not even so much the silence that is imposed on foreigners and slaves who cannot participate in self-rule, but the necessity of hiding one's thoughts, of having to cover or veil what one believes or knows to be true before another who is less wise. Thersites resurfaces. Indeed, the misery is not only to cover oneself, but to agree with what one recognizes as foolish, to be denied the opportunity to criticize the absence of wisdom in others. Polyneices' life as a foreigner in a foreign land is that of a woman who is silenced, that of the well-spoken Tecmessa, Ajax's wife, unable to speak to her husband of his folly.

The elevation of *parrhêsia* to the point of demarcation between those who are within the city and those who are exiles itself points to the longing for a freedom that allows for a self-exposure connected to the resistance to hierarchy. To be free within a city is to share in the critique of others without the fear of reprisals. Polyneices rebels against a shame that forces him to cover and restrain himself before others. As Polyneices explains, he must play the slave – unseen and unspeaking. This, he tells his mother, is against (his) nature (*para phusin*, 395). Not to say what one thinks is to be unseen and unheard, indeed to not be. To be a slave or a young woman (like the Pedagogus and Antigone in the first scene of the play) is to hide not only one's body, but also one's thoughts. Unable to express oneself, the foreigner, the slave, and the woman become invisible.

Eteocles arrives on stage as Polyneices laments the life of the poor well-born for whom "nature" provides no benefits. The contrast that emerges between Eteocles and Polyneices is stark. Polyneices, defending his decision to come home in order to take his turn ruling in Thebes for a year and then to yield that rule when the year has passed, longs for a world grounded in a natural hierarchy, where Nature teaches an absolute truth of what is just. "The tale of truth (*ho muthos tês alêtheias*)," he tells his brother, "is (*ephu*) simple and that which is just does not need many-colored interpretations" (469–70). It is the sick "unjust speech (*adikos logos*)" that requires a "clever medicine (*pharmakôn ... sophôn*)" (471–2). Polyneices concludes his lengthy speech directed toward his brother by noting that he has not used the "multi-colored (*periplokas*) [techniques] of unjust speech" (494). Polyneices trusts in a world where speech on its own has the power to order, where even the absurd agreement that the brothers make to take turns ruling, ought to hold sway.

Eteocles, in contrast, envisions a world without the absolutes for which Polyneices yearns; he begins his response: "If for all, the beautiful (*kalon*) and wisdom (*sophon*) were by nature (*ephu*) the same, there would not be strife (*eris*) of uncertain words (*aphilektos*)" (499–500). Rather, Eteocles continues, "for mortals equality/fairness (*ison*) are not at all the same except in name; the deed (*ergon*) does not exist" (501–2). According to Eteocles, neither good nor bad are grounded in a permanent nature waiting to be revealed by the exercise of *parrhêsia*. There is no natural hierarchy of the well born to which Polyneices appeals. Eteocles, through his own shameless *parrhêsia*, respectful neither of traditions nor oaths nor family affirms simply and without qualification that truth comes from power. If this is the result of speaking freely, unconstrained by hierarchy or tradition or *aidôs*, what is the value of the *parrhêsia* that Polyneices (and the Athenians in general) had so praised?

Eteocles sets the challenge powerfully. To his mother he says that he will speak all openly, practicing the *parrhêsia* that Polyneices longs for: "I speak, mother, hiding nothing (*ouden ... apokrupsas*)" (503). Shamelessly he tells her that he would go up to the stars or down into the earth to have the greatest of divine things, power in the city, tyranny (506). "This, mother, is the best and I am not willing to hand it over to another and not preserve it for myself" (507–8). This he says, despite oaths sworn with his brother before his father. The shame would be for him to yield to his brother for fear of the arms he brings with him. Thus, he will not yield the scepter despite his mother's pleas and despite the oaths he has sworn. If no equality, no fairness lives beyond speech, as Eteocles asserts, then those who possess power, in Eteocles' exposition, affirm the meaning of words. Eteocles as the ruler in Thebes, openly and shamelessly, we can perhaps say, expounds without hiding his praise of tyranny. He speaks from a position of power and is uninhibited by the fear of reprisals or the castigating looks that restrain

Antigone and her Pedagogus. Nor is he awed by a world of supposed justice. He would do anything, he tells his mother, to preserve the power he currently has. It is to Polyneices, Eteocles claims, coming to lay waste to his father's land, that shame (*aischunê*, 510) belongs.

Eteocles concludes his startling speech with a powerful oxymoron that matches the outrageousness of what has preceded. He says: "If it is necessary to be unjust, to be unjust for the sake of tyranny is most beautiful (*kalliston adikien*)" (523–5). The English translation does not capture the proximity of "most beautiful" and "unjust." No shame, *aidôs*, inhibits this expression of what he believes. His truth is uncovered, as ugly as it may be. Indeed, the chorus reacts with the affirmation of the conventional in response to this shocking proclamation: "It is necessary not to speak well upon deeds not well done; for this is not beautiful (*kalon*), but harsh (*pikron*) towards justice (*dikêi*)" (526–7). In deference to their sense of what is right, the chorus urges that Eteocles' speech not reveal, but hide, the shocking expression of Eteocles' own truth. They advise him to show respect for the noble and the just, to be controlled by shame and hide his thoughts. They wish him not to be himself.

Before Eteocles goes off to battle with Polyneices, he calls forth Creon to tell him assorted details about the attack. During this conversation, Eteocles informs Creon that he has sent Creon's son Menoeceus to bring Teiresias to Thebes so that they may learn from the seer of any prophecies concerning the welfare of the city (767). The oracle Teiresias brings, though, is one that Teiresias would rather not speak. When Creon questions him, Teiresias begins by affirming that while for Eteocles his mouth (*stoma*, 865) is always closed, for Creon he will speak – and so he does at length until he reaches that point when he has to name "another divine *mêchanê* of safety" (890). Then he hesitates, for to speak it is full of dangers and harsh to those who have the chance to give the city the *pharmakon*, the medicine, it needs to preserve itself. He prepares to leave and will not speak openly for, he says, to do so is "unsafe" (890–5). Hierarchy rules here since what he has to say will bring down the anger of the one with power over him, but his timidity covers the truth as well. Uncovering the truth will lead to harm for some and good to others. Speech (as in the *Thesmophoriazusae*'s women's portrait of Euripides) is ambiguous in its consequences – aiding and harming, clarifying and obfuscating.

The speech that uncovers all in this case leads to the tragic death of Creon's son. The speech that does not conceal brings on tragedy especially for Creon, but it is Creon himself who demands this exposure and its consequences when he bids Teiresias to speak before his son, though Teiresias had requested that Menoeceus be led away (911–14). This insistence on public speech uncovers the unconscionable choice that Creon must make – whether to kill his own son for the sake of the city. The naked truth is too much for Creon. He cannot endure the revelation from Teiresias: "Oh, many evils have you spoken in a brief moment...I heard not, I listened not" (917–19). He pleads with Teiresias to be silent with what he has revealed: "Do not speak these words to the city" (924). Teiresias refuses: "You bid me be unjust. I would not be silent (925)...let it be spoken by me...save either your son or your city" (951). The terrible truth has been revealed to Creon by Teiresias. And Creon's reaction now is not to speak: "Creon, why are you silent (960)," ask the Chorus. "What would one say, *ti d'an tis epoi*?" Creon asks in return (962) and resolves that he "like all human beings" will not slay his son (965). The scene ends with Creon urging Menoeceus to flee, lest the city fulfill what the father cannot.

Some of the tension of the scene between Teiresias and Creon repeats itself when the messenger reports to Jocasta about the battle at the Theban gates, which left both her sons still living and Thebes still standing. Rejoicing at this report, she then asks for news concerning the future, "What after these things is to be done by my sons?" (1208). The messenger responds: "Let go the rest (*ea ta loipa*)" (1209), but like Creon, Jocasta insists on the unveiling powers of speech that will for her – as for Creon – uncover unspeakable tragedies. In Creon's case, the unveiling speech led to the unbearable choice of whether to kill his son for the safety of the city; in Jocasta's case, it leads simply to foreknowledge of an unbearable fate that will precipitate her suicide. She rebukes the messenger: "You hide some evil and cover it closely with darkness" (1214). The messenger, unable to escape, speaks and reveals the duel that has been arranged between the brothers, the duel that will in turn lead to the death of both her sons and herself. Creon, Jocasta, Oedipus: this is a family that pursues the truth and that wants speech to reveal and uncover, but that always ends by regretting when the speech they so forcibly demand reveals the truths they would rather not hear. The uncovered truth can be harsh, exposing the vile and ugly (for example, fratricide, incest, and the bloodthirsty gods who demand the sacrifice of a young boy) as well as the beautiful.

When Antigone arrives on stage fresh from witnessing the deaths of her brothers and mother, she is no longer the timid young woman burdened by *aidôs* who had appeared in the first scene nor is she the modest child who had not wanted to leave her "maiden room" when her mother ordered her to go to the battlefield. "I am ashamed before the crowd (*aidoumeth' ochlon*)," she had said at that point in the play (1276). And to that her mother had responded: "There is no shame (*aischunê*) for you" (1276). What Antigone has now seen of death within her family dissolves all modesty and shame. After her excursion to the battlefield, she affirms, there will be no covering (*prokaluptomena*) of the delicate curls hanging over her cheeks nor any reddening on behalf of a maidenly modesty; there will be no blush (*eruthema*) on her cheeks nor will she feel shame (*aidomena*, 1485–9).

No more surreptitiously climbing the walls of the city, escaping the notice of the citizens, Antigone now plunges – without shame, as she herself says – into the middle of the city's events. She sings her dirge, displays herself without respect for the city (or even, perhaps, for the gods), drags forth her blind father from the house into the light and openly debates with Creon about his decision to follow Eteocles' demand that Polyneices not receive burial. Creon remarks to Oedipus (not without a certain irony): "Do you see (*eides*) how daringly she scorns and upbraids me?" (1676). From the silence imposed upon her at the beginning of the play, she moves on to a confrontation of the boldest sort, speaking boldly without deference before the male ruler in the city about the injustice of denying burial to Polyneices, refusing to wed the man chosen for her according to the customs of the city, insisting on leaving her proper place in the palace in order to follow her father into exile, and rejecting that father's concern that attending a blind father in exile would be shameful for the daughter (1691). The play ends as father and daughter head for Colonus, lamenting their fates but resigned to them.

The multitude of themes, not to mention characters and scenes, give this play its "overstuffed" quality; yet drawing out just the single theme of the practice of free speech, or daring speech, we see Euripides again exploring the consequences of this peculiarly Athenian practice: exclusion for some like Polyneices who had been thrust into a foreign land, tragedy for others as the frank speech of the characters brings on disaster for themselves. But ultimately it is Euripides himself whose play forces his audience (who, seeing only the public role of *parrhêsia*, may have on some recent occasion voted to name a state ship *Parrhêsia*) to assess more deeply the consequences of this political practice when it intrudes on their lives outside the Assembly. Ambiguous in its consequences for the lives of individuals, *parrhêsia* as a political practice may serve the city in its deliberations, but as the plays suggest an unmoderated exaltation of *parrhêsia* on stage reveals gods who are vengeful, who evoke fear rather than worshipful admiration, or as in Aristophanes' comedy, women who are duplicitous. *Parrhêsia* can sometimes harm and oppress, and as the debate between Eteocles and Polyneices reveals, a commitment to *parrhêsia* may ultimately require a commitment to a world in which there is a truth to be revealed lest it simply become a tool for the exercise of power rather than an expression of human daring and equality. Eteocles had offered a world where speech defines rather than discovers truth, a world where *parrhêsia* reveals and practices a "beautiful injustice."

Socrates' *parrhêsia* in the *Apology* in contrast to Eteocles' is committed to the unveiling of truths that the city itself has hidden from itself by its false speeches and resistance to the examined life. Socrates' *Apology* speaks frankly in an effort to release the city from its own false speeches, speeches that have prevented it from discovering its true self. The playwrights enjoying so much freedom on the stage, nevertheless, question the consequences of the practice of free speech in the lives of their dramatic characters.

7

Thucydides' Assemblies and the Challenge of Free Speech[1]

"[T]here were two circumstances in the working of the Athenian democracy which imparted to it an appearance of greater fickleness without the reality: – First, that the manifestations and changes of opinion were all open, undisguised, and noisy: the people gave utterance to their present impression, whatever it was, with perfect frankness: if their opinions were really changed, they had no shame or scruple in avowing it: Secondly – and this is a point of capital importance in the working of democracy generally – the *present* impression, whatever it might be, was not merely undisguised in its manifestations, but also had a tendency to be exaggerated in its intensity." Thus wrote George Grote in the middle of the 19th century.[2]

Thucydides' *History*, renowned for the sharpness of its analysis of relations between states, for the exposition of a "realism" that openly admits that "the strong rule where they can," includes within it descriptions of a series of deliberative Assemblies where citizens discuss among themselves the future actions that the city will take. Whether the speakers there spoke "with perfect frankness" and "had no shame" should their opinions change, as Grote writes, is the question for this chapter. Thucydides records speeches from four such democratic Assemblies for our consideration. This chapter will look at three of those Assemblies, the Athenians deliberating about the punishment to be inflicted on the rebellious island of Mytilene, the Athenians deliberating about whether to set sail for the conquest of Sicily, and the Syracusans deliberating about whether they should prepare for an attack from the Athenians.[3]

---

[1] Parts 1 and 4 of this chapter draw in part on Saxonhouse (2004), though the theoretical emphasis there is on deliberation rather than the freedom of speech.

[2] Cited by Demetriou (1999: 113).

[3] The fourth Assembly not discussed here is that at Sparta when the Spartans consider whether to respond to the speeches of the Athenians and Corinthians concerning a declaration of war on the Athenians. That Assembly does not take place in a regime that considers itself a democracy or has pretenses to *parrhêsia*, though see Socrates' description of the parrhesiastic

In his detailing of these assemblies, Thucydides presents us with characters caught up in the practice of democratic deliberation as imagined in the quotation from Grote. Their speeches investigate, each in its distinctive way, the viability of the practice of *parrhêsia* within the Assembly. In previous chapters we saw the ideals of *parrhêsia* as they came to be expressed in the literature and culture of the time. In Thucydides' *History* we have the reporting of Assemblies where *parrhêsia* was supposed to have been practiced. And what we find is that the practice was more problematic even in the fifth century (well before Socrates came up for trial) than the ideology of the plays, the rose tinted recollections of the fourth-century orators, and the florid language of George Grote might suggest. A question is whether there can be this ideal of free speech in the Athenian (or any) political system. The Assemblies portrayed in Thucydides' *History* raise concerns about the possibility of *parrhêsia*, the daring exercise of truth telling, as a political practice. The challenge posed is whether we are doomed to practice deceit rather than *parrhêsia* in political deliberative settings as Thucydides' character Diodotus concludes. Is *parrhêsia* simply a figment of idealistic dreaming or an ideological tool that has no relation to the practice of politics? Is it appropriate for the Socratic philosopher, but impossible in the venue of political life? Thucydides' Assemblies put *parrhêsia* to the test and offer a very different story from Socrates' *Apology* with its portrait of Socrates' philosophic uncovering of oneself. This chapter drawing on Thucydides, then, is a response in many ways to Chapter 5 on Socrates' speech before the jury.

Grote in the passage that introduces this chapter suggests a democratic Athens governed by frank speaking in the Assembly and explains away the notorious Athenian "fickleness" by attributing it to the frankness with which the Athenians were willing to express all their opinions. Thucydides' portrait is not quite so forgiving, but neither is it as damning as Hobbes' analysis when he writes in his Introduction to his translation of Thucydides: "For his [Thucydides'] opinion touching the government of the state, it is manifest that he least of all liked the democracy" ([1628] 1975: 13–14). Rather, Thucydides presents us with the challenges that deliberative assemblies pose for the practice of free speech: that is, can, ought, do ecclesiasts speak frankly and openly to express their views, or must the deliberative process be shaded by the calculated veiling of what one may know, the covering of what is true? A ship named *Parrhêsia* may enshrine the concept as an exclusive and favored

---

Spartans in the *Protagoras*, to be discussed in Chapter 8, pages 189–91. Though Archidamus speaks wisely, his opponent Sthenelaidas practices the laconic art of speech, calling in the briefest of speeches for his fellow citizens to be like the Athenians and act rather than ponder (1.85–7). There are also a number of occasions when Thucydides uses indirect discourse to describe such debates, but these occasions do not capture the complexity of the issues that emerge from the detailed "recorded" speeches. Both West (1973) and Lattimore (1998) provide valuable lists of all the direct and indirect speeches in Thucydides' *History*.

practice of Athenian democracy, the Athenians may identify *parrhêsia* as the practice of a free people, but does the practice function effectively and helpfully within the democratic Assembly of antiquity?

1. FREE SPEECH AND THE HISTORICAL METHOD

Near the beginning of his *History*, Thucydides explains his historical method. He complains that men take what they hear, but do not test it. He offers as examples the lack of care that people exhibit in evaluating what they hear by reference first to the popular – but incorrect – version of the story of the tyrannicides Harmodius and Aristogeiton and then to the belief that the Lacedaemonian kings have two rather than one vote, so careless, he says, is the search for the truth among the many (*hoi polloi*, 1.20.3). He, Thucydides, in contrast, depends on spoken evidence (*ek eirêmenôn tôn tekmêriôn*), accepting which "one does not make a mistake (*hamartanoi*)." He relies, he tells us, on the most manifest signs (*ek tôn epiphanestatôn sêmeiôn*, 1.21.1). These are the investigative principles that he applies to the study of this greatest of movements, the war between the Athenians and the Lacedaemonians. Behind his *History*, then, is the testing and evaluation of the evidence he has acquired largely through the speech of others; this means, in particular, that he must evaluate the speeches – the *logoi* – that he has heard from others, for he must rely on what others report in order that he himself may report correctly to his readers the vast details of the war. Earlier in Book 1, Thucydides had reflected that if Lacedaemonia were to be deserted with only the temples and the foundations of the structures left standing, men would be unbelieving (*apistian*, 1.10.1) of her power or that her fame matched her power, though she controlled, at the time that Thucydides writes, two fifths of the Peloponnesus. On the other hand, Thucydides remarks, if Athens were to suffer the same fate, it is likely that the appearance of the city would make her seem twice as large a power than she is at Thucydides' time. So much for the reliability of sight as the basis for accurate knowledge about the power of cities. Instead, Thucydides offers speech as the tool for revealing the true power of cities.

Thucydides, while dismissing as pleasurable amusements the stories Homer and Herodotus tell, reveals his own dependence on the stories of others as he moves in his methodological paragraph to clarify the status of the speeches that he records. Though some speeches he claims to have heard himself, others (most?) were told to him from other places (*tois allothen pothen emoi apaggellousin*, 1.22.1). With precise recording obviously impossible, Thucydides famously writes that the speeches in his *History* are pretty much what is needed (*ta deonta malista*, 1.22.1), deducing what was necessary given the circumstances. With this language he assures the reader of his concern with precision – but he also reveals a dependence on his own imagination to discover "that which is necessary." For the narrative, he repeats, he relied on what he saw, but also on what others saw and later reported to him, that is, again on speech. But, and this is the passage I wish to stress, it took "a great effort" or was "a great burden" (*epiponôs*) to sort out what he was told, given that those who were near the actions did not always say the same things about those events, burdened as they were by the prejudices and faulty memories (*tis eunoias ê mnênês echoi*, 1.22.4) that shaded the stories retold to him. Eager to offer his readers an understanding of *why* the war happened, he laments that the "truest" cause (*tên . . . alêthestatên prophasin*) is also the one that is "most unrevealed" by speech (*aphanestatên de logôi*, 1.23.6). The challenge, as Thucydides understands it, is to make speech revealing rather than concealing. The historian such as he is caught in a world of speeches that mask and cover the truth for individual reasons. To write a history one needs the skills to see beyond the coverings, or what we today might refer to as the subjectivity of the speech of his informants, in order to learn also what is not said.

When Thucydides acknowledges that the stories told to him are encumbered by prejudice and the uncertainties of human memory, he acknowledges as well that he must perform the same intellectual exercises that must go on in democratic assemblies. Precisely because, as he shows, speakers do not practice *parrhêsia*, uncovering what is true, those engaged in deliberation must evaluate and test, just as Thucydides does, the biased speeches spoken before them. Adam Parry in a path-breaking article expresses a certain impatience with Thucydides (who for decades had been so revered as the objective, scientific historian)[4] for not being more open about this aspect of his historical method: "[Thucydides'] very reluctance to speak of himself, his way of stating all as an ultimate truth, is . . . one of his most *subjective* aspects. When you say, 'so-and-so gave me this account of what happened, and it seems a likely version,' you are objective about your relation to history. But when, without discussing sources, you present everything as *auta ta erga* [the deeds themselves] . . . the way it really happened, you are forcing the reader to look through your eyes, imposing your own assumptions and interpretations of events" (1972: 48). Thucydides does not draw us into the assessment process in the way that Herodotus does. We do not see him testing the speeches that he hears. The great effort in which he engages to sort through the stories is invisible in the product he presents to us. Instead, though, in his portrayals of political assemblies he captures for his readers the difficulty both he and those who sit in assemblies have when faced with speeches that may or may not have been spoken with *parrhêsia*.

---

[4] Since Parry's time, veneration for Thucydides has appropriately shifted and readers now acknowledge and admire his interpretive intrusions. The literature is vast, in contrast to when Parry wrote his classic article. See, for example, Orwin (1984a; 1984b; 1994); Rood (1998); Ober (1994; 1998: chap. 2).

Socrates, in Plato's *Protagoras*, describes the experts who advise the ecclesiasts sitting in the Assembly: "I see that whenever we speak together in the
Assembly, and the city has to deal with a matter of building, builders are
sent for to consult about building; and whenever it concerns shipbuilding,
shipwrights are sent for, and other things of this sort" (319b). Aristotle in
Book 3, Chapter 11 of the *Politics* remarks on the benefits of the wisdom
of the many; like a potluck dinner, each participant brings some advantage
to the deliberations in the Assembly. But neither Plato nor Aristotle in these
contexts explores the problem to which Thucydides is so sensitive: how do
we know whether the experts and the people speaking before the Assembly
are exercising *parrhêsia*, speaking frankly and uncovering what is true? How
do we know whether the expert is giving advice to help or harm the city,[5] or
whether the multitude contributing to Aristotle's potluck express their views
openly without subterfuge? It is Thucydides, so aware of the self-interested
passions that drive the behavior of humans and of cities, so often called the
father of realism, faced with sorting through self-interested speeches in his
efforts to record the "greatest movement," who recognizes the need not just
to listen to what the experts say or what people claim to have seen or heard,
but to understand those claims as tinged by biases, as not being spoken freely
without shame or pretense.

Deliberation in the Assembly and the researches of the historian require
more than expert advice and the blending together of various opinions. They
require the awareness of human nature that a historian like Thucydides
employs in the reading of his sources, an awareness that speakers do not
always aim at the truth. Those at the Assembly listening to speeches,
Thucydides' book indicates, face the same challenges and must resolve the
problems in the same way that he does in developing his own historical
method. The plight of the democrat arises from the failure of others to practice the *parrhêsia* for which the Athenians were renowned. It is a plight that
affects the ecclesiast, the historian, and as we shall see in the next chapter, the philosopher. The failure to practice the free speech that arose in the
democratic culture of Athens appears at first to inhibit the success of deliberative assemblies. Yet, as becomes apparent from the deliberations I discuss
in the following sections democracies retain the capacity for reevaluation as
a check on the effects of the absence of words spoken freely. Indeed, Thucydides' *History*, so dependent on the words spoken to the historian, and the
Assembly of those attending to the political speeches both retain the capacity
to change, to amend the words written and the choices made as the result of
those words.

The text of Thucydides's *History* indicates that Thucydides never com-
pleted it; a wide range of scholars have speculated at length about the

---

[5] Consider Socrates' discussion with Polemarchus in Book 1 of the *Republic*, 331d–340b.

chronology of the composition of the text. Not only does the *History* end virtually in mid-sentence with Tissaphernes, a general in the Persian army sacrificing to the god Artemis, but the text itself is plagued by multiple inconsistencies and evidence that the work was composed over three decades with ample time for reevaluation and reappraisal. Such a text open to constant revision has frustrated scholars caught up in the challenges of the so-called *Thukididesfrage*, the question of what revisions were made when and what this may indicate about Thucydides' changing view of the war about which he writes.[6] Scholars, always eager for a moment of completion, anguish over this, but perhaps we can also read the openness of Thucydides' text as the unending search for what is true. Thucydides' possession for all times (*ktêma . . . es aiei*, 1.22.4) is itself, as he writes, hardly an unchanging document. Thucydides regularly reassesses the stories he had been told and the conclusions to which he had come. Textual revision is Thucydides' tool for dealing with the inaccuracies of the speeches he heard during his investigations as well as allowing for the wider vision that a greater distance from the emotion of the events may give him and his informants. Political revision by the democratic assembly is not a fault but a response to decisions similarly based on speeches that in their failure to be given frankly and openly require constant retesting and reassessment. The case of the Mytilenean Debate is Thucydides' prime example of democracy reversing itself – revising, so to speak, the text of political action. It is also the debate that explores most powerfully the place of honesty in political assemblies. Thucydides gives to this debate a searing emotional and dramatic power that makes it stand out amidst the usually reserved prose of his work.

2. THE MYTILENEAN DEBATE

In the fourth year of the war between the Athenians and the Peloponnesians, the oligarchs from Mytilene on the island of Lesbos prepare to unify the island and lead the Lesbians in a revolt from Athens.[7] In response to information leaked by their informers, the Athenians, though wearied from the plague and the other pressures of war, send forty ships to Mytilene and Lesbos. Despite a powerful plea by the Mytileneans to the Lacedaemonians

---

[6] See, for example Konishi (1980). Orwin (1994: 5–7) provides some background for this debate. More recently, Rood (1998) turns what others saw as a "problem" or "question" into a part of Thucydides' narrative style.

[7] I consider the Mytilenean Debate in detail also in Saxonhouse (1996: chap. 3), but there my primary focus was on the capacity of democratic assemblies to change their minds and the benefits that accrue to democracies from that capacity. The focus here on free speech and the place of past and future in the process of deliberation gives a very different texture to the discussion. Certainly, one of the best discussions of the Mytilenean Debate remains Orwin (1984b), but see also Connor (1984: 79–91) and Mara (2001: 825–32).

for support and the Lacedaemonians' acceptance of an alliance with the Mytileneans, the desultory prosecution of the war by the Peloponnesians, the strength of the Athenian resources, and internal treachery in Mytilene enabled the Athenians to enter the city, regain control of Mytilene, and subdue the islandwide rebellion. The Athenian general at Mytilene, Paches, sends back to Athens those oligarchs he considered responsible for the revolt along with the Lacedaemonian Salaithos who had arrived to help the Mytileneans. The Athenians put Salaithos to death immediately and then deliberate (*gnômas epoiounto*) in the Assembly about the other men sent to Athens by Paches, deciding, as Thucydides notes, "in anger (*hupo orgês*)" to kill not only those men who have been sent back to Athens as the instigators of the rebellion, but also all the Mytilenean adult males and, in addition, to enslave the women and children (3.36.2).[8] The Athenians send a trireme to Paches to inform him about what had been decided (*dedogmenôn*, 3.36.3) and tell him "to handle (*diachrêsasthai*)" (3.36.4) the Mytileneans as quickly as possible.

Thucydides records, however, that the very next day there was straightaway a change of mind and a reassessment (*metanoia . . . kai analogismos*) about the decision (*bouleuma*) – great and savage (*ômon*)[9] as it is – to destroy the whole city rather than just those who were the cause of the rebellion (3.36.4). The rethinking comes from both horror at the greatness of the punishment and reflection on the justice of punishing those who were not the cause (*aitious*, 3.36.4) of the revolt. Another Assembly is called without delay and the Athenians reconsider the decision of the previous day. Assorted opinions were expressed, but Thucydides reports only two speeches, that of Cleon, the most forceful of the citizens (*biaiotatos tôn politôn*, 3.36.6), and that of Diodotos the son of Eucrates, described by Thucydides as the man who had spoken most against killing the Mytileneans in the earlier Assembly (3.41). Though Thucydides does not mention – nor would we expect him to – the curiosity of the second speaker's name, Gift of Zeus, son of Good Power, nor would he be able to alert us to the fact that Diodotus appears nowhere else in the historical records of ancient Athens, we should not ignore

[8] As Orwin notes, little is made by Thucydides of the fact that it was the oligarchs who initiated the revolt and who then armed the people in the hope that they would support them in their resistance to the Athenians. He reads Thucydides' silence on this issue as an indication that "he has bigger fish to fry" (1984b: 486).

[9] Thucydides includes the word ômos in his narrative, thus leaving us uncertain as to whether it is Thucydides himself who describes the decree as "savage" or the Athenians. His comments about the success of the second ship sent by the Athenians at preventing the "horrible deed (*pragma allokoton*, 3.49.4)" from happening suggest, though, that ômos is the editorializing Thucydides. See Connor (1984: 82n5) for the significance of the word ômos, which originally means "savage" (in the sense of "raw") for the larger themes of Thucydides' work concerning the developing savagery of the war. Connor also discusses the significance of allokoton as a word associated with divine wrath or retribution (1984: 86).

these features of this particular speechgiver.[10] The two speeches Thucydides introduces into his narrative address many topics, but for my purposes here I will discuss how they address the possibility of free and open speech within the democratic Assembly and what emerges as a related concern for both speeches, whether we ought to live in a political community focused on past or future, a world that is restrained by what has been or one that leaves all open to a present-focused calculating humanity, free from the chains of the past. The *aidôs* of Protagoras' myth may require that restraint from the past, but the Mytilenean Debate uncovers some unsettling consequences of such restraint in Cleon's speech that, though, is no less unsettling than Diodotus' world of openness.

A. Cleon

Cleon speaks boldly; no shame restrains the expression of his views. In no way does he flatter his audience. Instead, he begins his speech to the Athenians sitting in the democratic Assembly with an attack on democratic Athens. "Often I have thought that a democracy is unable to rule over others, and especially so in your current change of intentions (*metameleiai*) concerning the Mytileneans" (3.37.1). Athens' democratic way of life, a life without fears and a life without internal conspiracies – (is he really speaking of Athens?) – hinders their understanding of human nature such that they are too trusting and allow the soft emotions like pity to blind them to dangers that await them. They do not see that their tyranny over others depends on the fear the allies have of Athenian strength, not on gratitude or goodwill (*eunoia*, 3.37.2) toward Athens. The tolerance of the democratic regime – described so vividly in Book 8 of Plato's *Republic*[11] – creates for its citizens, Cleon claims (in sharp contrast to others in Thucydides' *History* such as the Corinthians in Book 1 and Pericles in the Funeral Oration) the incapacity to act when needed and thus the incapacity to rule. Before an Assembly of democrats, Cleon invokes the failures of democracy. He calls on the vibrancy of democracy to give way to the stolidity of an oligarchy: "A city using worse laws that are unmoving (*akinêtois*) is stronger than one using good laws that lack authority (*akurois*), and ignorance along with moderation is more beneficial than sharpness along with intemperance, and the more dull-witted men (*phauloteroi*) for the most part guide cities better than those who are more

---

[10] Ostwald (1979) speculates on who Diodotus may have been, suggesting that he might have been serving as an officer responsible for collecting tribute for Athens' allies, but he remains hesitant to confirm such speculations. The disappearance of Diodotus from the historical record, though, is important for understanding a speech that critiques a city that honors speakers who speak well.

[11] See Chapter 2, pages 47–9.

quick witted (*xunetôterous*)" (3.37.3).[12] The unquestioned acceptance of what has seemed best to the many in the past is for Cleon the only grounds on which the Athenian regime can preserve itself.[13]

Challenging his democratic audience in this fashion, Cleon identifies just the problem an author like Wolin (1994) understands, though for Wolin this is not a problem.[14] Democracies, insofar as they rest on the momentary will of the many, are "formless" and thus variable (Saxonhouse 1998), not limited by laws or committed to follow earlier decisions – be they good or bad decisions. Constitutionalism is not necessarily democratic; it may oppose the decisions of the people. Cleon threatens democracy not so much by his demagoguery, for in no way does he flatter the people, but by a professed reverence for the past as a restraint. Decisions that were made in the past (even if it was only yesterday) must hold, he claims.

Cleon's most powerful appeal to the past comes in his call for the execution of justice. His justice is one that looks to the past, demanding recompense for past harms. In a perverted sense, Cleon shows *aidôs*; he reveres what has been,[15] and uses his (feigned?) reverence for what has been in order to limit the practice of *parrhêsia* and squelch deliberation.[16] The democratic assembly in principle always stands on the brink of the new and resists limits (the forms) imposed by past actions. Shamelessly, Cleon stands before this Assembly and speaks freely to them of the faults that come from this democratic openness. The democratic Assembly allows Cleon to critique its fundamental capacity to create, revise, and renew; it allows him to belittle the institution for which the past is not a standard free from reassessment by those assembled on the Pnyx.[17]

---

[12] The similarity between Cleon's speech and that of the Spartan Archidamus from Book 1 (1.79–85) is worthy of note here.

[13] Andrewes (1994: 39) makes the argument that in this way Cleon is a democratic speaker, defending the opinion of the *dêmos* *against* the sharp wit of the elites. He does not consider whether it was the sharp wit "yesterday" that also led to the decision concerning Mytilene.

[14] See the discussion of Wolin, Chapter 2, pages 49–50.

[15] Andrews (1994: 33) makes a good case for Cleon as devoted to a "traditional aretê," one consistent with the resolve involved in the Athenian decision to go to war and to annihilate the Mytileneans, one based on the notion of "surpass[ing] one's enemies in the harm inflicted." See also Saxonhouse (1996: 75).

[16] As Orwin writes: "Cleon's aim in eulogizing law is simply to discredit deliberation, by placing the result of yesterday's discussion beyond any further discussion" (1984: 315).

[17] As Gomme (1945–81: 2.300) and others note: "Kleon... is confusing *psêphismata* with *nomoi*. The laws of Athens would not be affected by the rescinding of an executive decree." A number of scholars, for example, Winnington-Ingram (1965: 71–2), have wondered about why Cleon speaks about "laws" when the previous day's decision about the Mytileneans was a "decree." See also Gomme (1945–81: 2.315) concerning the use of *hupeuthunon* in 3.43.4. I discuss the issue of the *graphê paranomôn*, a law instituted to hold accountable anyone who proposed to the Assembly a new law that would overturn the laws that had already been established, in some detail in Chapter 2, pages 44–5. When Cleon calls for the city to remain the same, though, he does not appeal to a *graphê paranomôn*. Thucydides is

Cleon's speech (like most of the speeches in Thucydides' *History*) is filled with irony. Speaking with absolute candor, with *parrhêsia*, Cleon urges the halting of *parrhêsia* because it is injurious to the welfare of a city that depends on restraints and unquestioned respect for the (day-)old. The vulnerability of democracy lies, in Cleon's views, precisely in this excess of speech (which he practices) and the capacity of those who so speak to manipulate his listeners rather than use speech to unveil a truth before the Assembly. Cleon taunts his audience: "I marvel at whoever ... will show (*apophanein*) that the harms done by the Mytileneans were beneficial for us, and ... It is clear that what was thoroughly decided was spoken in just the opposite way" (3.38.1–2). He mocks his audience, his fellow citizens: "You yourselves are the cause (*aitioi*) ... accustomed to being spectators of words and listeners of deeds ... trusting sight less than what comes through hearing,[18] giving honor to what comes beautifully from speech" (3.38.4). He calls these freemen, these democratic citizens, "slaves (*douloi*)" (3.38.5), imprisoned by their fascination with the novel and unexpected. The consequence, he complains, is that they sit in the Assembly "overcome by the pleasure of listening and seated as if attending the theater of the Sophists rather than deliberating for the city" (3.38.7). In his own dramatic speech, Cleon urges the Athenians not to make decisions on the basis of dramatic speeches. Let the rhetoricians with their pleasing words deal with more trifling matters, he argues, but not at a time when the city would pay a harsh penalty for brief pleasure (3.40.3). Practicing the most daring *parrhêsia*, Cleon faults the Athenians for allowing the freedom of speech to run amok in the Assemblies.

The core of this powerful man's speech lies in his demand for justice, justice understood as punishment for harms suffered. "Let them be punished," he demands, "in a way worthy of the harms (*adikias*) they have caused" (3.39.6). The speech is bold and outspoken in its appeal to the justice of vengeance. The Mytileneans deserve the punishment the Athenians decided upon in their moment of anger. In his unique moment of looking forward, Cleon urges expediency as well, affirming that the justice meted out to the

---

reporting a speech that supposedly took place in 428 BCE. The first attested example of the *graphê paranomôn* occurred in 415 (Munn 2000: 102).

Castoriadis captures the issues raised here when he writes about the Athenian Assembly: "[T]he *demos* was appealing against itself in front of itself: the appeal was from the whole body of citizens (or whichever part of it was present when the proposal in question was adopted) to a huge random sample of the same body sitting after passions had calmed, listening again to contradictory arguments, and assessing the matter from a relative distance. Since the source of law is the people, 'control of constitutionality' could not be entrusted to 'professionals' ... The people say what the law is; the people can err; the people can correct themselves. This is a magnificent example of an effective institution of self-limitation" (1991: 117).

[18] Consider Thucydides' own insistence on words rather than sight in 1.22; see discussion in Section 1 of this chapter, pages 148–9.

Mytileneans will terrify the other allies who will see in the case of Mytilene a paradigm (*paradeigma*, 3.39.3; 3.40.7) of what happens to allies who resist Athenian rule. Apart from this brief passage Cleon looks backward. Punishment focuses on the past and especially a past order that has been violated by the rebellious actions of the Mytileneans. Shameless before his fellow citizens, castigating and mocking them, deriding their institutions, Cleon ends his speech with a final plea to pay back the Mytileneans and set forth a clear example for the allies so that the Athenians can fight with their enemies and not their allies (3.40.7). Diodotus, the gift of Zeus and the son of good power, knows better than to speak with such mocking freedom before the Assembly of the Athenians. Diodotus knows better than to reveal before the Assembly what he really thinks if he wants his views to prevail.

B. Diodotus

Cleon had looked to the past for what is to be done now – even if the past is but a day ago. Decisions reached, deeds accomplished, words written become the milestone for his assessments, if not for his misguided fellow citizens. Cleon's focus (like the aristocracy from which Cleisthenes had freed the Athenians in the founding moment of Athenian democracy)[19] is on what has been. Within the aristocratic model, what is old serves as the guide to the present. Diodotus, Cleon's opponent in the Assembly as Thucydides chose to report it, is attentive to the future, not to the past. His speech is an abstraction from what has been and expresses what I have called a form of democratic amnesia. His willingness to forget the past, to exist at the moment of creation, free from any reverence for the past, correlates with a noble vision that he offers in his speech of an Assembly where participants debate honestly and rationally, without subterfuge or bias. Escape from the past and escape from a concern with how one appears before others, from the experience of shame, would enable the Assembly to function as a forum for full and frank participation that would be the fulfillment of a regime of *parrhêsia*. Initially, Diodotus pleads for such a utopian Assembly where those engaged in deliberation practice *parrhêsia*, but ultimately he must acknowledge the impossibility of such an ideal and so he himself must practice the subterfuge he had denounced. Diodotus' speech remains the most philosophic speech within the Thucydidean corpus; it is the one that, released from all conventions from the past, is the most open to the future, but it is also profoundly pessimistic in its admission that the unharnessed expression of views has little attraction for the many.

Cleon had found fault in an Assembly of citizens too enamored of speeches. They are the ones responsible (*aitioi*), he had said, when speakers

---

[19] See Chapter 2, pages 40–2.

eager for profit mislead them, for they are like theater goers (*theatai*) at spectacles. They consider future deeds from words, not taking into account what has been already accomplished, guided as they are by words more seriously than sight (3.38.4). With such an audience, those who speak do so with a view to charming it with novelty (*kainotêtos*, 3.38.5), rather than attending to what has been accomplished. And the Athenians, Cleon concludes, sitting in the Assembly do this all at the expense of their capacity to rule. Diodotus also criticizes his audience, but not as Cleon does because they are in love with what is novel rather than what is old. Rejecting Cleon's vituperation of those who brought the issues forward for further deliberation, Diodotus says: "I do not find fault with those who have placed before us the resolution (*diagnômên*) concerning the Mytileneans," nor does he praise those who find fault with the frequent deliberations over the most important things (3.42.1). None of the adoration of the "beautiful things discovered long ago" to which Gyges had appealed (especially if "long ago" is only yesterday as was the decree concerning the fate of the Mytileneans) limits Diodotus. Rather, Diodotus opposes the Assembly because those attending distrust their speakers and instill a fear in those speakers that inhibits free speech. As a result, Diodotus bluntly tells the Athenians, the only way that he (and other speakers) can address them is through deception. Both Cleon and Diodotus point to the absence of *parrhêsia* in the Assembly. Both blame the citizens themselves in their assembled state as the cause of its failure. But Diodotus, unlike Cleon, also gives us a vision of a city where such pretenses and lies would not be necessary.

Diodotus begins his own speech with a defense of speech itself against Cleon's assertions that speakers in the Assembly speak only for self-promotion and personal gain. According to Cleon speech is an impediment to action and especially an impediment to the city's capacity to rule over others. Diodotus responds: "Whoever [that is, Cleon] battles against speech (*tous logous*) as not teaching about affairs either is stupid (*azunetos*) or seeks something for his private benefit" (3.42.2). Diodotus is not subtle in his attacks on Cleon, though subtlety marks so much else of his speech. The "battler against words" is stupid, Diodotus tells us, because the future is always unclear and unknown; speech is the only way to assess it. Diodotus also recognizes the ability of those who are eager for their personal benefit to devise speeches that will manipulate the people so that the listeners (as Thrasymachus points out as well in Book 1 of the *Republic*) end up serving the interests of those who manipulate them. But, Diodotus also imagines an Assembly where *parrhêsia* is practiced, where there can be the expression of one's honest beliefs, where speakers are innocent of the personal agendas that turn speech from a clarifying practice into a deceptive one.

In a brief passage, Diodotus envisions a city where "the good citizen (*agathon politên*), not frightening those who speak against him, but from an equality (*apo tou isou*, that is, fairly) appears to speak better" (3.42.5).

In such a city, which Diodotus calls "moderate (*sôphrona polin*)" (3.42.5), those who offer the best advice are not honored excessively nor are those whose opinions fail to prevail punished or dishonored. In such a city, the moderate city of our dreams, there would be no incentive for those who can speak well to speak for the sake of prestige rather than with a view to what is best for the city. Glory and shame would not interfere with the exercise of free speech. Those speaking before the city would not say what they do not think (*para gnômên*) nor would they speak for the sake of causing pleasure (*pros charin*). In Diodotus' dream, those who do not have good fortune (that is, win the debates in the Assembly) would not therefore struggle to be pleasing (*charizomenos*) in order to take the many (*to plêthos*) along with them (3.42.5–6). Accuracy would be more important than the serving up of a pleasurable tale.[20]

Clifford Orwin rightly calls this description of the "moderate city" in Diodotus' speech "utopian" (1984a: 319). Diodotus dreams here of an Assembly in which all speakers feel secure knowing that they will not be held accountable if they speak what they believe according to their own minds without the intention of pleasing the audience. Deliberation in Diodotus' model is not practiced for the power of the self, but is necessary with an eye to the future welfare of the city. Practices that inhibit *parrhêsia*, such as honors granted to the elegant and successful speaker, dishonor for the one who fails to persuade, do not serve the welfare of the whole. Diodotus does not ask for consensus; his utopia is not a unified city of uniform opinions. That is what Cleon had longed for, an Athens committed to justice as he understood it. Diodotus asks only for an honest deliberative body. He argues for the arguments and disagreements that constitute debate. The speech of Cleon tried to bar that debate. Cleon demanded uniformity, not disagreement, submission, not freedom.

Though Diodotus may tell his audience of this dream Assembly, one of honest speakers practicing *parrhêsia*, he nevertheless acknowledges the inadequacy of such a vision when speaking before the Athenians. Whereas Cleon accused his audience of not being suspicious enough to rule an empire, Diodotus accuses the citizen body of being too suspicious. The Assembly assuming that the speaker always speaks with a view to private gain prevents itself from hearing those who may offer good advice. "We take away from the city a clear benefit (*phaneran ôphelian*, 3.43.2)" by such suspicions.[21] A city that is full of suspicions, where good advice is no less suspect than bad advice harms itself; the result is the destruction of *parrhêsia* and its benefits, to be replaced by deceit (*apatêi*) and lying (*pseusamenon*). Instead

---

[20] We cannot ignore here Thucydides' own insistence that he records his history not to give pleasure for the moment, but to enable men to "see clearly" (1.22.4). This is only one of a number of ways in which Thucydides aligns himself with this "gift of Zeus."

[21] See the discussion in Hesk (2000: 252–5).

of unadorned (*eutheos*) speech,[22] even the good adviser must develop the capacity to cover the truth if he is to achieve what is beneficial for the city (3.43.2). Speakers will speak ingratiatingly against their convictions, adjusting their speech to the expectations of those who listen. From such speech the city will get no benefit. An Assembly with individuals speaking frankly and freely of the sort for which Diodotus longs has been destroyed by an Assembly that understands speech not as the prelude to action, but as the resource for individual praise or blame. *Parrhêsia* was meant to be a collective endeavor where speech serves the welfare of the city. Speech in the Assembly in Athens, as both Diodotus and Cleon have come to see it, is that of the individual.

The tragedy of Diodotus' speech is that he recognizes the truth of Cleon's description of the Assembly as an audience of spectators enamored of words. Diodotus chides his audience: this practice of speaking openly what one truly believes is impossible in a city where the speakers, because of fear for themselves rather than a concern for the whole of the city, give speeches that they themselves may not believe. And, attacking the intellectualism of the Athenians that Pericles had so praised in his Funeral Oration, Diodotus notes that because of an "excess cleverness (*perinoias*, 3.43.3)"[23] speech in the Assembly thus must entail the art of deception.[24] As a result, the city is deprived for the most part of the open advice it needs to deliberate appropriately about the future.[25] Acknowledging this, he tells his audience that he himself must deceive in order to succeed.[26] With such explicit warnings that we are to recognize his own speech as shaped by the necessity of deception before an Assembly governed by suspicions, Diodotus proceeds to explain to his suspicious audience what will benefit the city, recognizing that the Assembly holds the speaker, not themselves, accountable for their

---

[22] Recall Socrates' promise to speak "without cosmetics" and "unadorned" right at the beginning of the *Apology* (17c).

[23] Gomme (1945–81: 2.315) notes that this word does not appear elsewhere in classical Greek.

[24] Elster (1998: 1) introduces his edited volume on deliberative democracy with a quotation from Pericles' Funeral Oration in which Pericles, praising the Athenians, remarks on their refusal to see words (*tous logous*) as a hindrance (*blaben*) to deeds, but rather as a necessary predecessor to action. Elster properly notes that despite this noble vision, "Athenian democracy was also the birthplace of the tendency to debunk discussion as sophistry or demagoguery," and concludes by comparing the debates before the Athenian assemblies to forensic speeches before juries rather than to the goal imagined by the advocates of deliberative democracy. As such Athenian democracy loses for him the focus on the moral life that deliberative democracy's advocates have tried to reintroduce to our democratic theories.

[25] I disagree with Mara here who suggests that "Diodotus also appears to serve justice only by subverting the processes of deliberative democracy" (2001: 828). It is not that Diodotus "subverts" the deliberations going on in the Assembly, but that the Athenians have perverted them by forcing speakers to deceive. The beginning of Diodotus' speech is one of regret that he has to rely on deception in order to serve the interests of the city.

[26] See Strauss (1964: 233).

decisions. How should the audience hear the words that Diodotus promises will be lies?

To help the city, he must defy the standard he sets for the practice of free speech. Gomme comments on Diodotus' speech that Thucydides "comes perilously close to questioning the *value* of free debate."[27] It is not so much the *value* of free debate that Diodotus ultimately questions, as the very possibility of its practice in a democratic deliberative assembly. Thus, his own speech is a brilliant deception presenting an argument to accomplish what is in the city's interest – and, incidentally, is also the humane action to take. Through his own manipulative speech he overturns what Thucydides himself, in a rare moment of editorializing, calls a "harsh/severe (3.36.4)" decree and prevents (again in Thucydides' words) a "horrific" deed (*allokoton*, 3.49.4), a word that invokes threats of divine retribution.[28] Deceptive speech accomplishes the deeds for which Thucydides uncharacteristically expresses approval.

While Cleon and Diodotus both see the failure of the Assembly as a venue for honest deliberative practices (albeit from different perspectives), they remain virulently opposed on the place of the past in the advice they each try to give to their imperfect assembled fellow citizens. Cleon expounds a slavish acceptance of the past, Diodotus the transcendence of the past with a focus on the future. Foresight, not memory, dominates the perspective of this advocate of the lost art of *parrhêsia*. It is in this context that he argues before the Assembly "not about the injustices of the Mytileneans," but about the "good counsel for ourselves (*tês hêmeteras euboulias*)" (3.44.1). Emphatically dismissing a concern with justice, with whether the Mytileneans caused harm to the Athenians, he asserts: "I think that we deliberate rather concerning the future (*tou mellontos*) than what is" (3.44.3). He takes from Cleon not his argument about what the Mytileneans deserve since that is backward looking, and focuses instead on Cleon's calculation that by executing the Mytilenean men and selling the women and children into slavery, the Athenians will prevent future revolts. No, says Diodotus, looking to the future (*peri tou es to mellon*) as he explicitly urges the Athenians not to consider justice. Admitting that Cleon's speech may be the "juster" one (*dikaioteros...ôn autou ho logos*, 3.44.4), he draws the opposite conclusion about incentives for rebellion: fewer rebellions will occur if the Athenians do not impose such a harsh penalty on Mytilene (3.44.4).

Finding in hope, not memory, the essential characteristic of human nature, and the incentive to action, Diodotus expounds a theory that explains the inefficacy of punishment, even punishment by death, as a restraint on actions that will harm others. Driven by the hope and the expectation of success, all men, Diodotus suggests, will venture forth to achieve their own interests. The fear of punishment as a deterrent stands no chance in Diodotus'

---

[27] Quoted in Orwin (1984a: 318, italics added) and in Strauss (1964: 232).
[28] See note 9.

version against the hope of success that all men share. Human nature, not the conventions men have constructed, determines the march of human history. Diodotus, in a rare (for him) look back at history to prove his argument, points to the history of change. "It is likely," he speculates, "that long ago the greatest injustices had punishments that were softer, but in time punishments moved to death" (3.45.3). Adaptation not stagnancy, change not reverence is the lesson Diodotus draws from history. Only when hope no longer clouds the perception of the future will the rebel or the lawbreaker calculate that submission may trump fighting to the end. But this will happen only if submission does not lead to the same punishment that would be meted out if one were to fight to the very end. If clemency awaits those resisting, they will submit when they realize that their resistance is doomed. Applying this reasoning to the allies, Athens would save herself the resources usually expended on the continued sieges and control over a subject city that has not been destroyed. Such preservation of resources, for sure, benefits the city of Athens making her even stronger against her enemies and more feared among her allies. With such cost-benefit calculations, Diodotus perhaps uses deceptive speech to persuade the Assembly to vote for the measure that is more just, punishing the guilty but not the innocent men, women, and children who did not cause harm to Athens.[29]

This is the language Diodotus uses to argue against the retributive justice of backward-looking Cleon. "So that it is necessary that we, not being judges (*dikastas*) bringing harm to those who have injured us, rather with a view to future time (*es ton epeita chronon*) punish moderately" (3.46.4). Indeed, Diodotus continues, the security on which the Athenians should rely is not "the awe-fullness of the laws (*tôn nomôn tês deinotêtos*) . . . but the vigilance over the deeds (*tôn ergôn tês epimeleias*)" (3.46.4). Justice belongs in the speeches of the courtroom, not the deliberations of the Assembly (Connor 1984: 84). The goal Diodotus establishes for the city is to avoid the need to punish actions taken and to protect against the allies ever even thinking of revolting in the first place. We might reflect on the full implications of that argument for imperial rule given the human resistance to rule.[30] Subtly, through deceit, Diodotus seems to question the Athenian empire itself. Such a question raised in the Athenian Assembly, for sure, would not bring pleasure to the citizens as listeners/spectators who had so recently been urged by Pericles to take such pride in the empire they and their ancestors had built

---

[29] Coby finds significant fault with Diodotus' argument here: "The argument of Diodotus that severity prolongs resistance gives insufficient credit to the argument of Cleon that leniency fosters rebellion. Diodotus' reply to Cleon does not add up to a perfect strategy of imperial rule but instead forces a choice between few rebellions meticulously planned because failure is fatal (Cleon) and numerous rebellions thoughtlessly chanced because the hegemon is wont to rationalize and excuse the attempt (Diodotus)" (1991: 88).

[30] The classic expression of this view is in Xenophon's *Cyropaedeia* (I.1).

and to preserve Athens' glory by defending it with their lives. To express such a view about the state of the empire would raise honest and frank questions that would only be welcome in Diodotus' utopian Assembly.[31]

At the end of his speech, Diodotus draws on the resources of justice that he had eschewed just moments before. If the Athenians kill the *dêmos* of Mytilene, those who did not take part in the uprising even after they received arms from the oligarchs, "you will be unjust killing those who did you a service" (3.47.3). But Diodotus does not rest his argument here; rather, he elaborates on his earlier point of how such an action harms the Athenians. If they do indeed kill the *dêmos*, in the future, the *dêmos* of other cities will side with the oligarchs, seeing that they will be killed whether they join the rebellion or not. The suppression of all such cities will be all that more difficult – irrespective of the justice or injustice of the punishment meted out by the Athenians.

Thus, Diodotus switches again quickly away from justice to benefit, returning to the issue of deceit with which he began his speech, for he argues now that even if the *dêmos* were guilty, it is necessary to pretend (*prospoiesthai*) that they were not in order that the *dêmos* in other cities remain allies rather than enemies (3.47.4). Athens' policy itself must also transcend truth through pretense, and justice must yield, on Diodotus' account to his suspicious audience, to that which is necessary for the common welfare: "This, I think, is by far more beneficial for the preservation (*kathexin*) of the empire, willingly to be unjust rather than justly destroying those whom it is not necessary [to destroy]" (3.47.5). Cleon had suggested at the end of his speech that the just and the beneficial are the same. At the end of his own speech, Diodotus concludes the opposite, but nevertheless offers a speech that deceptively accomplishes the unity Cleon has affirmed. Diodotus' speech works to keep justice and interest separate, and in their isolation from one another, he chooses, he says, to side with the beneficial, not with justice while in fact he unites them. Concluding his own speech, he asks the Assembly to attend to the good that awaits them in the future (*es to mellon agatha*, 3.48.2). The one who deliberates, thus, will be stronger against his enemies than the one who acts as if driven by senselessness. Backward-focused justice is senseless; forward-looking counsel freely offered without concern for praise or blame brings success for the city, if not to the individual who offers it. Diodotus, we must recall, disappears from public notice, neither honored nor scorned.

The demagogue Cleon brashly, unphilosophically, appeals to the old and condemns the exercise of speech as a hindrance to action. The soft-spoken gift of Zeus opens the door to what can be. Diodotus' break with

---

[31] This reading of Diodotus' speech argues against those who write of the cruelty of Diodotus' position, of Diodotus as the "preliminary stage to the unemotionally matter-of-fact philosophy of the Melian dialogue" (Wasserman 1956: 29).

the past expresses the philosophical potential of *parrhêsia* without *aidôs* –
the Socratic moments of the *Apology*; his opponent's demagoguery points
to *parrhêsia*'s dangers. In the construction of Thucydides' narrative, the
forward-looking advocate of free speech unrestrained by *aidôs* wins (though
not by much) in that his resolution passes (3.49.1) and the adult males of
Mytilene are not killed and the women and children are not sold into slavery.[32] But the restraint here is matched by a continued savagery stirred up
by Cleon. The Athenians vote for Cleon's motion to kill the thousand oligarchs who were sent back to Athens; the walls of the Mytilene are torn
down; the ships of the Myteleneans are appropriated; their land is redivided;
and much of that land is given to Athenian settlers (3.50). The Myteleneans
survive, but largely as "serfs" (Connor 1984: 87). Diodotus' resolution to
reverse the previous day's decision wins, but it is hardly the victory of the
"moderate city."

3. THE INVASION OF SICILY

A. The Context

Long after the Mytilenean Debate, after the events at Pylos, after the Peace
of Nicias has been agreed to, after the Athenians engage in a dialogue with
the leaders of the small island of Melos, the Athenians invade Sicily. All of
Books 6 and 7 of the *History* detail the story of that invasion. The Assemblies
that take place (as recorded by Thucydides) again offer insights into the
nature of *parrhêsia* in the political world of antiquity.

Book 6 begins the story of the Sicilian invasion: "During that winter the
Athenians resolved to sail against Sicily in order to subdue her" (6.1.1). The
expedition starts during the Peace of Nicias agreed to some six years earlier.
As prelude to the campaign, Thucydides describes in detail two Assemblies –
one in Athens, one in Syracuse. As in the case of the Mytilenean Debate, the
Assembly at Athens becomes a session devoted to a reconsideration of an
action decided upon at an earlier meeting.[33] The Assembly again – Wolin-
and Jefferson-like – expresses its independence, its freedom from the past as a
determinant of what it must do next. This Assembly occurs several days after
an earlier Assembly had voted to respond favorably to a request by the Egestaeans from Sicily for aid in their conflict with the Selinuntines. Thucydides'

---

[32] The irony remains that the speaker who says the Athenians should ignore justice is the one
who defends the humane policy – and does so with a speech that perhaps he does not believe
himself. His warning early on in his speech that in the Assembly one could not practice
parrhêsia without danger leaves open the question of whether he himself spoke frankly or
relied on deceptive speech to achieve his goals – or perhaps the question does not really
remain open.

[33] Connor (1984: 162n11) also notes how this ties the Sicilian deliberations to the Mytilenean
Debate.

narrative highlights the analogies to Book 1 when the Corcyreans had come to ask the Athenians for assistance against Corinth, a request that precipitated the war with Sparta (Ober 1998: 106; also Connor 1984: 159–61). The Athenians recognize that aid for the Egestaeans would provoke resistance from other cities, but they also anticipate the opportunities it would present to expand their empire, considerations not absent from their deliberations concerning Corcyrea's request reported in Book 1. In each case, concern for the empire rather than justice prevailed.

The Athenian Assembly, which Thucydides reports was originally called to assess the preparations necessary to embark on their naval expedition, under the influence of Nicias becomes instead a reconsideration of the decision to embark on the expedition in the first place. Nicias, though unwilling (6.8.4), had been chosen to serve as general on the expedition; he questions the wisdom of the expedition and forces the city to deliberate again about its earlier decision. Alcibiades defends the earlier decision and attacks Nicias' motives. The Assembly, supporting Alcibiades, reconfirms with still more enthusiasm than before the decision to set sail. Nicias, who could not persuade the Athenians to forego the expedition directly, next tries to dissuade the Athenians by enumerating the large number of ships, men, and money required for such an adventure. Nicias' plan backfires: the Athenians are only more encouraged by his speech and vote to put all the resources Nicias requests into the expedition, making the eventual defeat even more costly.

After describing the sendoff for the Athenian fleet to Sicily, repeating in more detail the story told in Book 1 of Harmodius and Aristogeiton, and reporting on the desecration of the hermae and the implications of these acts of impiety for the subsequent career of Alcibiades, Thucydides turns to the situation in Sicily and in particular the Assembly in Syracuse. The Syracusans deliberate whether their city is to respond to the stories about the impending Athenian expedition or whether the reports and the attention to them are part of an oligarchic plot to take over power in the city. Hermocrates urges preparations; Athenagoras, called "foremost (*prostatês*)" of the people by Thucydides (6.35.2), argues that the Athenians would never be so foolish as to invade Syracuse and leave behind a hostile and still powerful Lacedaemonia. It must, he claims, be the oligarchs eager for power who are circulating these rumors.

I shall argue that each of these speeches identifies the problematic nature of the practice of free speech – the shameless effort to uncover a truth in the context of the Assembly. With the striking exception of Nicias (who fails in his efforts to deter the Athenians from taking on the expedition) and though deference to hierarchy no longer controls speech, new concerns about the inadequacies of any pretense to knowledge and the effects of speech now surface.

B. The Athenian Assembly: Nicias versus Alcibiades[34]

Thucydides describes in as vivid detail as he gives anywhere in his *History* the departure of the Athenian fleet for Sicily. The whole throng of people, whoever was in the city, both city dwellers (*astôn*) and foreigners went down to the port together accompanying loved ones for the spectacle of the departing forces (6.30.2). The sight of the combined strength of ships and men creates in all a brief moment of dread at the wonder (*ta deina*, awefullness) that this expedition entailed. For readers who are aware of the sad conclusion to this expedition, *ta deina* resonates with foreboding, a foreboding that was not there when the Assembly voted to set sail. Why not? Does the foreboding come from a fear of their own arrogance captured best by the sight of how grand the expedition really is? Only by seeing the ships and the men gathered there do they fully sense the arrogance of the expedition they have voted on. It was an arrogance that the speeches of the Assembly did not convey when the people deliberated on whether to proceed with the invasion. Such pride, as Herodotus had shown frequently in his *Histories*, such crossing over boundaries, brings destruction for the transgressor; similar stories of arrogance confronted and frightened the Athenians when they attended the theater and watched an Oedipus or a Creon suffer on the Attic stage. The debates that take place in the Assemblies, unlike those debates that take place between states such as the Melians and the Athenians of Book 5 or the Plataeans and the Thebans of Book 3, though, do not draw on religious themes of *hubris* and punishment. The Assemblies draw on apparent calculation and rationality, on evidence and probabilities concerning the best interest of the city. No Melian appeal to divine laws that limit the actions of the stronger infect the Athenians' deliberation about whether to go to Sicily. The discussions in the Assembly concern whether it is in the interest of the Athenians to proceed with the expedition, not whether it is just. But, on what basis do they assess the potential benefits and potential costs? How do they calculate their interest and especially how do those speaking in the Assembly assist or hinder calculations the Athenians must make? How free is their speech in this setting?

Thucydides introduces the Athenian Assembly with some editorial comments. Within the very first sentence of Book 6, Thucydides tells us that *hoi polloi* were inexperienced (*apeiroi*) of the size of the island of Sicily and of the number of the inhabitants (6.1.1), making it seem as if the Athenians sailed to Sicily in ignorance. This contradicts not only his claim in 2.65.11

---

[34] Ober discusses in illuminating detail the debate between Nicias and Alcibiades (see especially 1994 and 1998); his focus is on the difference between historical and democratic knowledge according to Thucydides. I question, however, how different these two forms of knowledge are (Saxonhouse 2004).

where he writes that the failure of the expedition rested as much on the lack of support given to those whom the Athenians had sent forth as on error in judgment; it also contradicts the information he gives us about the Athenians sending envoys to scout out Sicily (5.4–5). In Book 6 Thucydides records the results of his own learning, his *historia* about the peoples of Sicily,[35] but we learn later that the Athenians were not so derelict in their efforts to learn about the situation at Sicily as Thucydides at first would make us believe. As a result of the importuning of the Egestaeans whom the Athenians heard speaking frequently (*pollakis legontôn*) in their Assemblies (note the plural) of the need for Athenian assistance against the Selinuntines, the Athenians had voted still earlier to send envoys to Egesta. The envoys were to scout out (*skepsomenos*) how much money the Egestaeans held in common and in the temples in order to assess the Egestaeans' ability to support the expedition and to determine whether the Egestaeans would be valuable allies in the future (6.6.3).

The problem with getting information about Sicily lay not in the democracy's failure to seek knowledge, but in the reliability of the reports they received. The report of the Athenian envoys who returned from Sicily, Thucydides tells us, was full of enticements (*epagôga*), but it was not true (*ouk alêthê*, 6.8.2). The ambassadors – to put it simply – had lied. Cleon's accusations come home: the Athenians were too trusting in this case and did not question the veracity of their envoys. They assumed speech adequately captured what was seen; they did not take into account the *eunoia* about which Thucydides had warned his audience. While Thucydides in Book 1 had acknowledged how the reports he heard were always slanted by *eunoia*, favoritism, prejudice, and therefore – according to his methodological exposition – must always be tested against other reports, the Athenians had sent only one embassy and did not ask (except for Nicias, 6.13.2) the *cui bono* question when they received information from their delegates: in whose interest is it to bring these favorable reports from Egesta? Both in the Assembly and in the practice of history, Thucydides alerts us to the need to question those who tell us stories: do they speak frankly or not? Do they reveal a truth or cover it? The Egesteans had covered the truth.

While the Athenians did not ask the *cui bono* question of their own ambassadors, it is in fact this question that resounds through the deliberations about the expedition. The speakers in the Assemblies of Book 6 all question the motives of the opposing speakers and thus especially the reliability of

---

[35] It is a matter of scholarly debate whether Thucydides ever went to Sicily himself or whether he needed to rely on the reports of others. The probability is that he did not go; if that is the case, we must be attentive to how much his presentation of the "facts" about Sicily depends on reports, *logoi*. In 6.2 Thucydides says that he will leave information about ancient things to the poets. This was not the strategy he followed in Book 1 when he revised the Homeric account of the Trojan expedition (I.9).

the information they transmit and the action they propose. The problem of deceptive speech is at the core of the debates and Diodotus' utopian vision of the parrhesiastic Assembly is long forgotten. In the Assemblies of Thucydides' *History*, the participants do not speak freely. The trust displayed with regard to the ambassadors is not – contrary to Cleon – the mode of behavior in the Assembly. Nicias questions Alcibiades, Alcibiades Nicias, Athenagoras Hermocrates, and Hermocrates Athenagoras. We see the suspicions of others' motives that Diodotus had told the Athenian Assembly (as well as Thucydides' readers) would hinder effective deliberation in the Assembly and engender its own need for deception, even by those eager for the common welfare – and perhaps even justice. This is a lesson that Nicias, the author of the peace treaty, does not understand at first, and when he does, it is too late for him to be effective.

Thucydides introduces Nicias' speech by commenting that Nicias thought that the city "had not deliberated correctly (*ouk orthôs bebouleusthai*)," but had based its decision on a slight excuse, the request for aid from the Egestaeans (6.8.4). Nicias' speech immediately picks up the concern about the quality of deliberation that has led to the decision to attack Sicily: "It seems to me that it is still necessary (*eti chrênai*) . . . to explore (*skepsasthai*) this issue, if it is better to send out the ships, and not to be convinced to choose war with such brief consideration (*bracheiai boulêi*) about great things" (6.9.1). Affirming his stature as the appropriate speaker on these matters, Nicias reassures his audience (as the son of good power Diodotus had not): "Never from a concern with honor in a previous time have I spoken what was contrary to my opinion (*para gnômên*), nor do I do so now, but I say what I know (*gignôskô*) to be best" (6.9.2). No deception is promised; he has had no tutoring from Diodotus. Nicias speaks frankly, making transparent his views about the plans of the Athenians. Nothing holds back his speech: not shame, not reverence for the decisions of the Assembly – nor political savvy. Yet, as he speaks openly and honestly, his argument becomes a complex of contradictions that undercut his own position. He claims to recognize that his words will be weak against the character of the Athenians (6.9.3), and yet he speaks to the Athenians as if he and they were Spartans (Connor 1984: 166), urging that they remain quiet (*hêsuchazontôn*, 6.10.2). He talks of restraint and assumes that the explication of the difficulties the Athenians will face should they launch the proposed expedition will deter rather than challenge them.

While the quiet that the Athenians currently enjoy comes from the peace treaty Nicias arranged, he points to the treaty's numerous flaws and explains why the Athenians should not count on their security. Their enemies were made (*poiêsontai*) to sign the treaty because of their own misfortunes and with greater disgrace/shame (*aischionos*) than the Athenians (6.10.2), a shame that makes them even more eager to make the Athenians falter in their endeavors (6.11.6). And further, there are those who never accepted the agreement Nicias arranged in the first place (6.10.3). He does not speak favorably of his own accomplishments, nor does he flatter the Athenians with their own. He speaks to them, ruling citizens of a great empire, and tells them it will be difficult to be able to rule over Sicily "because of the distance and many men" (6.11.1). To the Athenians proud of their accomplishments, men who have been told by Pericles at the beginning of the war of the memorable achievements of their empire spread wide across the world, Nicias now speaks of defeat. Disparaging not flattering them, Nicias proceeds to try to persuade them of their own inferior stature and incapacities telling them that it is senseless (*anoêton*) to go against men they cannot hold (6.11.1). Their victory over the Lacedaemonians was neither due to their great skill nor to their character, but was "beyond reason (*para gnômên*)" (6.11.5). They should not expect such successes *para gnômên* so quickly again.

Nicias does not lie or flatter in his speech, but he recognizes that others may. His speech moves in this direction by focusing first on the exiles from Egestaeans for whom he tells his audience "it is useful to lie beautifully (*pseusasthai kalôs*)" (6.12.1). But the exiles are not his target; Alcibiades is. This is the Alcibiades who "considering only himself (*to heautou monon skopôn*)" would be delighted to be chosen to lead the expedition, especially since he is still too young for such a position of rule (*es to archein*, 6.12.2). Nicias turns this attack on Alcibiades into a contest between the old and the young, between deference for age and submission before the eagerness of youth, between the past and the future. He looks to the hierarchy of age and warns about an Alcibiades and his followers who undermine those undemocratic hierarchies, advancing without respect or deference for the old and their past. Thus, he chastises not only the young for embarking on the adventures toward which Alcibiades urges them, but also the older men who, because they feel shame before the lively young, fail to vote in a way that they know will serve the welfare of Athens. "I make my appeal to those who are older (*tois presbuterois*) that they not be ashamed (*kataischunthênai*), even if they are sitting next to some one of them [the followers of Alcibiades], lest he seem to be soft (*malakos*) if he should not vote to go to war" (6.13.1). The regime that Nicias describes with the old intimidated by the scorn of the young calls to mind again Socrates' description of the democratic regime in Book 8 of the *Republic* where "the father becomes accustomed to be like the son and fears him, and the son is accustomed to be like the father and shows no shame (*aischunesthai*) nor fears his forebears" (562e). Nicias' Athens has reversed the ancient order. We now have a city where the old hold no stature against the youth, where *aidôs* does not preserve hierarchy, but in the democratic redefinition shatters it. But this does not transform Athens into the city of Pericles' Funeral Oration where inequalities came from worth and citizens lived freely without the castigating glances of others. Now, fear of the gaze of the young controls the actions of the old who dare neither speak what they believe to be true nor vote freely in the Assembly.

Thucydides tells us that most of the speakers in the Assembly spoke in favor of the expedition and not for undoing what had been voted for (*epsêsmena*, 6.15.1), though some spoke against it. The one who spoke with the most enthusiasm in favor of the expedition was the totally shameless young Alcibiades, the one who may revel in the gaze of others and is not controlled by it. He desires prestige but acquires it by flaunting the expectations of the society in which he lives. He is a mass of contradictions, attentive to what will bring him fame and what brings fame is also what makes him stand out, transcend the norms and customs of the community in which he lives. From Thucydides we hear of Alcibiades' extravagances for horses and for luxuries, of his ambition that makes him want to lead the expedition to Sicily, of his hostility to Nicias especially because he recalled how Nicias had spoken slanderously of him (*autou diabolôs emnêsthê*, 6.15.2). And yet we hear as well of how he frightened the many (*hoi polloi*) with the greatness of his violations of the laws/customs (*to megethos tê . . . paranomias*), both with regard to his body and his mind (*dianoias*), accomplishing all he imagined in his mind. They feared him as one eager to set up and acquire a tyranny for himself (6.15.4). Nevertheless Alcibiades appeals to the Athenians: they should free themselves, be forward looking and unrestrained in their vision of themselves by the castigating glances of others. Alcibiades captures their own dangerous shamelessness.[36]

Alcibiades' speech begins with an effort to show himself as distinct from his fellow citizens – distinct and greater. Scorning the egalitarianism of Athenian democracy, he plays on his inequality, his unique gifts to the Athenians (his victories, for example, in the Olympic games) that go well beyond the speeches he might give as one of many in the Athenian Assembly. Like Socrates, he does not adjust to the city in which he lives (as Protagoras' Zeus might prescribe), but rather insists that the city adjust to him. As the *Apology* was Socrates' uncovering of himself, so too is this speech Alcibiades' brazen uncovering of himself, of his ambitions, of his expectations, of his superiority in a city of equals. Alcibiades, like Socrates, manages to dazzle while heaping scorn on his listeners. He – the one who has won all those victories at the games, the one who provides choruses for the city – shines brilliantly (*lamprunomai*), he tells his listeners. It is natural (*phusei*) that the townspeople (*tois astois*) – as he derisively refers to his fellow citizens – are jealous (6.16.3), but it is not unjust (*oude ge adikon*) that he should have great thoughts about himself, he who is not equal to the others (6.16.4). Rather, they should accept the arrogance of the one who is successful.

---

[36] Compare the description of Alcibiades' personality to the Corinthians' description of the Athenians. See Forde (1989) for a development of Alcibiades' relationship to the Athenian regime.

"I know that such men and those who stand forth with any brilliance (*lamprotêti*) give grief to men in their own lifetimes, most especially to those who are their equals (*homoiois*)," Alcibiades, standing forth with such radiance, says (6.16.5). Appropriately, he follows these claims with examples of his successes in providing for the public welfare (6.16.6). Though the townspeople in their narrowness may not give him the admiration he deserves, Alcibiades himself exults in his own successes. He boldly speaks of his own "brilliance" to those who will be pricked by his arrogance. Bowing neither to shame nor to deference does he hold back his assertions of superiority that justify his claims to authority and power in the city.

Alcibiades' speech turns at this point to a series of detailed claims about the conditions in Sicily in which he contradicts all that Nicias had said about the people of Sicily. Alcibiades calls them a "mixed mob" (6.17.2) who easily change regimes. He says that they do not care about their own country and that they have no arms or settled homes. We do not know the grounds on which Alcibiades makes these claims, although he professes to know by hearing (*egô akoeî aisthanomai*, 6.17.6), a phrase that Nicias will use as well in his next speech (6.20.1). Each speaker affirms that he has knowledge, but the Assembly is left to decide which one to believe and is given no clear guidance as to how to weigh the reports each brings to the discussion. Which speaker uncovers what is the true state of affairs in Sicily and how is the Assembly to assess their claims?

Unlike Nicias who had spoken to the Athenians against their character by urging moderation (6.11.7), Alcibiades encourages action and warns that quiescence (*hêsuchia*, 6.18.2, 3, and 6; also *apragmosunê*, 6.18.6 and 7) will lead to their destruction. Melding the Periclean warning that they cannot give up the empire that they have acquired with the un-Periclean advice that they not restrain themselves, he pleads from probabilities that are far more consistent with the lessons of Thucydides' *History* than are Nicias' assertions. Predicting the actions of the Syracusans, he claims: "One (*tis*) does not only defend against an attack, but so that the attacker may not come, one strikes first" (6.18.2). And he concludes by focusing on the active character of the Athenians, calling on a unity between the young and old who in their aggressive stance will rejuvenate the city. In a clear response to Nicias' plea to set age over youth, Alcibiades says: "Realize that the old and the young without one another accomplish nothing." He proceeds from here to erase all distinctions between the worthless (*phaulôn*) and those who belong in the middle and those who are especially gifted. Only by bringing them all together will the city be able to be especially strong (6.18.6).

Though Alcibiades' knowledge of Sicily is based on reports that he has heard (or claims to have heard) that may be inaccurate, what he possesses in contrast to Nicias is a knowledge of the character of the people to whom he is speaking, an understanding that may come not so much from a testing of facts in an effort to discover what is true, but from an individual sensitivity – and a similarity – to the citizens among whom he lives.[37] It is an understanding of human nature paralleling Thucydides' that might have served him well had he had the chance to serve as general in Sicily. Since he was recalled, we will never know.

The contrast between Alcibiades' ability to understand the people to whom he speaks and Nicias' failure to do so is nowhere captured better than in Nicias' subsequent speech. Thucydides prefaces this speech by indicating that Nicias, acknowledging that the Assembly would not be moved by the "same *logoi*," thought that he could change their opinions if he spoke of the magnitude of the preparations that would be required for carrying out the expedition (6.19.2). Thus, Nicias details the enormous resources that he claims are necessary, but these details are part of a strategy, not an effort to reveal what he considers to be true. But, he misunderstands the Athenian character and fails to recognize that this will incite rather than deter. Using the same words as Alcibiades (*akoêi aisthanomai*, 6.20.2), he presents information opposite to that of Alcibiades.[38] The cities of Sicily are great (*megalas*), not subject to one another, nor in need of change (6.20.2). The reports of the two speakers differ and the Assembly has no way to judge the differences. What makes the difference in this deliberation are not the "facts" of the case, the uncovered truth, but the character of a people. Especially given Thucydides' suggestion that the decision to sail to Sicily was not so evidently the "wrong" decision, the significance of democratic deliberation in this Assembly is not so much its distance from historical knowledge (to which it may be closer than Ober [1994], for example, gives it credit), but the dependence of deliberative decisions on knowledge of the character of those to whom one speaks. Nicias' failure to acknowledge the character of the Athenians makes him a poor speaker in the Assembly. Neither his willingness to speak frankly at first nor his subsequent willingness to say what he believes to be false succeeds. The Assembly here is indifferent to *parrhêsia*. Understanding of character rather than the open expression of what one truly believes wins the debate.[39]

---

[37] This raises the further question of the need to attend to one's audience, whether one is the speaker in the Assembly or the historian writing the story of a war. The old vision of Thucydides the universal, apersonal, writer has been rightfully subject to considerable questioning of late; the issue of audience needs to be part of that reassessment.

[38] Ober remarks: "Nicias initiates a contest of facts: Alcibiades' information about Sicily versus his own" (1998: 113).

[39] Scholars are not of one mind about whether the expedition was itself foolhardy – or simply badly handled. Connor, for one, accepts what he sees as the general scholarly view that it was not a mistake, though he recognizes that "at the beginning of book 6 Thucydides emphasizes the folly of the decision itself" (1984: 158n2); see also Rood (1998), Orwin (1994: 118–19, 122–3); Dover (1987: 81) and Yunis (1996: 108) argue that the trip was misguided.

C. The Assembly in Syracuse

The Assembly at Syracuse is distinctive in Thucydides' *History*; it is the only time that Thucydides describes deliberations in a democratic regime other than Athens.[40] Previously, Thucydides presented Syracuse as the analogue to Athens, a rising power, possibly threatening the independence of the surrounding cities. Paralleling in several ways the debate at Athens described just a few paragraphs before, the debate at Syracuse is even more epistemologically explicit about the sources of knowledge and whether to reveal them. Hermocrates asserts that, based on reports he has heard, the Athenians are coming; the Syracusans must prepare for the invasion. Athenagoras, speaking from probabilities about human nature, says that the Athenians are not coming. Similarities between Athens and Syracuse certainly exist, but the power of Thucydides' presentation is that the similarities are not simplistic. They point instead to the varied texture of political speech and political knowledge. In this debate the moderate Hermocrates urges action, arguing against the fiery Athenagoras who counsels Spartan quiescence. Each speaker claims access to knowledge. Book 6 had begun with the Athenians' being inexperienced about Sicily and then deceived when their own ambassadors return from an expedition especially undertaken to acquire knowledge. In contrast, the Syracusans did not need to send out envoys. Reports had come from many places about the impending Athenian expedition, but, Thucydides tells us, for a long time they were not believed (*ou mentoi episteueto*, 6.32.3). Belief or trust (*pistis*) becomes the theme of the debate in the Syracusan Assembly. Thucydides summarizes the Assembly by noting that among the speakers some believed (*pisteuontôn*, 6.32.3) the reports about the Athenian expedition and others did not. Who speaks frankly? Who lies? How are we to know? These are the questions the Syracusan Assembly raises. Political action is always based on trust that the speaker urging action (or inaction) practices *parrhêsia*. But how can the members of an Assembly know to whom they should grant belief (*pistis*)?

Thucydides introduces Hermocrates as one who "thought he knew clearly about these things (*saphôs oiomenos eidenai*)" (6.32.3). Thucydides had in his discourse on his historical method identified his goal as enabling men to see clearly, *saphôs*. Hermocrates, we know from Thucydides' description of the Athenian preparations for the expedition, does indeed see "clearly"; he trusts the reports that *we* the readers know from Thucydides accurately reflect the actions of the Athenians. But *why* does he believe the reports? Because they are numerous? Because he admires the reporters? Because,

---

[40] Connor remarks on the analogy this offers between Athens and Sicily. The two Assemblies "underline ... an essential similarity in the political life of the two cities. Up to this point we – and the Athenians – have seen Syracuse as a remote Dorian city and have not penetrated beyond the simple collective label 'the Syracusans' to look at the nature of the political life within their city ... We have traveled to Syracuse and found Athens" (1984: 171).

as Athenagoras argues, Hermocrates is plotting an oligarchic take over of Syracuse? There is no indication that Hermocrates believes the reports because he has himself seen the armaments. He must rely, like Thucydides, on the speech of others to reach his conclusions, but (just like Thucydides) we are not privy to how he weighed the reports he received from others, how he came to his "true" speech. Hermocrates' speech, I would suggest, is a blind for Thucydides' own speech throughout the history. Both endeavor to help others see clearly. Both test the speeches of others. Hermocrates correctly describes what he does not see. Thucydides claims the same for himself.

The first word of Hermocrates' speech is *apista*. He is concerned that he will not be believed, that he will seem unconvincing when he speaks the truth (*tês alêtheias*) about the impending Athenian expedition. He knows, he says, that those speaking that which is not believed (*mê pista*) are not only not convincing (*ou peithousin*), but considered to be fools (*aphrones*). Forms of *pista* appear three times in a few short lines (6.33.1). He speaks frankly, but nothing ensures that others will see his speech as such. What becomes the basis for decision making in deliberative bodies? Hermocrates continues forcefully: he is persuaded (*peithôn*, again) that he knows the matter more clearly (*saphesteron*)[41] than anyone else (6.33.1). He does not use the language of *parrhêsia*, but says that the clarity of his understanding gives him the courage to say what he is convinced he knows. He speaks against prejudices among men who may not wish to believe what he says – and he speaks, he claims (though Athenagoras disputes this), for the sake of his city. He is committed to expressing what he knows to be the truth based on the reports that he has heard. He takes on the mantle of the parrhesiast. But to speak frankly does not ensure that others will accept the truth offered. Trust instead becomes an issue of character both of the speaker and the audience.

The challenge that Hermocrates faces is to convince the Syracusans that the Athenians are acting contrary to what seems "reasonable." The expedition of the Athenians is unreasonable since with Sparta still hostile, with the limited ability to bring provisions with them or acquire them in Sicily (all points raised shortly by Athenagoras), who would believe that the Athenians would so foolishly set out for Sicily? Who would believe that Athenian impetuosity would trump human rationality? Thucydides had emphasized the role of eros, a desire for adventure and for wealth (6.24.3), in the decision of the Athenians to set sail for Sicily. Hermocrates, the rational one, with the emphasis on *gnomê*, understands the passions that would drive the Athenians to Sicily; Athenagoras, the fiery orator, focuses on what is rational. The truth of human nature as both Hermocrates and Thucydides know lies in those passions, not in reason.

---

[41] See 1.22.4 where Thucydides dedicates his work to those who "wish to see clearly (*to saphes skopein*)."

Though Hermocrates may be correct about the reports concerning the Athenian expedition, the power of his speech must depend on his theories about human nature and his affirmation that (in Thucydides' language) the same things happen over and over again (3.82.2). Hermocrates knows what had happened in the Persian Wars; he can project what happens when a small city defends itself against the overwhelming forces of a powerful empire that attempts to conquer lands far from home without adequate supplies. Hermocrates tries to communicate the lessons of Herodotus' history, but though he speaks with complete candor about what he believes he knows, he cannot spur the quiet Syracusans into action. They, unlike the Athenians, are limited, Hermocrates warns, by a characteristic quietude (*dia to zunêthes hêsuchon*) that makes them slow to be persuaded (*hekist' an oxeôs peithoisthe*, 6.34.4).

On the basis of his own speculations concerning human nature, Hermocrates proposes that the Syracusans send off a fleet to meet the advancing Athenians at Tarenteum. He expects that the Athenians, taken aback by the sudden show of force, would spend time deliberating about what to do and would want to assess the number of the Sicilians resisting; this would delay their trip across the open sea until the moment for such travel would have passed and the Athenians would then return home. The proposed scenario is highly speculative and Gomme and the subsequent editors of his magisterial work on Thucydides are firm in their conviction that it would never have worked, that the outcome would have been "the annihilation of the Sikeliot fleet and the rapid imposition of Athenian rule on Sicily and South Italy" (1945–81: 4.299). We will never know, but Hermocrates proposing his grand defensive action to the Syracusans is the model democratic deliberator blending the *logoi* (speeches) he has heard with deductions about human nature, speaking frankly without deception. The analogies with Thucydides' conception of his own task and accomplishments resonate throughout Hermocrates' speech. As readers of the *History*, we know that Hermocrates' reports are accurate. The ecclesiasts, though, must rely on a faith that what he says is true. All he can offer is what "I believe (*hêgoumai*)" as a result of his calculations (*toutôi tôi logismôi*, 6.34.6). Thucydides as the author of Hermocrates' speech reconfirms for the reader the accuracy of Hermocrates' information, when he has Hermocrates report to the Assembly that he has heard (*egô akouô*) that the general with the most experience (that is, Nicias) unwillingly became the general for the expedition and that he would grasp at any excuse to abandon it (6.34.6).

When Hermocrates explains his Tarenteum strategy to the Assembly, he remarks: "We would be reported with exaggeration," and "the minds of men steer to what they hear" (6.34.7). The Athenians are attacking because they think that the Syracusans are unprepared. They based this judgment, he suggests, on their inference from the Syracusan failure to help the Lacedaemonians. By a sudden show of force, Hermocrates claims, the Syracusans would be daring beyond expectation (*para gnômên tolmêsantas*, 6.34.8). The Athenians still in Corcyrea would then be influenced more by the reports of the Syracusans' strength at Tarenteum than by the actual numbers or facts behind those reports (*têi autou tou alêthou dunamei*, 6.34.8), that is, the Athenians would be misled by misrepresentations in unreliable speech. Hermocrates' strategy depends on the Athenians believing the exaggerated reports of Syracusan strength for his Tarenteum plan to work, but we the readers (and presumably the Syracusan ecclesiasts) are left to wonder about his speech. If the Athenians will be influenced by exaggerated *logoi*, and if the minds of men "steer to what they hear" even if what they hear is untrue, why does Hermocrates not worry that the *logoi* he has heard may likewise be exaggerations? Again, how does he (like Thucydides) know who speaks the truth and who does not?[42]

The profound irony of this speech as Hermocrates keeps making clear is that we rely on the speech of others for what we ourselves cannot see. To rely on speeches and reports, as Hobbes recognized and argued so well, limits us to the subjectivity and potential for deception from those who speak their stories to us. Hermocrates' practical suggestion depends on the shock value of the *logoi*, reports that would not be in accord with the facts of the case, where the *logoi* have not been adequately tested. His plan depends on the uncertainty of knowledge and speech, which in turn he must deny in order to be persuasive himself. Asking that the Syracusans believe his speech, he proposes a plan that shows the limits of all belief in what others say. Speaking as the parrhesiast, he sees a world full of believed untruths.

Ending as he began, Hermocrates again calls on the Syracusans to be convinced (*peithesthe*, 6.34.9). He can do no more than appeal to the belief that he speaks the truth. Hermocrates knows well (*eu oid'*, 6.34.9) that the Athenians are coming, but his knowledge is based on the *logoi* that in his own speech he says can be exaggerated.[43] Reactions to Hermocrates' speech among the *dêmos* at Syracuse vary from thinking that what he said about the impending Athenian invasion was not true (*oud' alêthê*) to ridicule to the few who found Hermocrates' warning persuasive (*to pisteuon*, 6.35.1). To speak the truth, to speak frankly and openly without deceit is not the same

---

[42] Cartwright claims Hermocrates relies on "real facts" (1997: 239). I am not sure what "real facts" means in this context.

[43] Hunter comes to a similar conclusion: "The reader is witness to a genuine dilemma. How can the Syracusans . . . distinguish truth from error? Unless they are as convinced of the facts as Hermocrates, i.e., have some absolutely trustworthy source of information about Athens' aims, what intrinsic superiority has one logos over the other? Any choice between the two must be subjective . . . Thus are revealed the limitations of logoi." See also p. 160 where she comments: "Hermokrates . . . has learned from experience. But just as important, so have his listeners. Previously they had no means of determining which logos was intrinsically superior. Until news of the expedition was confirmed by eyewitnesses as saphe, the assumptions and predictions of both logoi were mere eikota" (1973: 155).

as ensuring the success of speech, as Diodotus has made so clear several Books/years earlier. Though Thucydides has given the reader reason to sympathize with Hermocrates' efforts to persuade the *dêmos*, it remains unclear why the Syracusans should be moved by his claims to have heard accurate reports of an event that he himself has not seen or why the *dêmos* should be persuaded by him to act against their customary quiet. Our knowledge based on reading the earlier sections of Book 6 is not available to the ecclesiasts sitting in the Syracusan Assembly. Speaking freely truth as one sees it does not ensure trust. Hermocrates has not studied with Diodotus.

Athenagoras, "most trusted (*pithanôtatos*)" (6.35.2) by the many, gives the speech opposing Hermocrates. Thucydides uses terms similar to those he had used to describe the Athenian demagogue Cleon back in Book 3 (Gomme et al. 1945–81: 4.301) and Athenagoras like Cleon has not fared well in the scholarly commentary. Hermocrates asked to be trusted, but it is ultimately Athenagoras whom the many believe. Accusing those Syracusans who warn about the advancing Athenians of having private motives and being hostile to the city, Athenagoras speaks to the citizens of Syracuse of human nature and disregards the *logoi*, reports. He speaks of the Athenians as *deinoi* (skillful) and experienced in many things (*pollôn empeiroi*, 6.36.3). What, he asks, would men of this sort do? It is not likely (*ou gar . . . eikos*, 6.36.4) that they, leaving behind the Peloponnesus without fully ending the war, would begin willingly another war of equal size. Athenagoras, rather than claiming to know the truth from the reports of others, calculates what the sane man would propose and vote for when he knows that his city's powerful enemy (Sparta) is eager to retaliate for an ignominious defeat and treaty.

The passionate Athenagoras argues that men act rationally and only irrationality would bring the Athenians to Sicily. Given that rationality governs human actions, Athenagoras continues, those warning that the Athenians are on their way can only be acting out of self-interest with a desire to take over the city and establish an oligarchy. Athenagoras predicts the future on the basis of rational self-interest – whether he describes his enemies within the city or outside it. Unlike Hermocrates, and unlike Thucydides, Athenagoras ignores *logoi*; they, as Hermocrates himself admitted, can be unreliable in comparison to the truths that come from a knowledge of human nature. "You will deliberate well (*eu bouleuêsthe*) not when you calculate what is likely by considering the messages brought in, but by considering what skillful men and those experienced of many things – just like the Athenians – would do" (6.36.3). The choice as Thucydides presents it in this debate is between uncertain speeches and deductions from human nature. The deliberative process, always based on uncertainty about both the future and the past, is caught between these two poles. The former depends on *parrhêsia*, the full revelation of the truths one knows; the latter relies on a knowledge of human nature that can function freed from the speeches of others. Ironically,

Thucydides appears to side with the character who offers uncertain speech rather than deductions from human nature.

Athenagoras continues by explaining that even if the Athenians came, numerous factors would thwart their success, factors that Nicias too had noted as he warned the Athenians about the huge costs of the expedition, and so Athenagoras turns from the realm of probabilities to claims of knowledge. Thus, Chapter 38 begins with the assertion *eu oid'* (I know well) that the Athenians know their limitations and want to preserve their own welfare. He calls men like Hermocrates "story-makers (*logopoiousin*)" (6.38.1) of what is not and what will not be and he warns his listeners about these "story-makers" who use stories to frighten the people into turning the city over to them. Stories become an oligarchic weapon, in Athenagoras' own story. Inverting Hermocrates' criticism of Syracusan quietude, he notes that on account of these storymakers, the *logopoientes*, the city seldom is at rest (*oligakis men hêsuchaze*, 6.38.3). Movement – the absence of *hêsuchia* – comes from internal conflict fostered by false speeches and taletellers rather than from a natural drive for external expansion as at Athens.

Thucydides inserts into Athenagoras' speech a defense of democracy: "Someone will say that a democracy is not wise nor equal, but that those having money are also those best able to rule in the best fashion." In contrast, Athenagoras asserts: "I say first that the *dêmos* is all . . . while the wealthy are the best guardians of money, and the clever (*zunetous*) are the best at giving counsel (*bouleusai*). The many who listen are the best at judging (*krinai*)" (6.39.1). Unlike Cleon who had accused the people to whom he spoke of fostering false speeches by their love of the theatrical, Athenagoras praises the people to whom he speaks, extols their capacity to judge speeches, and tries to persuade them with appeals to their ability to reason and calculate probabilities. He lays the provocation of excitement and emotion at the doorstep of his opponents who rely on false reports and not on reason. In a classic twist of Thucydidean irony, it is the character who extols the Assembly's critical powers of analysis and who dismisses provocative speeches (of the sort he himself gives) who is the favorite of the many. Athenagoras does warn the people that they risk being most unwise (*azunetôtatoi*) and unlearned (*amathestatoi*) and unjust (*adikôtatoi*) if they listen to Hermocrates, but he does not begin by accusing them (as Cleon had, and Diodotus assumed) of being all these things (6.39.3). The most believed man in the city asks of this Assembly to use reason so that they will not depend on whether the speakers speak truthfully or not. Unfortunately for all, a reliance on calculations from human nature in this case did not lead to the truth, for it failed to understand the irrational – eros – as a profound component of human drives. For that understanding one needs the narratives and the speeches of Thucydides' *History*.

While from the outside we the readers know that Hermocrates' reports are accurate, Athenagoras concludes by attacking the reports as not being true (*mê...alêthes*, 6.40.2) and sees them as a mechanism for enslaving the city. He assures the Assembly that even if the reports were true, the Syracusan generals would be able to respond. If the reports are not true and the people listen to the warnings of the potential tyrants, the city, having stirred itself up into a panic, will have chosen for itself servitude. He warns those who threaten the city with these reports that the city looking to itself will judge (*krinei*) the "words as deeds" and will protect its liberty (*eleutherian*). The frightening speeches of Hermocrates (6.40.2) will not lead to the loss of their freedom.

A third unnamed Syracusan general speaks briefly after Athenagoras has finished. He urges the Syracusans to leave off the ad hominen attacks that characterized both Hermocrates' and Athenagoras' speeches and instead attend to the messages that have come from outside – whether they are true or not. For him the role of speech as revelatory or as potentially enslaving is irrelevant. Rather, he urges that the Syracusans prepare defenses against those who may be coming. If it turns out that the preparations were not necessary, "no harm (*oudemia blabê*)" is suffered (6.41.3). This unnamed general takes no stand on the *logoi*, whether they are true or the work of storymakers eager to gain power in the city.

Thucydides ends his description of this Assembly by remarking that the Syracusans disbanded from the Assembly without taking any actions. The debate appears almost irrelevant for the Syracusans. Yet, it shows Thucydides' readers the difficulties *parrhêsia*, understood as honest and daring speech, faces in the deliberative setting. Diodotus has relied on deception to achieve his noble goals. Hermocrates cannot persuade the Syracusans to believe what is true with his honest speech. The stature of *parrhêsia* as a civic ideal may be powerful in the Athenian self-presentation, but Thucydides' Assemblies identify the problem such a practice faces when applied in the settings of democratic decision making. In the next chapter I take *parrhêsia* out of its ambiguous political setting and look at it in the philosophic world of a Platonic dialogue.

8

Protagoras' Shame and Socrates' Speech

It is time now to turn to the Platonic dialogue that gave us the *aidôs* of Protagoras' myth, the dialogue that takes Protagoras' name for its title and presents a Socrates skillfully and engagingly sparring with his sophistic interlocutors. Other dialogues such as the *Gorgias* and the *Laches* address more directly the practice of *parrhêsia*.[1] In the *Gorgias*, Socrates appeals to Callicles to carry on a dialogue with him since Callicles as an Athenian enjoys *parrhêsia* in a way that Socrates' foreign interlocutors do not; with this freedom, Socrates claims, Callicles can be a true touchstone to Socrates' arguments (486d–8b). In the *Laches*, as Foucault (2001: 91–101) points out, Socrates becomes the practitioner of *parrhêsia* and in turn serves as a touchstone to those who come to discuss the education of their sons with him. Nevertheless, while the explicit language of *parrhêsia* is not present in the *Protagoras* as it is in the *Gorgias* and the *Laches*, quite early in the discussion Protagoras introduces *aidôs*. This emotion that curiously melds reverence and shame, deference to the old as well as an awareness of and concern with the gaze of others, shapes political communities into coherent bodies and transforms them into peaceful wholes rather than sites of constant warfare – at least according to Protagoras. The irreverence of speech spoken freely without deference for the old, without any concern with the judgment of others, however, marks the Socratic style of discourse as we saw in the *Apology*. Socrates speaks without the shame Protagoras has identified as the source of political stability. The subtle (and often not so subtle) power struggle between the two main interlocutors leads to the exploration of whether it is possible to use the revelatory powers of speech without the dramatic disruptions that arise when one practices *parrhêsia* without *aidôs*. Can Socrates find an alternative resource for the preservation of

---

[1] I refer the reader to Monoson (2000: 155–65) and Foucault (2001: 91–101) for provocative and insightful readings of the role of *parrhêsia* in the *Laches* and *Gorgias*: Monoson for both dialogues, Foucault for the *Laches*.

community at the same time that he dismantles the foundation of *aidôs*? Is there something besides the deceit practiced by the gift of the gods, Diodotus?[2]

The *Protagoras* has been largely read as a work concerned with whether we can teach virtue, whether the virtues themselves are one or many, and whether the good is the same as pleasure. As the dialogue proceeds, though, limits placed on the speakers come from the conditions of dialogic intercourse. These limits on how the interlocutors are to speak replace the backward-looking, other-regarding *aidôs* presented to humans by Hermes on behalf of Zeus so that they might live together in cities. The god-given *aidôs* restrains the questioning and the uncovering to which free speech – and Socratic philosophy – leads us. The controls that Socrates sets on speech, though, still allow for an uncovering. Content-laden sources of *aidôs* drawn from a reverence for the past and for traditional hierarchies are replaced by contentless rules that allow for a democratic (and philosophic) forward-looking perspective. In some ways the story of the *Protagoras* replays the debate between Cleon and Diodotus discussed in the previous chapter. Socrates replaces Protagoras' backward-looking *aidôs* that ensnares individuals in the encircling gaze of others with forward-looking practices that recall the guidelines for speech that Diodotus proposed. This replacement, though, is not necessarily accomplished by Socrates without the deception that Diodotus also needed in his efforts to secure a justice that went beyond Cleon's demands for revenge. In the discussion of the *Protagoras* to follow, what I shall call "patterns of dialogic/democratic speech" replace shame as the limit on the practice of *parrhêsia*. Lost is the emotional engagement that *aidôs* produces, but gained is an openness that belongs to both democratic practice and philosophy.

I. THE DIALOGIC CONTEXT

Socrates is the narrator for most of the dialogue, but the structure of this dialogue is actually a nested narration. The dialogue begins with two characters – Socrates and an unnamed companion – whose conversation is recorded in direct discourse. Socrates then takes over and narrates the lengthy tale of his encounter with the Sophists at the home of Callias.[3] The companion to whom Socrates initially speaks begins the dialogue by

---

[2] What follows is not in any sense a full reading of this complex and challenging dialogue. It is one rich in ambiguity and vivid in dramatic detail. My attention is given only to a few select passages, but they are ones that help us reflect on the relation between shame and free speech. For thorough readings of this dialogue see, e.g., Coby (1987); Cropsey (1995); Weiss (2006: chap. 2).

[3] For an engaging, if occasionally excessive, study of the importance of always remembering the narrative role of Socrates in this dialogue see Berger (1984).

suggesting the whiff of a sexual scandal. He asks Socrates where he has come from and then quickly answers his own question: "Or is it clear that [you have appeared] from the hunt after the sight of Alcibiades?" And before Socrates can admit or deny, this companion continues that he himself had been "watching Alcibiades and thought him as a man (*anêr*) still beautiful (*kalos*)." Yes, he confirms for himself, a "man (*anêr*) since he has quite a beard already." The companion seems to be whispering these thoughts to Socrates since he assures Socrates that his questions and his responses to his own questions are "just among ourselves" (309a). Before Socrates takes over the narration of the dialogue, the companion uses the first person plural, asking Socrates to "lead us through an account of the get together" at Callias' home, to which Socrates immediately replies that he will be in their debt "if you [plural] listen (*akouête*)" (310b). More than one companion will hear Socrates' report of his encounter with the great Sophist.

The comments from Socrates' initial interlocutor about Alcibiades' pubescence are not to be spoken openly before the others. It is a hidden topic, this implied sexual pursuit of the already hirsute Alcibiades.[4] The whispering, the sexual innuendo of "hunting" a youth, the unseemly pursuit of a bearded youth all indicate a companion aware of sexual mores, one who cares about keeping private what perhaps should not be open to public discussion. In his own salacious way, he reveres the customs of the Athenians concerning what should be hidden and not open for all to see. The *aidôs* he shows, though, by speaking "just among ourselves" does not appear particularly attractive in the early moments of the dialogue.

Socrates, however, will have none of this salacious talk. He will not be shamed into whispering with this companion. "So what?" he basically responds to mention of Alcibiades' now growing beard, and he quotes for his interlocutor Homer's praise of the gracefulness of a youth whose beard is just beginning to appear. The friend, expecting a whispered reply, persists and wants to know whether Socrates has been with Alcibiades and how the youth was inclined toward him, but Socrates shocks the companion by ignoring the persistent sexual innuendoes. And so no descriptions of a sexual conquest fill Socrates' response. Instead, Socrates offers the happy report that Alcibiades has treated him very well indeed, not by responding to sexual advances, but rather: "He spoke many things on my behalf." This is not the story the companion had initially hoped to hear. Socrates admits that he barely noticed the beautiful young man who defended him; at times his presence even completely escaped him though they were just together. The companion can only assume that the presence of someone who was still more beautiful than Alcibiades – an "unlikely prospect in this city" – could

---

[4] Coby (1987: 21) comments on the "impropriety of a bearded lover."

explain such forgetfulness of Alcibiades' attractions (309c). Socrates thinking of the beauty of wisdom rather than of a body that may grow a beard at a certain age explains that yes, there was someone more beautiful "if Protagoras seems most wise to you" (309d).[5]

The companion struck by the news shows as much enthusiasm at the prospect of hearing about Socrates' encounter with Protagoras as he did about hearing about the pursuit of Alcibiades and at once asks Socrates to take the place of his slave and sit beside him so that he may recount his time with Protagoras. The salacious pleasure expected from the tale of Socrates' conquest of Alcibiades is to be replaced by the story of Socrates' meeting with the Sophist. Thus, Socrates launches into his uninterrupted recitation of that encounter, narrating the rest of the dialogue himself to tell of his conversation with Protagoras and the other Sophists at the home of Callias. From sexual pursuits we move to the contest of wits, a tale Socrates portrays himself as only too happy to report. "I shall be in your debt if you will listen," he says (310a). The "business" that in the middle of the dialogue he tells Protagoras draws him away (335c) is readily forgotten (or, more likely, never existed).[6] All the following speeches and descriptions of dramatic interactions now come through the medium of Socrates' voice.

The initial setting of the dialogue introduces allusions to what is hidden and surreptitious, the sexual escapades of old and young men, but quickly leaves those titillating concerns behind to uncover another scandalous event, the hidden conversation of Socrates within the well-guarded house of Callias that Socrates now reports to his companion. This secret world Socrates gladly brings out into the open for his companion (and perhaps the others who are with him) to hear. Socrates expresses no shame about his own life; he hides nothing despite his companion's initial surreptitious efforts to draw secrets out of Socrates. In this sense, Socrates speaks and acts freely, without a dependence on the customs from long ago, without deference for age, without any concern with external approval. Socrates exists impervious to sexual scandals, impervious to the traditions within his community as well as to the attractions of political power that Protagoras claims to offer. He is beyond *aidôs*. He has broken from the ties of the past and looks forward (with one notable exception that I shall discuss later). Thus, he lives freely. We begin this dialogue, then, the one in which Protagoras says that shame is the glue of the city, with an emphasis on the freedom of Socrates from shame and the castigating glances of others. Socrates accepts his companion's request for the story of his encounter with the famed Sophist and replaces the slave boy sitting near his anonymous companion.

[5] Throughout this dialogue we must constantly keep in mind Socratic irony. In this particular passage the important word is "if (*ei*)."

[6] See page 195.

2. YOUTHFUL SHAME

Socrates begins: the impetuous young man Hippocrates had come into his home just before dawn, shouting to Socrates "Are you awake or sleeping?" (310b). There is only one possible true answer that Socrates can give to this question.[7] Hippocrates does not want to deal with the potential complexities and ambiguities in Socrates' speeches. He almost seems to want to eliminate Socrates' freedom by allowing only a single answer to the question.[8] Socrates, though, resists this young man's effort to enslave him; preserving his freedom to ask questions rather than respond with the only possible answer, he does not make life as simple as the youthful Hippocrates might wish. Hippocrates has come to find Socrates in this impulsive fashion to tell him that he had learned late the night before that Protagoras is in town. He had not learned of Protagoras' presence earlier because he had been pursuing a slave who had run away. Hippocrates does not see himself in this instance enslaved by his slave. (Socrates, we should remember, has just taken the place of his companion's slave.) Hippocrates, after getting some sleep himself, has come so early in the day to ask for Socrates' help in gaining access to the Sophist Protagoras; he is eager to become a student of Protagoras.

Socrates questions this enthusiasm made without much foresight and urges Hippocrates to think of the future by asking: "Who will you become after you go to Protagoras?" In response, Hippocrates blushes (*eruthriasas*, 312a). Hippocrates had come to Socrates so early in the morning that it was still dark when he arrived, but Socrates reports that "now a bit of day appeared" (312a) and he was able to see that reddening of Hippocrates' cheeks, that unique human response to the gaze of another, the physical manifestation of the desire to be unseen, to hide – namely, the blush. Suddenly, with Socrates' simple yet unsettling question, Hippocrates, who had been so enthusiastic about studying with a much-praised man whom he has neither seen nor heard, is forced to imagine the future, to look at himself as he will appear in the eyes of another, to see himself observed, caught up in the web of social relations. The blush he experiences acknowledges on the one hand the presence of Socrates looking at him, but also the community that seems to detest the Sophists who train others to become teachers of deceptive, hiding rhetoric. He is caught, no doubt, between his desire for political precedence promised by the arts of Protagoras and his democratic experience of egalitarianism within the city of Athens.[9] Socrates, the one executed by the Athenians for corrupting the young, will lead him to reject the former.

---

[7] I am grateful to Tracy Strong for this point.

[8] The obvious contrast here is Crito finding Socrates asleep in his prison cell. Crito, a man of Socrates' age, lets Socrates sleep.

[9] Mara (2001: 832) sees him as "ashamed . . . before the Greeks, presumably due to the bad reputations that the sophists have as subverters of civic values."

Socrates, though, will not let Hippocrates hide from the implications of what he desires and will not allow him to offer answers as simple as the one that needs to follow the question "Are you awake or asleep, Socrates?" Instead, Socrates continues: "Would you not be ashamed (*aischunoio*) to put forth yourself as a Sophist among the Greeks?" (312a). Socrates pushes Hippocrates to see himself not only in relation to the Socrates who walks beside him, or even his own city of Athens, but in relation to all the Greeks and the mores of that community of men. He is asking Hippocrates to judge himself not by himself (as Socrates ignoring the gaze of others would). He is putting Hippocrates right into the social context of all of Greece. This is not a dialogue that will take the individual out of the social and political world as perhaps the *Republic* does with its emphasis on the ordered soul. Rather, it is a dialogue that understands the political context of our speech and our aspirations, recognizing the restraints that context places on what and how we can speak to others of our own city and beyond. Socrates initially is asking Hippocrates to subject himself to the gaze of the Athenians and then the Greeks, but not to himself.

Hippocrates' blush, however, does not abort the journey to Callias' house and the interview with the renowned Sophist within. It is at the home of the wealthy Callias that Protagoras and a number of other Sophists are lodged during their time at Athens. Before Socrates and Hippocrates enter the house, though, they must deal with the Charon-like eunuch who guards the entrance to the house. The activities of these foreigners within Callias' house are not open to the gaze of the many. These are Sophistic foreigners without the *parrhêsia* enjoyed by Athenian citizens (*Gorgias*, 487ab). They do not speak before the city as a whole and those young Athenians who are with them secret themselves behind well-guarded doors. Socrates' narration to his unnamed companion(s) unveils what the Sophists themselves and those with pretensions to political power wish to keep hidden behind the walls of the wealthy men of Athens. This is a small group of individuals from all over Greece who have crossed their own cities' borders to create a new community that exists outside the familiar sources of shame. Withdrawing from their own cities, they escape the bonds of *aidôs* within those cities. The group is free from the shame implied by the scandal-seeking questioning of Socrates' initial interlocutor, and yet shame, the concern with how one appears before others, as we shall see, still functions to knit together this community of speech behind Callias' walls.

3. PROTAGORAS' SHAME

Once inside Callias' house and in the majestic presence of Protagoras, Socrates reports that he approached Protagoras to tell him that he and Hippocrates had come to see him. Before even hearing why they want to see him, Protagoras – ever sensitive to his audience – asks whether Socrates wishes to carry on the conversation with him alone (*monôi*) or along with others (316b). The gaze of others weighs heavily on him; throughout the dialogue Socrates reports Protagoras' many moments of discomfort under Socrates' often biting critiques. Even though Protagoras may be staying well within Callias' house, he sees himself as a foreigner under observation in Athens. As a foreigner and outside the restraining circle of *aidôs* that cements the particular community of the Athenians, he nevertheless acknowledges how Sophists such as himself appearing in Athens threaten the internal security of the city. "A foreigner going into great cities and persuading the very best of the young men in these cities to leave their other associations, both family and foreign, both old and young, so as to become better through being together with oneself, someone doing these things must be careful (*chrê eulabeisthai*)" (316cd; cf. 317b; 351d). Protagoras is scared. Throughout the dialogue, he speaks with care for his own safety, not with the freedom of speech exalted by the daring practitioner of *parrhêsia*. He has come to Athens to undermine the *aidôs* he identifies in his great speech as one of the two critical emotions that allow for political life. But he does not engage in this practice openly, for such activities make for him enemies of those who are eager to defend the city. Thus, not only does his speech praise an *aidôs* he is eager to undercut, but we find that the guard at Callias' door and the walls of protection around the house are not adequate to secure his safety. He always takes care before he speaks, and despite frequent protestations, Protagoras does not court danger with his speech nor risk being shamed (333c).

Socrates at first responds to Protagoras' query as to whether they should speak alone or have an audience by affirming his own (and by inclusion Hippocrates') daring and saying: "To us it makes no difference." After explaining to Protagoras why they have sought him out – because Hippocrates wishes to be distinguished in the city – he throws back to Protagoras the question Protagoras had just asked of whether they should discourse about these things alone (*monos*) before themselves alone (*pros monous*) or along with others (*met'allôn*, 316c). Socrates claims to remain indifferent; he does not distinguish between what is public and what is private, what is spoken before others or in isolation (*monos*), what is the speech of a foreigner or a citizen. Shedding *aidôs* as Candaules' wife sheds her clothes, Socrates presents himself as standing naked shamelessly before others, indifferent to their gaze, just as he does in the speech before the jurors (at least according to Plato's version of the speech). He rejects whispering "among ourselves" as the unnamed companion wanted to do. His own words and actions are no different whether he is seen by others or not, whether he speaks in Athens or (let's say) Thebes. Socrates without shame speaks openly for all to hear. His speech so constant, at least in its pursuit of uncovering what is hidden, whether in the homes of the wealthy, the prison cell, or the courtroom of Athens, comes from his nature, irrespective of the wishes of his auditors. Protagoras often squirming in the presence of others, adjusting to the presence of the few or the many, enacts the relativism he expresses as his philosophical stance. That Protagoras even asks the question about who the audience is to be suggests that he neither lacks shame nor speaks all things in the open for all to see. Protagoras despite all his professions to the contrary, does not practice *parrhêsia* but is restrained by shame and by fear. His constant concern with his own safety ensures that his speech is never daring.

For Socrates, the one without shame, what is true is never relative. While his speech may differ when he engages in conversation with a young Hippocrates or an old Protagoras, he remains the same political and social character that his interlocutors – who blush and care about whether they speak before others – are not. The goal of his speech is to uncover others, not to hide himself. As we saw in the *Apology*, Socrates does not share in the shame Protagoras' myth says humans need in order to live in peaceful cities. By repeating Protagoras' query back to him, Socrates reminds his audience of Protagoras' sensitivity to the dictates of shame and the limits the gaze of others might place on his speech. Socrates, in contrast, by his apparent indifference to the audience before whom he speaks suggests that he himself speaks freely – and daringly. Protagoras, always questioning whether to speak before others or alone, fearful of the consequences of speaking his views openly and looking to what it is safe to say, does not.

Before addressing Protagoras' question about whether they are to converse in the presence of others or not, Socrates had explained that Hippocrates has come to see Protagoras because he longs to gain renown in the city. Hippocrates who comes from a distinguished family is eager, just like the other Athenians present in this dialogue, for the precedence in a city of equals that the skills the Sophists teach will give him.[10] The gathering behind closed doors at this mock Hades is precisely for those who are not content with the egalitarianism of Athenian democracy. These men are driven by a desire for the individual glory that is in conflict with the ideology of equality governing the city in which they live. No wonder the doors to Callias' house are shut. No wonder Protagoras questions whether they should speak alone or before others. Once Protagoras learns the purpose of the visit by Hippocrates and Socrates, he offers a curious speech intended to explain why he is so circumspect about who hears his speeches. Acknowledging Socrates' foresight (*promethêi*, 316c) in asking whether they should speak before others, Protagoras tells a tale of the Sophists of old. Protagoras begins: the Sophists of ancient times (perhaps not having homes such as Callias' in which to hide) devised other ways of hiding their craft from the view of others, using pretenses (*proschêma*) and dressing up their speeches (*prokaluptesthai*,

---

[10] The cast of characters present in Callias' house is a *Who's Who* of the illuminati of Athens. Besides Alcibiades, there are the future tyrant Critias, the soon to be famous playwright Agathon, and the renowned doctor Pausanias, among others.

316d) – just as (he somewhat surprisingly claims) the poets Homer and Hesiod and Simonides did with their poetry. He points specifically to Agathocles, "a great Sophist" from Athens who with many others made pretenses (*proschêma* for a second time in 316) in order to escape detection by those who were powerful in the city (316e). Deception and disguises marked the speeches of these early Sophists. They did not follow the practice of the Athenians themselves, speaking freely when they visited Athens. Instead, according to Protagoras, they wisely worried about the prosecution that would follow if they boldly proclaimed their intentions. They did not see Athens as a tolerant society welcoming the speech of foreign Sophists, especially those who threatened to undermine the practices derived from Zeus' gift of the cohesive emotion of *aidôs*.

In contrast to the ancient Sophists who hid their teachings in the mysteries of poetry and other forms of discourse, Protagoras claims that he bravely (from the comfort of Callias' protective custody)[11] announces that he is a Sophist and that he teaches men. "I have taken the entirely opposite road and admit that I am a Sophist and that I educate men and I think such care (*eulabein*) is the better of the two: to admit rather than to deny" (317b). In the *Gorgias* Socrates initially welcomes his conversation with Callicles. Recalling the exclusionary aspects of *parrhêsia* that we saw especially in the plays of Euripides, Socrates remarks that Callicles as a fellow citizen has the *parrhêsia* that the foreigners do not. Protagoras, from the security of Callias' house, claims to have the same *parrhêsia* that Socrates suggests in the *Gorgias* is denied by the Athenians to foreigners. With this appropriation of Athenian *parrhêsia*, then, Protagoras claims to be free from the need to cover his speeches with myth and ambiguity. No subterfuges for him, he assures us, sheltered as he is by carefully monitoring to whom and before whom he speaks; indeed, no subterfuges for him, especially since (as he reveals in his descriptions of what the Sophists of old suffered) they do not seem to work. In fact, those screens and pretenses made those who used them even more hated and treated as evil doers or rogues (317a). Protagoras will, he deceptively assures Socrates, speak openly – unlike the Sophists of old. Protagoras here embodies the fourth-century orators' complaints about the transformation of *parrhêsia* into rhetoric. The free speech they practice now is not for the sake of truth, but for the sake of covering. The daring for the benefit of the city is lost and the interest in self-promotion and self-protection is paramount.

Reading all these remarks by Protagoras about the old Sophists, one almost has the sense that Protagoras is foreshadowing Leo Strauss' essay "Persecution and the Art of Writing" where Strauss unveils his own theory of an esoteric writing intended to communicate through hidden meanings

---

[11] See also 351d; he answers Socrates' questions with a view to what is "not less safe (*ou ... asaphesteron*)," i.e., "safer."

what one feared to speak openly. The screens of language enable men to speak what they dare not say for fear of a society's intolerance for the unconventional. "Persecution, then, gives rise to a peculiar technique of writing, and therewith to a peculiar type of literature, in which the truth about all crucial things is presented exclusively between the lines. That literature is addressed, not to all readers, but to trustworthy and intelligent readers only" (1952: 25). In Protagoras' version of this argument, the absence of free speech, the fear of jealousy (*phthonos*) of others, and the dread of persecution forced the Sophists from ancient times to use the assorted covers derived from poetry and music – "to write between the lines," in Strauss' language – in order to communicate their views. Hidden within their poetry were the lessons they could not express openly.

There were indeed fetters on the tongues of these Sophists, but these fetters came not from the community-building *aidôs* as in Protagoras' myth, but more powerfully from the fear of persecution and *dikê*. As he explains the strategy of these Sophists, Protagoras hardly is the democrat some find him to be (Farrar 1988: chap. 3; Nussbaum 1986: 100–6). Instead, we see a Protagoras perched in the house of the wealthy Callias who is scornful of the many: "Since *hoi polloi*, so to speak, perceive nothing but simply sing as hymns (*humnousin*) whatever the [powerful] tell them" (317a), the Sophists did not and do not fear what the many might do were they to speak freely.[12] Rather, they feared the leaders, those with power in the city, those whom the young men in attendance at Callias' house hope they themselves will become. Protagoras' comfortable myth of the political community united by *aidôs* shatters in his articulation of his own role as a foreigner in Athens. He comes not only as one disrupting the circle of *aidôs* by taking the young away from their family and friends as he had told Socrates earlier (316cd); he comes as a competitor to challenge those powerful citizens who have the many sing the songs they write for them. These powerful men, through their own deceit, control and manipulate the many who "perceive nothing," those weaklings who are chained by *aidôs* and the lessons of reverence perpetuated by the powerful for their own self-interest. Protagoras appears in their city to undercut the control of those who traditionally held power and to introduce new songs for the many to sing.

The beautiful myth expounding a politics of equal engagement in the life of the polity where men share in *aidôs* and *dikê* and where all enjoy a political *aretê* or excellence, is a pretense to lull the many (and, he hopes, Socrates)

---

[12] See also 352b where Protagoras wonders whether he and Socrates must attend to the opinion of the many (*tên tôn pollôn doxan anthropôn*) when they speak just whatever happens to come to their mind. Weiss (2006: chap. 2) catalogues the hostility to the *dêmos* expressed by Protagoras. Socrates in contrast sees in the speech of the many something that will bring them closer to finding how courage is related to the other parts of virtue (353b).

with dreams of a god (Zeus)-given reverence for the old.[13] Protagoras himself knows better and so he tells his beautiful stories to soothe the many and teach them reverence for the old while giving his own students those techniques that enable them to train the many to sing their songs. Protagoras, grandly concluding his own lecture on the esoteric speech of the early Sophists, affirms: "It is by far the most pleasing for me, if you wish something, to speak about all these things before those who are present within (*endon*)" (317c). Grandly, he heroically claims free speech before all – or rather the small circle who are "within" the very narrow walls of Callias' house.

Socrates obviously knows better than to believe Protagoras' myth as anything more than the Sophist's subterfuge and is not fooled by Protagoras' pretenses, screens, and beautiful speeches that attempt to hide the meaning and intentions of his words. And Socrates knows well the psychological needs of his deceptive interlocutor. The beautiful young Alcibiades may be present, but as Socrates told his unnamed companion he barely noticed him with the preening peacock Protagoras – speaking of esoteric and exoteric speech – before him. "I suspected that he wished to display himself and make himself appear beautiful (*kallôpisasthai*)" (317c). And so Socrates draws together a greater audience than he and Hippocrates could provide. While we have not the city of *hoi polloi* who perceive nothing and who are so scorned by Protagoras, we find an assembly of listeners, Prodicus and Hippias and the young men from distinguished families who are eager for individual power and prestige in the city of supposed equality. As we shall see later in the dialogue, Protagoras, the one who now has claimed for himself the daring *parrhêsia* of the Athenians, gives speeches inhibited not only by the same fear of persecution that haunted the early Sophists, but also by a fear of the loss of stature before the small audience in Callias' home. Despite vaunting claims to speak openly, concern with his appearance before others nevertheless manages to work its power over him.

Considerably later in the dialogue, Socrates offers a startling response to Protagoras' surprising story concerning the esoteric Sophists when in the middle of the discussion about how to interpret a poem by Simonides he offers an equally peculiar tale about the laconic Spartans, a people hardly known for their free speech, much less any pretense to philosophy. In a passage as fanciful as Protagoras' *muthos*, Socrates envisions a Lacedaemonia populated by the philosophic (!) Spartans (342). In order to develop this astonishing image, Socrates removes from the Spartans their reputation for a natural taciturnity. They are, it turns out, no less loquacious than the Athenians. Socrates explains that the Spartan restraint on speech is only a cover or pretense (*skêmatizontai*, 342b) making explicit the analogy to Protagoras'

---

[13] A persistent theme in the dialogue is that of age – the young Hippocrates and the aged Protagoras with Socrates somewhere in between (310b, 314b, 317c, 318b).

Sophists in this regard. Socrates' Spartans (like Strauss' esoteric writers and Protagoras' early Sophists) limit their speech strategically in order to hide the true source of their power, which, it turns out – contrary to all report – is their wisdom. That way the Spartans fool others into thinking that their power comes from their military strength when in fact it really comes from their philosophizing. Within the city and among themselves, the Spartans speak freely once all the foreigners have been expelled. The expulsion of foreigners (*xenêlasia*) was a well-known and often remarked-upon practice of the Spartans[14] – but not usually (or, indeed, ever) interpreted as Socrates does here. Unobserved, so Socrates tells us in his own myth, the Spartans speak freely with their own Sophists (342b); they philosophize (342de) and through the practice of philosophy, far more than through gymnastics, they secure their political power over others.

What a story! What an outrage to the conventional wisdom that attributed free speech and philosophy to the Athenians! As Pericles had said in an effort to point out to the Athenians how special they were: "We philosophize without softness" (Thucydides 2.40). Not so, says Socrates. It is really the Spartans who philosophize without becoming soft – far more effectively than the Athenians, though unlike the Athenians, the Spartans have the sense to hide this source of their power rather than flaunt it before all of Greece as Pericles does. Socrates' tale is engaging precisely in its absurd opposition to all the conventions concerning Sparta, the stolid, unphilosophic, xenophobic city whose regime focused on training the body to encourage an unthinking valor (*Laws* Book 1; Xenophon, *Constitution of the Spartans*, passim).

Yet, in offering this perverse picture of the Spartans, Socrates suggests an alternative understanding of political power. The military world of the conventional Spartans demands devotion to common principles and the subordination of the individual entirely to the rules of the society and to the expectations of others. *Aidôs* rules the conventional Spartans for whom reputation in battle and self-restraint is of primary significance. They are the extreme expression of a society governed by Protagorean *aidôs* in the cohesion achieved by their reverence for the past and their concern with what others see. This is the city renowned in Greece as preserving their laws over seven hundred years. This is the city of the Spartan general Archidamus who appears in Book 1 of Thucydides' *History* to remind his fellow citizens as they debate whether to go to war: "Holding on to these practices which our fathers handed down to us we have benefits through all things; let us not let them go" (1.85.1). He further admonishes his audience that: "We are orderly (*eukosmon*), with *aidôs* partaking of the greater part of moderation (*sôphrosunês*) and we take care so that we are educated with the lack of learning that would make us arrogant before our customs" (1.84.3).

---

[14] See, e.g., Pericles' praise of Athens for making the city open to all for learning and seeing (Thucydides 2.37.1) and Xenophon's *Constitution of Sparta* (14.4.2).

Such respect for the old as reported by Thucydides is, in Socrates' tale, only a pretense among the Spartans and in fact has nothing to do with the power and the success they enjoy as a military power and as a city. The *aidôs* so praised in Protagoras' speech is, in Socrates' tale, mocked by the military leader of Greece. Socrates takes Protagoras' *aidôs* away from the Spartans and introduces an unexpected openness among themselves – a daring *parrhêsia* uninhibited by the past that was thought to characterize only the democratic world of the Athenians and in which the Athenians expressed their unique pride. In this fanciful vision that Socrates offers, the Spartans have power because in the privacy of their own city they practice *parrhêsia*. In the privacy of their city, they are forward looking, not grounded in an unchanging past. *Parrhêsia* and philosophy go together in Sparta. Despite Pericles' noble portrait of the Athenians living freely both in private and in public, they fail to philosophize. In contrast to the wise Spartans, the Athenians show off their *parrhêsia*, that is, they demonstrate that they care about their reputation for free speech among the Greeks. Yet, they condemn those who do engage in philosophy to death, unaware that it is the power of free speech and philosophy that secures the military strength of the Spartans.

In Socrates' story the Spartans, having expelled all foreigners, speak freely and courageously among themselves in their pursuit of wisdom. Protagoras, even with the "foreigners" expelled cannot, like these imagined Spartans, enjoy both *parrhêsia* and philosophy. In his extended explanation of why he had queried Socrates about whether to speak before the many or the few, Protagoras suggested why he himself has not followed the restraint and artifice practiced by the earlier Sophists. He does not do so, in part, he explains, because he thinks that it is not possible to escape the notice of those who have power in the city, even if the many – the *hoi polloi* (317a) – would be oblivious. Thus, in an effort to allure rather than offend the strong within the city, he claims he has been open, admitting that he is a Sophist and that he educates (wealthy, young) men. So far, he assures Socrates, he has suffered nothing dreadful (*deinon*, 317b). As a result, he would be most pleased if Socrates prefers to have the discussion before all the others in Callias' house (316c), hardly an audience of Athenians – and all potentially powerful and all eager to learn from him except Socrates.

Socrates – the narrator and well in control of the impressions created here – remarks on how Protagoras' desire to speak before others coincided with his desire to show off (*kallôpisasthai*, 317c). Protagoras' awareness of how others perceive him dominates his willingness to speak "openly" before others. As Plato has Socrates present it, Protagoras' open speech is his own effort at subterfuge soon to be uncovered by Socrates. He does not recognize the wisdom of Socrates' taciturn Spartans whose power depends precisely on not showing off, on knowing what knowledge to keep secret (Coby 1987: 107). So concerned with his appearance and as such embodying the emotion of shame, Protagoras reveals his dependence on others. He is not the autonomous individual of later philosophy that he projects himself to be; rather, he is constrained by the search for the good esteem of those who surround him. It is that concern with appearance that limits the openness of his speech and turns him into a slave of his own audience. Despite himself and against all his pretensions, he behaves as those governed by *aidôs* about whom he talks in his myth, though he may see himself as teaching others to escape its power.

In the introductory section of the dialogue, Socrates had assured his unnamed companion that Alcibiades had spoken up for him. This defense occurs during one of the numerous dramatic interludes of the dialogue when a somewhat flustered Protagoras resists continuing participation in the discussion. Alcibiades is putting pressure on Protagoras to persist. Socrates notes that Protagoras, at least as it seemed to Socrates, was "embarrassed (*aischuntheis*)" by the blandishments of Alcibiades and Callias and of all those gathered there (348c). Here, Socrates alerts us to Protagoras' own "shame" and Socrates sets Protagoras' subsequent assurance that he speaks truthfully (*egô alêthê legô*, 349d) about the parts of virtue into an ironical context. Socrates harkens back to Protagoras' speech about his difference from the early Sophists when he says to him that Protagoras is an excellent interlocutor for "while others hide (*apokruptomenôn*) their craft, you openly announce yourself among all the Hellenes that you are called a Sophist and teacher of *paideuseôs* and virtue" (349a). The complex tension between shame and free speech surfaces here as it is now shame that supposedly forces Protagoras to speak openly, to practice the *parrhêsia* that he resists and to reveal his true beliefs before Socrates and the others at Callias' house.

In contrast to Protagoras, Socrates as narrator and indeed in control of all the speeches of all the characters, reports himself as saying near the beginning of his conversation with Protagoras: "I shall not say to you anything other than what I think" (319b). Socrates neither practices the supposed laconic restraint as subterfuge nor does he find himself propelled by the Protagorean desire for renown. He speaks fully and freely before outsiders such as Protagoras and Hippias (unlike the Spartans) as well as before his fellow citizens who have managed to gain access to Callias' house. Saying what he thinks in an effort to uncover what is true before whatever audience there happens to be, he separates himself from the demands and constraints of a political community.

At one point in the dialogue Socrates and Protagoras find themselves debating whether the pleasant and the good are the same thing. In this particular discussion Protagoras yields leadership to Socrates: "It is just (*dikaios*), he said, that you lead (*hêgeisthai*) since you initiated the discussion (*tou logou*)" (351e). And so Socrates openly directs the conversation by introducing a rather peculiar analogy. He posits an individual who is eager to assess someone else's health and is not satisfied with only seeing the uncovered hands and face and asks the individual to uncover (*apokalupsas*) as well his chest and back in order that he may examine him more clearly (*episkepsômai saphesteron*, 352a). Similarly, Socrates says to Protagoras that he must uncover (*apokalupson*) the views he holds concerning knowledge (*epistêmê*, 352b). As a condition for speaking with Socrates, there is to be no hiding of the thoughts, no esoteric speech, and no shame. In the Socratic dialogue, all must be shamelessly uncovered for a public viewing, just as if one were undressing for a doctor concerned with assessing the health of a body – or for a lover. Socrates demands revelation in discourse; it is an openness that the proud and shame-driven Protagoras resists. Protagoras pretends to be eager for openness, but only when it enhances his reputation. Socrates in his turn demands the nakedness achieved by *parrhêsia* in speech and by undressing before doctors. Only then can the proper medications be administered to the soul and to the body. Only then can the philosopher and the doctor practice their arts.

4. SOCRATES' SPEECH

The issue of secret writings, of hiding one's teachings and not speaking openly, introduced early in the dialogue by Protagoras and later by Socrates' discussion of the supposedly wise and not at all laconic Spartans, alerts us to a question that faces all of us reading the conversations reported by Socrates in the Platonic dialogues, namely, the degree to which the characters in the dialogues are themselves allowed to speak freely. We must always be aware of the control that Plato as author and Socrates as narrator have over the characters in the dialogues. The dialogues are not deliberative Assemblies where the herald rises to ask "Who wishes to speak?" The dialogues are carefully constructed literary works. And within the crucible of the action and discourse of the dialogue, Plato offers his readers examinations of the consequences of the limits and potentialities of free speech. Hippocrates who had blurted out with all the enthusiasm of a young man his desire to study with Protagoras blushes when he becomes aware of how others will understand what he freely revealed about himself. Had he allowed shame to control him first, he might not have expressed so openly his longings. His sensitivity to the gaze of the Athenians and even the Greeks would have limited his speech. He cannot openly proclaim in a city of equals his desire to become their ruler and manipulator with the skills he hopes to learn from the Sophists. His blush admits the discomfort produced by the obvious answer to Socrates' question about what he would become were he to study with Protagoras. In his discourse with Hippocrates Socrates invokes shame as the restraint that should lead to a deeper questioning of incentives, but the restraints on speech that he who prides himself on speaking freely imposes within the context of the dialogue can take on a variety of forms and this becomes one of the prevailing leitmotifs of the *Protagoras*. Socrates moves beyond shame and the blush of Hippocrates to the formal restraints that ensure the progress of the dialogue.

For example, after Protagoras has given his great speech defending the proposition that the virtues are teachable and after Socrates has begun to probe whether the virtues are one or many, thereby unsettling the confidence of a Protagoras who has started to bristle at Socrates' questions (333d), Socrates interrupts the flow of the conversation by complaining about a rather brief – at least in comparison to other earlier speeches both by himself and Protagoras – comment by Protagoras. In the speech that triggers this interruption in the flow of the discussion, Protagoras had presented the theory of relativism for which he was so well known. Explicating the theory that what benefits some can harm others, Protagoras had remarked: "There are foods and drinks and drugs and thousands of other things that are sometimes beneficial and other times not" (334a). He offered examples to support his claims: dung, good for the roots of trees but destructive on branches; or oil, bad for the hair of animals but good for the hair of man (334b). Protagoras concluded this speech of less than a page by noting that the good is multicolored and many-sided (*poikilon . . . kai pantodapon*, 334b). Socrates remarks that Protagoras' speech here had met with a loud response (*anethorubêson*) from those listening. They shouted that Protagoras, defending relativism, had spoken well (*eu legoi*, 334c).

Socrates mitigates the effect of the group's enthusiasm when he does not respond directly to Protagoras' advocacy of relativism. He ignores the content of the speech and instead cautions that he is unable to remember long speeches. He made (we must note) no such complaint when much longer speeches were given earlier in the discussion, most obviously the great speech that included the myth of the distribution of skills. Now, suddenly at this point in the dialogue, Socrates says: "I happen to be a forgetful (*epilêsmôn*) sort of man and if someone speaks at length, I forget (*epilanthanomai*) what the speech was about" (334cd). (This is the "forgetful man," we must remember, who is reciting virtually the entire dialogue, and who on another occasion reports the entire and far longer conversation from that evening in the Piraeus at Cephalus' house.) Socrates in the *Protagoras* uses the analogy of a man who is somewhat deaf: a speaker must acknowledge the disability of the deaf man and address himself more loudly to him if one wants to be heard. Given his forgetfulness, then, Socrates suggests Protagoras must cut short his speeches (334d) in order for the conversation to continue. Protagoras' speech is suddenly to be restrained by Socrates' *pretense* of being unable to remember. In this case, Socrates, like the Sophists of old, creates screens and hides his real meanings. And by doing so eventually comes to control the mode of discourse employed in the rest of the dialogue.

Protagoras, well schooled in the relativism he has just preached, asks in response to Socrates' request: "Too long for whom and what is to be the measure of long and short." Trying to prove his earlier point about the subjectivity of the good and the ambiguities entailed in the notions of measures, Protagoras asks (according to Socrates' report): "Are my answers to be what seems best to me or what is according to you?" (334e). Who is to be the judge of the proper length? The speaker or the listener? Does the power over speeches belong to the speaker who determines what and how something is said or to the listener who decides what to hear? Protagoras seems to be confused here: he assumes the speaker is in control. This is the basis for his role as a teacher of the art of rhetoric, but the speaker as Socrates so well understands is always subject to the power of the listener. The listener need not listen – no matter how long or short the speaker speaks. Euthyphro, Anytus, and a whole host of others can walk away when they do not like listening to the questions that Socrates poses for them. Not only may speech be free, but so too is listening. The listener need not hear the speech as the speaker intended. Glaucon laughed off the *bêma* in the Athenian Assembly learned that lesson the hard way (Xenophon, *Memorabilia*, 3.6.1). Here, within the structure of Plato's works Socrates tries to teach Protagoras the same lesson about the priority of the listener to the speaker. Protagoras is not as good a student as Glaucon whom Socrates saved from his political ambitions. The question "Who wishes to speak?" asked in the Assembly brings with it no assurance that the members of the Assembly will listen.[15] In the Platonic dialogue, Socrates can control the speaker by defining the terms under which he, Socrates, will listen but he cannot force others to listen.

Instead of responding directly to Protagoras when he asks about the appropriate length for speeches by saying that yes, there is a measure, or that the length of speeches is to depend upon either the speaker or the listener, Socrates tries to flatter Protagoras by remarking that "reputation has it that you can speak long and short" (334e), suggesting Protagoras' own indifference to length or measure. When these efforts to appeal to Protagoras' vanity fail to move the Sophist, Socrates reports that he prepared to leave: "Since you are not willing [to speak briefly] and there is a certain business that awaits me and I am not able to remain here . . . it is necessary that I leave. I shall go." This is Socrates lying in order to control the flow of the discussion, in order to limit the form of speech within the dialogue. We the readers know from the introductory passages of the dialogue that Socrates jumps at the opportunity to give his companion a long version of his encounter with the Sophists at Callias' house and that he is not, as he claims, "without any leisure *(tis ascholia)*" (335c). He uses this speech as a deceptive ploy to reengage Protagoras in dialogue, drawing along with him the others in the room who in their turn use force to continue the performance of the two main characters of the dialogue.

[15] The same is ultimately true in the courtroom as well. Consider the number of times that Socrates must ask for the attention of the crowd listening to his speech before the jurors.

Socrates threatens to leave since Protagoras will not promise to give brief speeches, but he is restrained by Callias. In a reprise of the beginning of the *Republic*, Callias "with his right hand took hold of my hand and his left hand of my threadbare cloak and said 'we will not release you, O Socrates'" (335e). The debate that follows about how to proceed finally ends when Socrates consents to stay, but only after all agree to follow his preferred method of discourse. Pointing to Protagoras' supposedly lengthy style of presentation, Socrates had remarked: "I thought being together (*to suneinai*) carrying on dialogue with one another was different from demagoguery" (336b). Socrates is eager to remove political speech from the speech within the house of Callias, but the wealthy Callias responds by objecting to Socrates' demand for brevity in Protagoras' speeches. He instead proposes complete freedom for the speaker: "It seems to be just (*dikaia dokei*) that Protagoras be allowed to speak as he wishes (*hopôs bouletai*) and Socrates to speak as he wishes (*hopôs bouletai*) and you how you wish (*hopôs... su boulêi*)" (336b). Democracy is the regime in which one does as one wishes as Socrates had suggested in the *Republic* and Aristotle repeats frequently in the *Politics* about some forms of democracy (*Politics* 1310a33). Callias now proposes such freedom for the conversation taking place at his house, that each "speak as he wishes." Socrates does not accept the democratic model of doing "whatever one wishes" and demands restraints before he agrees to continue to engage in the ongoing dialogue.

This is the point in the dialogue referred to at the very beginning of the *Protagoras* where Alcibiades shows his friendly feelings for Socrates and interjects himself in support of Socrates: "'You do not speak well, Callias,' he said," Socrates reports (336b). Alcibiades (who generally, after all, has little truck with the principles of democracy) argues against Callias' claim that it is just for everyone to speak as he wishes. Praising Socrates and well aware that Socrates is playing (*paizei*) when he says that he is forgetful, Alcibiades calls Socrates' proposal for brief speeches more fair (*epieikestera*), since it is necessary that each one reveal (make visible) his thoughts (*tên heautou gnômên apophainesthai*, 336d). That lengthy speeches hide rather than reveal is the implication here. Alcibiades finds "justice" not in everyone doing/speaking as he wishes, but in the undoing of whatever may hide one's thoughts. Uncovering one's thoughts, accomplished more effectively by the brief speeches Socrates insists on, is what Alcibiades proposes to the group as the proper measure for speech. Alcibiades here is defending *parrhêsia* as practiced by the democratic Athenians, not the practice of "doing whatever one wishes" that the democratic ideology also appropriated.

Hippias, so silent up to this point, intervenes into this discussion about how the conversation is to proceed and proposes a middle way: elaborating on Callias' suggestion, he urges that they let each speak as he wishes, but they also should set over themselves an "umpire" or "overseer" or "ruler" (he is not clear which) who will ensure that the length of the speeches is appropriate for each one (338ab). He requests that Socrates "not seek a precise form (*akribes touto eidos*) of dialogue with excessive brevity, if it is not pleasing (*hêdu*) to Protagoras, but allow the speeches to enjoy a loose rein" (338a). Protagoras, in Hippias' flamboyant language, is in his turn urged not "to let out his sails so far that he flees into an ocean of words, hiding (*apokrupsanta*) the land" (338a). Socrates rejects Hippias' mediating proposal on the grounds that it would be shameful (*aischron*, 338b). It would entail giving an inferior person authority over those who are better; or if this imagined overseer were the equal to Protagoras and Socrates, he would be doing just the same as each would do himself.

Thus, appealing to the antiegalitarian proclivities of the group assembled at Callias' house, those who would oppose rule by ones inferior to themselves, Socrates offers yet another method by which they will carry on the discussion already begun – a method that picks up on a different democratic principle, that of individuals changing roles, of ruling and then being ruled: first Protagoras will ask the questions and Socrates will respond, and then they will change roles and Socrates will ask and Protagoras will answer. Socrates concludes this proposal by remarking to the entire group that in this way "there will be no need for an overseer, but you all in common will oversee (*pantes koinêi epistatêsete*)" (338e). Socrates thereby transforms the community gathered in Callias' house into a self-ruling democracy, all engaged in ensuring that their "being together (*tên sunousian*)" (338d) yield discussion of the sort he prefers to the speechifying advocated by the Sophists present.

From the hierarchy proposed by Hippias where a ruler of sorts would assert a standard of evaluation and judge the conformity between the speeches and their length, Socrates moves the group to a more democratic model of self-rule and exchange – even if (just as in the courtroom) it does not allow one the freedom to speak for as long as one wishes. Appropriating the language of the democratic Assembly, Socrates reports: "It seemed best to all (*edokei pasin*) that it ought to be done in this fashion" (338e). And all appear happy with this resolution – all, that is, except Protagoras who was "forced (*ênagkasthê*)" (338c) to agree to ask questions and then in turn to answer Socrates' questions. In other words, Socrates with his dubious claims about his faulty memory succeeds in controlling the flow of the speech in the dialogue. He achieves in the Platonic literary construction what he cannot do in the city of Athens: he constructs the form that the speech making of others shall follow.

With Alcibiades' assistance at first and then with the communal agreement of the rest of the group, Socrates has now appropriated for himself control over how his interlocutors are to speak, not with regard to the content, but with regard to the form. He has – with the blessings of his companions – prevented others from speaking as they might wish. While he himself gives

long answers in the subsequent pages of the dialogue,[16] he manages to sup-
press the long answers Protagoras might have given were he to speak as he
wishes, indeed turning his speeches into almost monosyllabic responses, if
even that. The author of the dialogue and its narrator ensure that our sympathies lie with the memory-challenged Socrates rather than with the pompous
Protagoras, but we should not ignore the role of Socrates as the manipulator,
the one who praises the Spartans for hiding the true source of their strength,
namely, their unrestrained speech and philosophizing among themselves.

Under Socrates' guidance the democratic Athenian practice of *parrhêsia*
when understood as saying just what one thinks, whatever (in Adeimantus'
language regarding democracy) comes to one's lips, encounters restraints.
By asking for brief speeches Socrates sets limits on the *form* (the *eidos*, as
Prodicus says) of expression; he establishes a structure for the conversation,
but neither *aidôs* as respect for what has been said in the past or for one's
fellow citizens nor the fear of persecution that the early Sophists according to
Protagoras felt serves as the source of constraint. We can say that through the
agreement among themselves, the group at Callias' house established certain
institutions to be enforced by all. The institutions affect only length, not content, but the form in its turn determines and limits what can be spoken. The
practice of the dialogue, where speech is clipped and defined by questions
and answers, replaces the *parrhêsia* that was so much a part of the Athenian
political and ideological landscape. In the narrow context of the dialogue,
then, the openness of the political practice encounters the Socratic/Platonic
practice and the latter prevails transforming what had been public speaking into the private speech of companions "being together" and the private
speech of Socratic philosophy. The "form" of discourse that Socrates has
instituted is independent of any attention to the past and the customs that
have developed over time. *Eidos* replaces *aidôs*. And the patterns of dialogic/
democratic speech protect the interlocutors from the prison of the past and
of the gaze. In the democratic world of the Assembly, there were the limits
on speech that came from institutional needs, not from a respect for the
past nor for the hierarchy of individuals present. As a result, the practices of
the Assembly and of Socrates' "brief speech" can focus on an indeterminate
future rather than a past defined by traditions and hierarchies. Because of the
brevity imposed by Socrates' manipulative deception, though, the freedom
from *aidôs* and from the hierarchies grounded on past relations does not
dissolve into the formless and bombastic rhetoric of Protagoras.

In a schematic sense we can say that the *aidôs* so praised by Protagoras
as a gift of Zeus focuses on the customs inherited from the past and on
the castigating gaze of one's fellow citizens in the present. The Athenians
reveling in the deference-smashing *parrhêsia* are nevertheless unable to live

---

[16] For some of Socrates' longer speeches see 342a–7b and 354e–6c; in contrast, the speech by
Protagoras about which Socrates complains goes from 334a–c.

in a world without boundaries and set institutional limits on who could speak when, on the topics to which they could address themselves in their Assemblies, and yet they resist *aidôs*. Procedures governed speech in the Athenian Assembly and in the courtrooms. And Socrates' dialogue likewise captures the limitations *parrhêsia* requires if the conversation devoted to the discovery of moral truths about the genesis of virtue is to protect itself from becoming a setting for the sort of political harangues to which *parrhêsia* had deteriorated in the fourth century.[17]

If we return to our early story of Herodotus' Gyges, *aidôs* was there enmeshed in the "beautiful things discovered long ago" by which most of the barbarians understood what was to be seen and what unseen. The barbarians found limits to their actions and adventures with the admonition not to look upon what was not their own. Such limits on what one can see protected "the beautiful things" from comparison with "the beautiful things" that others in other places may see and the community preserved itself secure in the beauty of what was its own. The practices of the past are revered as what ought to be. Protagoras' myth about the origins of cities lies within the confines of such an understanding about political foundations, but within the dialogue his story faces a biting critique by his fellow Sophist Hippias. Unwilling to be left out during the interlude devoted to how the interlocutors are to carry on their discussion, Hippias intervenes, claiming to regard those assembled in Callias' house from the various parts of Greece as "all fellow citizens by nature (*phusei*), not by law (*nomôi*)" and he warns in an oft-quoted phrase: "Law (*nomos*) is a tyrant over human beings and forces many things against nature" (337d). Hippias asks that they turn to a nature that can unite men not from the same cities, not sharing the same beautiful things from long ago. It is those beautiful things, the *nomoi*, that divide humans from one another. *Aidôs* has no place in Hippias' world – nor in Socrates'.

Socrates' limits on speech come not by looking back in history to the ancestral customs, the *nomoi*, that Hippias so scorns as he appeals to nature. Socrates accepts Hippias' plea that he find in the "form, *eidos*" the inherent shape to which speech must adapt itself. As Hippias himself had suggested, Protagoras' "open sail" hides rather than reveals. Socrates' "precise form" of brevity resists the tyranny of the *nomoi* and aims for the unveiling of a nature that lies behind the customs that divide men. With *aidôs* shed, there is indeed the uncovering of nature; the doctor demanding to see the body in order to heal it needs to strip the body bare in order to see its true form. Candaules insisted that Gyges would not see the true beauty of his wife, her form (*eidos*, 1.8), unless he saw her without the cover of her clothes. A woman in Lydia sheds her *aidôs* when she sheds her clothes, Gyges had said. But only then does she reveal her nature, her *eidos*. Protagoras had

[17] See Chapter 4, pages 91–3, 97.

in his myth defended the *aidôs* that hides and had himself hidden behind the wide sails of long speeches what, if anything, he believed to be true. Socrates, again like Candaules, disregarded the *aidôs* that counseled one not to uncover what is one's own, but it is the long speeches that hide, the short ones that reveal. Insofar as the dialogic speech allows for the escape from *aidôs*, it recaptures the democratic amnesia on which the future-focused democracies depend.

5. "FREE" WORDS

For many reading the *Protagoras*, a dialogue that seems to address mostly the question of the teachability of virtue and the unity of the virtues, the inordinate amount of time spent on the interpretation of a poem by Simonides is an annoying and unsatisfactory intrusion. One distinguished recent reader remarks: "This episode has often been an embarrassment to admirers of Socrates" (Kahn 1996: 210). Another scholar tries to explain away the "textual oddity" as a later interpolation (Frede 1986: 731, 747–8).[18] The quibbling that goes on over the difference between "becoming good" and "being good," what is hard (*chalepos*, harsh, bad) and what is good, takes on the texture of a tedious English class where the petty distinctions at first seem pedantic and ultimately become meaningless. The energy expended on the interpretation of the poem occurs because Socrates has won control over the "form" of the conversations in Callias' house. Now that it has been agreed that the speeches are to be short and that Socrates and Protagoras are to take turns asking and answering questions, Protagoras – after asserting that it is the greatest part of an education to develop skill with regard to the words (*epôn deinon*, 338e) of the poets – asks Socrates to reconcile an apparent contradiction in a poem by Simonides.

The preciousness of the discussion is foreshadowed, though, by Socrates' aside at the very beginning of the discussion. Having agreed that Simonides' poem is finely crafted and that a good poem will be consistent with itself, he admits in the heat of the moment that when Simonides writes that it is hard to become a good man he says the same thing as when he shortly thereafter criticizes Pittacus for saying that it is hard to be a good man. Socrates confesses to his anonymous interlocutor (still listening, we assume, raptly to the recitation of this conversation) that he fears that Protagoras may have had a point in noticing an inconsistency here (*ephoboumên mê ti legoi*, 339c). Socrates may have spoken too quickly and admitted to too much and thus ensnared himself in a web of his own making. The strangeness of this section arises, in part, from that loss of freedom that this precommitment (or "the past") imposes on him, from the fetters that tie him to a claim

---

[18] Frede (1986: 737) includes a helpful list of those who have addressed the peculiarities of this passage.

he has made without forethought. This is an Epimethean (or, shall we say, "Cleonic"?) Socrates, bound as he is by a position that he has staked out, who justifies rather than explores the validity of what has been. He is not the Socrates who rejects the unexamined life, but rather one who is trapped at first into defending a speech already given.

As justifier, though, he is faced by a new challenge posed by the "freedom" of words to signify many things. His own speech now dedicated to defending the consistency of Simonides' poem may not be free, but the words that he uses to escape the trap he suggests that he has fallen into are free – and that poses a challenge. After the initial exchange about Simonides' perplexing poem, Protagoras (who cannot resist answering his own questions) offers his reading of the poem that contradicts Socrates' assurances about coherence. Socrates finds himself at a loss. He feels like one, he says, who has been hit by a good boxer and ends up seeing stars. With an irony certainly apparent to his readers, if not to those with whom he is conversing, he remarks that he cannot fight on his own and thus he appeals to Simonides' fellow citizen the Sophist Prodicus for assistance.

Prodicus' appearances throughout the dialogue are emphatically comic. When Socrates and Hippocrates had first entered Callias' house, Prodicus was stationed in the storehouse that had been emptied out to serve as a guest room for him. There, wrapped in blankets, he pronounces – about what exactly is not evident. This man who later in the dialogue is so precise about the distinctions between words speaks in such a deep voice that it echoes in the room, making his words unclear (*asaphê*, 316d). Despite this blending of words in the echoing storeroom, Prodicus shows an obsession with precision during the interlude when the participants debate the form of speech to be followed. He thus enlightens his audience about the difference between listening to speakers commonly or impartially (*koinous*) but not equally (*isous*), "for they are not the same (*estin gar ou tauton*)." Similarly, he had urged Socrates and Protagoras to disagree (*amphisbêtein*), but not to get into a conflict (*erizein*). Talking with each other in that fashion, Prodicus said, they will be respected (*eudokimoite*) but not praised (*epainoisthe*) – and on and on (337a–c). The distinctions appear both plodding and comic, but they also foreshadow Socrates' appeals to him to clarify the distinction between becoming and being (340b).[19]

Prodicus' response to Socrates' plea for help, however, points to the more serious problem of trying to capture or ensnare words, not to let them wander freely through assorted connotations in the relativistic way that Protagoras would find compatible with the theory he articulated just moments earlier. Words are grounded in history and place in Prodicus' reading and

[19] The fundamental irony of turning to the Sophist Prodicus for a distinction between *to genesthai* and *to einai*, given the importance of those terms in such dialogues as the *Republic*, should not be lost.

Socrates' questioning of Prodicus is directed specifically to identifying that grounding. The meaning of *chalepos* may be "hard" if Simonides is using his own dialect but "terrible" (*deinos*) in Pittacus' dialect (341a–d). "Free" words with multiple meanings and multiple uses undermine community. The different dialects to which Prodicus refers reveal the divisions among the Greeks whom Hippias had considered to be his fellows. The dialects reveal the power of *nomos*, the power of *aidôs*. There are communities, each with an understanding of what is their own. Obviously, we cannot imagine words with *aidôs*; *aidôs* is a human emotion, but Prodicus is appealing to just that respect for what ties one to the traditions of one's community when he urges precision in the use of words, tied as they need to be to their conventional usage. Words cannot mock and dismiss the authority of the past in their interminable flexibility as do the words of Protagoras' relativistic thinking if there is to be communication.

Elsewhere in Greek literature we find the fear of words without shackles and without history, without (if we can say it) *aidôs*. Thucydides describes the rebellion at Corcyra where floating words mark the complete breakdown of the society. "Unreasoned daring is thought to be courageous love of friends, looking forward (*promêthê*) with care cowardly preparations, moderation is an excuse for cowardliness" (3.82.4). In language resonant of Thucydides', Socrates describes words in the democratic regime in Book 8 of the *Republic* where they float without an anchor, free as the citizens practicing *parrhêsia* who use them. Democratic words take on multiple meanings (just as in Athens citizens take on multiple roles) so that (in an evident recollection of Thucydides' Corcyra) moderation is called cowardice, arrogance good education, anarchy freedom and so on (560d–e).

Nevertheless, Prodicus' plea for precision is strangely at odds with the tone of Socrates' reading of the poem, which plays with the ambiguity of speech. Socrates' own interpretation of the poem is both mischievous and multileveled. It tries to put a stamp on the text and the words that are used, but Socrates also undermines his own analysis with the cuteness of the interpretation. It is in the course of his efforts at interpretation that he praises laconic brevity in an exceedingly long speech and concludes by suggesting that Simonides may be praising tyranny (albeit unwillingly) in his poem about being and becoming good. This weird and multifaceted interpretation (followed by Hippias' eager [but declined] offer to present his own original reading) is possible only because words are ambiguous, because in the dialogue, in the Assembly of citizens, in the conversation in Callias' house they lack the chains that Prodicus is so insistent on putting on them. And yet, without fetters on the words we use, obviously, there can be no communication. Socrates, taking on the mask of the literary interpreter, manipulates language freely and, we might say, shamelessly; he plays in this section of the dialogue the role of the complete democrat with language, releasing words from the fetters with which Prodicus (but not Protagoras) may be eager to enslave them. The history of words is missing. When speech is completely free like the words that comprise it, the consequence will be absurdity and social chaos. The capacity for discourse and dialogue would collapse if words could indeed escape their history and if humans could as well live without a view of the past, without *aidôs*. The Socratic dialogue becomes an effort to give words a "new past," to reconstitute the vocabulary of virtue that like a democracy resists the confinement imposed by the "beautiful things discovered long ago."

Recall that in Protagoras' myth, Prometheus steals both fire from Hephaestos and wisdom (*sophia*) from Athene. Thus, Protagoras tells us man had *ton bion sophian* (the wise life), but that was not enough for humans to survive; they still lacked, according to Protagoras, *hê politikê*, the craft of politics. That art Zeus kept well guarded in his fortress. In Protagoras' story the wisdom of Athene is useless without *aidôs*. The story Socrates tells through the narration of this dialogue is quite different. Wisdom in Socrates' story would be constrained by *aidôs*.[20] Thus, *aidôs* is the virtue excluded when the discussion turns to the unity of the five virtues – "wisdom and moderation and courage and justice and holiness" (349b). *Sôphrosunê* (moderation) replaces *aidôs*. The virtuous man in Socrates' version does not need the other-directed *aidôs* in the same way as, for instance, he needs *sôphrosunê*.[21] *Aidôs* enslaves him to a past from which virtue will free him. And once he practices this virtue he will be in a position to pursue the *eidê*, the truths grounded in nature, not the conventions inherited from long ago.

6. CODA

In the second chapter of this volume I suggested that free speech in its denial of *aidôs* and its daring rejection of the chains from the past and the traditions of hierarchy is a foundational principle of democracy – as well as the prerequisite for philosophic discourse. Part of the Socratic endeavor throughout Plato's dialogues is precisely to free words (such as virtue, justice, courage) from their conventional usages, to free them from their particular histories in the dialects of specific communities and to find for them a grounding apart

---

[20] These differences are, of course, consistent with the stands they take concerning the unity of the virtues. Socrates is leading us to the unity of the virtues while Protagoras is arguing for the differentiation. Thus, for Protagoras *dikê* can come to humans after wisdom/*sophia* has been stolen by Prometheus from Athene; such sequential gifts would not be possible in Socrates' vision.

[21] I believe that this is why *aidôs* gets lost in *sôphrosunê* as the dialogue progresses. They are not the same. The social and archaic quality of *aidôs* is replaced by *sôphrosunê*, which does not depend on a social context or the gaze of another. See further North (1966: esp. 92), who in reference to Xenophon's *Cyropaideia* notes Cyrus' comment that "those who possess *aidôs* refrain from what is disgraceful in public, while those who possess *sôphrosune* restrain themselves even in secret."

from the traditions of this city or that, what in other dialogues appears as the "forms," the *eidê*. But philosophy like democracy also admits to the need for its own limits; the artificial patterns of speech, the brief questions and answers that Socrates tells his interlocutor he imposed on the discourse in the *Protagoras*, provide a governing structure to the discourse, just as the procedures in the Assembly do. What both democracy and philosophy reject are not the forms and the limits on speech that come from the architecture of discourse, but rather the archaic and backward-looking *aidôs* that leads in Protagoras' world to the dependence on the gaze of others and the unquestioned "truths" lying contentedly in what has been. What both democracy and philosophy reject is the fear of uncovering oneself, of the nakedness before the gaze of others, a nakedness that scorns hierarchy and exalts the freedom of speech.

Lost with this rejection of *aidôs* by both philosophy and democracy, however, may well be the civility that gives to words their ability to serve as markers in dialogue and to the political community the coherence to which Protagoras appeals. Prodicus comically appealing to precision in the midst of the debate also warns us about the Socratic enterprise, the dialogue that tries to give new meaning to words, to turn the word courage into the same word as wisdom, to dismiss a past and introduce a new world of words that are not deeply embedded in the dialect of the community. Socrates' goal in raising the question of the unity of the virtues, of forcing Protagoras to admit that courage is wisdom, is nothing less than to release the words from their bondage and to transform the way in which we speak. As suggested in Chapter 2, the democratic regime is always on the precipice of change (Wolin 1994). The Socratic philosopher is ever eager to lead us to that precipice. Underlying the comic playfulness of this dialogue is the dark question of what exactly is the role of the shame that Protagoras had praised in our social lives and whether we can indeed live – and speak – without it. The unencumbered words that flit through the interpretation of Simonides' poem are just a faint indication of the challenges that face the groundlessness of practices of *parrhêsia*, democracy, and a Socratic philosophy devoted to the forward-looking undermining of the old.

Judith Shklar, remarking on the death of political tradition at America's founding, writes of tradition's replacement. She refers us back to James Madison in the *Federalist*: "In principle the new government did not need traditions, just social science" (1998: 175). It was a social science that was new, that was abstract, that was universal. Likewise, when Socrates concludes his debate with Protagoras over whether political virtue is teachable, he turns not to Protagoras' *aidôs* and *dikê* engraved in the hearts of mankind, but to a wisdom that in this dialogue is understood as calculation and measurement (357bc), a wisdom that like democracy frees one from a bondage to the past and looks for the truths elsewhere. For Madison in Shklar's account it was social science; for Socrates it was *eidos*.

Of course, a Platonic dialogue is not an Assembly. The practices of *parrhêsia* that fill the Athenians' experience of self-rule do not transfer easily into a literary representation of speeches far removed from the Assembly. But the daring willingness to use speech to uncover is as important in the Socratic dialogue as it is in the Assembly. Protagoras does not speak in order to uncover, but to hide himself behind the protective shield that words can often supply. The reliance on *aidôs* arrogantly professed by Protagoras turns one backward to the unexamined life of community values. The games Socrates (and Plato) play with speech turn the reader, the interlocutor, the citizen, and the human into an examining, questioning being, uncertain that the beautiful things discovered long ago are indeed beautiful. Engagement in the Socratic dialogue turns the reader into a democratic character trying to break from the chains of the past in a search for a truth unbounded by time.

Conclusion

Four Paradoxes

PARADOX 1: ANCIENTS AND MODERNS

This book, while extolling the freedom of speech that aligns itself with democracy and Socratic philosophy and that entails a rejection of the chains of the past that hinder a forward-looking truth seeking, nevertheless turns for guidance to the past, to the literature and history of a small city that flourished two and a half millennia ago. This ancient city and its literature have taken a powerful hold and placed their own chains on the contemporary imagination. Many in the last two centuries have exalted with eloquence and commitment the experiences of a democratic Athens; some in earlier centuries who feared the tumults of the democratic regime and some more recently who condemn a city that granted freedom only to a handful of men and no women have excoriated those experiences. I have tried neither to exalt nor to excoriate Athens in this volume; yet, the literature and practices of that ancient city for sure control what has transpired. To borrow the language of Sheldon Wolin (1989), the past is indeed present throughout this book, although I have throughout connected democracy (like Wolin) with a willing amnesia. Rather than seeing the past as a chain upon the present, a past that must be shed as was the aristocratic structure of pre-Cleisthenic Athens in the "founding" of democratic Athens, the ancient practices and the ancient texts become the tools whereby we can question our own practices and legacies, our own past – even that bequeathed to us by ancient Athens.

Thucydides records the events of the Peloponnesian War, he tells us, to enable his readers "to see clearly" (1.22.4). He rejects Herodotus' goal of recording the marvelous works performed by the men of the past lest these deeds be forgotten and lose their power to inspire his readers. The past for Thucydides serves neither as a model nor as a chain on current deeds; rather, it opens up the present and reveals the future. Thucydides contends that the past has this potential to enable us to see clearly both present and future because events "more or less" repeat and reflect what has been; or rather, they will do so as long as human nature remains the same (1:22.4; 3.82.2). Today, we might rephrase Thucydides' claims of perennial recurrence with the language of "perennial questions," those paradoxes and challenges from which we can never escape, no matter how much we try to forget the past. Questions that every political regime faces – the place of freedom within order and especially the balance between the two – will never leave us. For sure, as Jefferson noted so strongly in the passage cited in the Prologue to this volume, as Benjamin Constant insists when he writes of the differences between the liberty of the ancients and that of the moderns, much has changed and political founders and practitioners who return to the glamor of a world long past for instruction in current practices risk enslaving a new regime to models that no longer fit. Machiavelli warned in his chapter on Fortuna from *The Prince* that those who are wedded to the past and cannot change with changing circumstances are doomed by the destructive forces of nature and history. Athens and her democratic practices and her political theories cannot be such a chain on our understanding of the political world.

And yet, as I hope that the discussion in the earlier chapters suggests, Athens and those who wrote during the peak of her democratic experience are precisely the resources from the past that enable us to break away from the chains of our own past and free us from the legacy of the language that surrounds contemporary discussions of freedom of speech, whether it be the language of the rights of a people to protect themselves from oppression, or of the marketplace of ideas, or even the currently popular terminology of the "safety valve." The language drawn from our own legacy of freedom of speech blinds us to the egalitarianism and shameless self-revelation that the Athenians saw in their own practice of free speech, of saying all. Free speech for them was not the protection from an oppressive government; it was not the affirmation of individuality; it was not a psychological necessity that prevented a dissatisfied *dêmos* from resisting political control. Rather, it affirmed the rejection of an awestruck reverence for the hierarchical ordering of a society and the ancient traditions that supported it. *Parrhêsia* captured the full meaning of freedom, not as a private possession enjoyed by the isolated individual, but as the embrace of a world where all could freely reveal themselves before others without the fear of suffering from the blows of Odysseus' staff that had raised the welts on Thersites' back and drawn forth tears from Thersites' eyes. Ancient Athens and the texts discussed bring the past into the present not as a chain, but as an opportunity to rethink our own future. In this case, the past furnishes the means to release us from the legacy of the past. An amnesia that deprives us of those resources would deny us an avenue to freedom.

PARADOX 2: DEMOCRACY AND FREE SPEECH

Throughout this volume I have suggested the connection between the Athenian practice of *parrhêsia* and democracy, of speaking without *aidôs*, and a regime that breaks from the reverence for what has been and focuses rather on the present and the future. The new democratic regime constructs its own order, freed from the hierarchy that has been. The language of the Athenians extolling their own regime is filled with praise of this freedom as we saw in Chapter 4. On the most material level, the Athenians name a boat *Parrhêsia*, but the practice itself permeates the political life and sensibilities of the Athenian citizens. Forty times a year their Assemblies met and began when the herald asked: "Who wishes to speak?" Aristophanes in the *Thesmophoriazusae* captured the iconic significance of this beginning for the Athenian Assembly when he portrayed his own Assembly of women on stage mimicking those of their male counterparts. These women too have the sacrifices that initiate the meeting; these women too curse those who threaten the city; and they too have their "heraldess" who asks of those assembled: "Who wishes to speak?" (379).

And yet, *parrhêsia* becomes a problematic practice precisely because it opens the opportunity to shed *aidôs*, to speak without a reverence for what has been. Adeimantus' comment in the *Republic* that equated the freedom of democracy with saying whatever one wishes (563c) warns us about the potential for blasphemy that goes along with this freedom. *Parrhêsia* cultivated its own abuses. While initially entailing the convention of uncovering what one truly believes and courageously speaking those beliefs before others without regard to differences of social stature, *parrhêsia* also left open the potential for deception and manipulation by those controlled by the longing for power and freedom rather than for equality and truth. The art that the Sophists taught flourished in a regime that fostered this freedom. The practice that incorporates democracy's fundamental principles also harbors its share of self-destructive elements.

The familiar freedom to manipulate language through the art of rhetoric allowed those skilled in this craft to create a new hierarchy replacing the one that had been overthrown with the founding of democracy. This is the crux of Hippocrates' blush in the *Protagoras*; he is the young man eager to learn the art of the Sophists, an art that will enable him to be dominant in a regime that treasures equality. *Parrhêsia* degenerates from the "saying all," from the freedom to express – Thersites-like, Diomedes-like – what one truly believes in the face of social superiors, and becomes instead the practice of covering up what one truly believes in order to become foremost in the regime in which one lives. This new form of free speech violates that egalitarianism toward which *parrhêsia* was initially directed and for which *parrhêsia* was initially so acclaimed in the democratic regime.

This is the dilemma perhaps most powerfully expressed by Thucydides in the Mytilenean Debate where the wise Diodotus recognizes that *parrhêsia* is the practice not of democracies, but only of utopias. In democracies, a man like himself who cares for the welfare of the regime and does not seek individual fame learns not to speak by defying the traditions of the society, not to speak truthfully and boldly about what he believes. Rather, he comes to understand and inform the readers of Thucydides' work that one must speak with a view toward manipulation and control through the skillful exercise of deceptive speech. Democracy, Diodotus discovers, cannot endure the practice to which it gave birth and in which its citizens express such pride.

While Thucydides may perhaps lighten the dark prospect of the abuse of *parrhêsia* with the hopeful vision of a Diodotus speaking in the Assembly, the tragedian Euripides offers no such comfort. For him, that practice so favored by the democrats merely repeats the hierarchical orders that the regime was supposed to overthrow. Thersites may enter the deliberative circle, but the Athenian democracy and in particular the practice of free speech continues to exclude. Now it is the women and foreigners who cannot speak without fear before their superiors. Now it is the women and foreigners who live the lives of slaves unable, in Jocasta's words, "to say what one is thinking" (*Phoenician Women*, 392). Euripides finds even greater tragedy in this favored Athenian practice when his plays point to the devastation that can occur when one does speak freely, when one uncovers for friends the "true things" that cause them the harshest suffering. For Euripides, *parrhêsia* is not only the escape from slavery; it can also be a curse.

Aristophanes in the *Thesmophoriazusae* transforms such revelations from Euripides' tragedy into comedy when he finds Euripides guilty of divulging too much about the nature of women. In the end, however, Aristophanes offers a yet more serious critique of *parrhêsia* as the effort to uncover what is true by suggesting the extent of the poet's control over truth, appearances, and representation. Aristophanes thereby raises the uncomfortable question of whether there is any sort of truth that speech can uncover. Perhaps, all is illusion manipulated by the speech of the poet and we live in the shadows of Socrates' cave. Both Aristophanes and Euripides are only too aware of the challenges that a commitment to *parrhêsia* poses to the pursuit of truth and of happiness. Neither is as sanguine as the Persian Chorus of Aeschylus' play about the freedoms that attend the practice. Both, while exercising *parrhêsia* in the plays they write challenging the traditions and dogmas of Athens, also provoke reflection on and concern about just the freedoms they enjoy.

The purity of the practice of free speech may threaten the freedoms and ideals of the city. The tragedy that the writings of the ancients uncover for us is that it takes a Diodotus (the Gift of Zeus, the Son of Good Power) or the Socratic philosopher to understand the challenge of maintaining a democratic *parrhêsia* that preserves the welfare of the communities in which they live. Diodotus must lie to the Assembly in order to foster the political virtues of democratic self-rule in the city – not to mention a basic humanity. The ancients provide no solution to the paradox of free speech and democratic practices, to the self-destructive aspects of opening speech to all and releasing it from the power of *aidôs*, but they warn us of the potential for tragic consequences that may result from ignoring the dangers of the amnesia on which the freedom of speech is based without the discovery of alternative limits for its practice.

The possible exception here would be Plato with his *eidê*, but the story of Callipolis in the *Republic* suggests how the actual philosophical access to the *eidê* would end all *parrhêsia* and self-rule, a cost that is far too high for today's world. The paradox coming to us from the ancient world about free speech is not the so-familiar contemporary battle between individual rights and the community's welfare, but the transformation of a founding principle into a practice that undermines the theoretical commitments, in this case equality, of the regime itself.

PARADOX 3: SOCRATIC PHILOSOPHY AND THE DEMOCRATIC REGIME

The philosophic analogue of the paradox that emerges from the practice of free speech as the foundational principle of the democratic regime repeats itself in the life of Socrates and the Platonic dialogue. *The Apology of Socrates* with its emphasis on Socrates uncovering himself before the entire city, on the transparency of the defendant who insists on speaking only true things (*t' alêthê*) to a regime that supposedly embraces such openness, confronts the portrait of Socrates offered in the *Protagoras*. The regime, it turns out, cannot endure such openness and the effort to transform a shame that relies on the gaze of others into a democratic shame that looks to oneself leads to the guilty verdict from the majority of the Athenian jurors. Rejecting the principles out of which the democratic regime emerges, they condemn the parrhesiast to death.

We discover, as well, that Socrates cannot always play the role of the democratic parrhesiast standing naked before his interlocutors. In the dialogues of Plato, the philosopher does not speak with the openness that Plato's Socrates extols in the *Apology*. In conversation with the likes of those such as Protagoras he must employ "lies" and pretenses (what is sometimes more generously and euphemistically called "irony" [Vlastos 1991: chap. 1]) in order to uncover and reveal the true things he longs to impart. The self-serving speeches of Protagoras must be punctured by Socrates' ability to manipulate and structure the form of dialogue between them. And he can do this only by false presentations of himself, for instance as a forgetful man who cannot remember a speech of a few lines and as a man with "business" to attend to that would take him away from a conversation about the most important things, namely the nature of the virtues and whether they/it can be taught. The open speech challenging the traditions of the Athenians, so powerful when Socrates used it in the courtroom (even if it did not lead to his acquittal) disappears into the controlling language that conquers Protagoras and leaves the audience (especially the young Hippocrates) in that state of confusion so essential to their philosophic education and progress.

Open speech, the saying of all, does not simply uncover nature and reveal true things as Socrates may suggest during his trial; rather, speech is to be the instrument used to incite others to engage in the investigations that will lead them to the transformation of their own character. The Platonic dialogues that often appear as the casual and free conversations among clusters of interlocutors are the carefully controlled productions of the Platonic craft and Socratic direction. Socrates understands, just as the semidivine Diodotus does, that the *parrhêsia* he so praises in the *Gorgias* (486d–8b) as the prerogative of Athenian citizens must itself serve as a tool of control rather than of the freedom to say all things. Only then can it transform the certainties of the past into the uncertainties of the present, uncertainties that are essential to the task of uncovering the truths that lie beyond the practices of the past and the present.

When Socrates practices *parrhêsia* as the Athenians understood it, the bold affirmation and shameless articulation of what one believes to be true, the Athenians vote to execute him. When Socrates speaks not at all with a view to uncovering himself, but to controlling those who converse with him in the Platonic dialogues, he can move citizens like Hippocrates to the critical perspective and self-restraint that Socrates makes us see lie at the core of human virtue. This is a virtue that does not depend on a Protagorean *aidôs*, but on the shameless self-reliance that had governed the language of the *Apology*.

PARADOX 4: SHAME AND AMNESIA

In order to write about the egalitarianism that democracy has introduced into the modern world Tocqueville invents a new word to describe the sensibility that this egalitarianism has created: individualism ([1835–40: II.2.2] 2000: 482). This recent expression captures a new emotion that arises, Tocqueville says, from the loss of connection with the past: "[N]ot only does democracy make each man forget his ancestors, but it hides his descendants from him" (484). The new democratic man loses ties with the land, with the history of his family, and with the past. Though Tocqueville may see this individualism as a new emotion different from the egoism or selfishness of earlier ages, it recalls the amnesia of democratic foundings that permeated our discussion of the Cleisthenic beginning of Athenian democracy and of democracy as specifically understood in this volume.

The casting off of the past by these new democrats of Tocqueville's analysis allows for the egalitarianism of democracy, but it also threatens to undermine the cohesion of the society, leaving each individual isolated in a world of his or her own. Tocqueville, in some of the darker passages of *Democracy in America*, describes the absence of honor in a democracy, the regime in which the individual lives isolated from those who surround him. In the constraining world of the aristocracies, "no one can hope or fear not to be seen; he encounters no man placed so low that he has no theater, who will escape blame or praise by his obscurity" ([1835–40: 11.3.18] 2000: 598). It was in the aristocracies that democracy is now replacing that Tocqueville found the *aidôs* of Protagoras' speech, the emotion that sets the individual into a matrix of history, of reverence, and especially the gaze of others. No man, however lowly, could live free from the censuring looks that Pericles initially said had been banned from his democracy. The new democratic individualism that Tocqueville first finds in America, however, allows for the amnesia that enables one to dismiss the power of that gaze and threatens the cohesion that Protagoras affirms arises from that power. Famously, for Tocqueville, new resources must be found in the "secondary associations" that can reinstitute what has been lost with the demise of honor and the power of the gaze and the past. Tocqueville's response to the dangers of that demise poses precisely the challenge the ancient authors recognized – that the death of *aidôs* in the construction of democracy creates space for the unattached individual, for the resurgence of what we moderns have come to call the state of nature. Protagoras had described the condition of mankind before Hermes delivered Zeus' gifts: they were unjust toward one another for they did not yet have the political craft (*Protagoras*, 322b). Caring about the gaze of others, being susceptible to the blush, constitutes the political craft that Protagoras says Zeus gives to men so that they can escape the chaos of their lives as individuals looking only for their own self-satisfactions.

The democratic citizen's relation to shame is ambiguous. Democracy involves the effort to reject the past and commit to the present, to free one-self from the "beautiful things from long ago" to which Gyges had initially been so eager to defer. The democratic citizen is released from these bonds, able to speak and act as he or she wishes, to recreate the city without deference for what is old. But the dismissed *aidôs* had served as the glue about which I spoke in Chapter 3. It is the cohesive force that ties the community together, creates a public where individuals have the capacity to blush, and where the gaze matters. As pompous and bombastic as Protagoras may be in Plato's dialogue, the story of *aidôs* that he tells encapsulates the paradox that has governed this book. Protagoras' *aidôs* captures that reverence for our past, our history, and the submission to the gaze of others. It is a reverence that restrains through ancient hierarchies and traditions, but nevertheless fuses individuals into a community. In contrast is the amnesia that lies at the heart of a future-focused world distinguished by the egalitarian practices of *parrhêsia*, practices that see the truth in what will be shamelessly uncovered, not in what has been.

In the democracies of today, *parrhêsia* has tended to and most likely will continue to trump *aidôs*, but the experiences of an ancient city and the texts that emerged from that city point to the dangers in the too-ready dismissal of *aidôs*. The rejection of those bonds of respect enables free speech to become itself manipulative and enslaving rather than liberating, moving toward new forms of inequality rather than equality. The story of free speech and shame in Athens and today does not end with a tidy package or aphorism. The "unbridled tongue," so praised by the Persian Chorus as the symbol of freedom from tyranny and so central to democratic Athens' self-conception, challenges hierarchy, affirms an egalitarianism, and opens a vision of the future. It powerfully allows for the Socratic and Thucydidean search for truths that can transcend particular times and places. But it also can harm, exclude, and dissolve community. It demands a replacement for *aidôs*, perhaps a sort of "democratic *aidôs*" to replace the democratic amnesia from which democracies emerge. The Socratic replacement of *aidôs* with *eidos* in the *Protagoras* may work within the narrow confines of the private dialogue where, like doctors in Socrates' image, we uncover and scrutinize speeches as if we were, in Socrates' language, doctors examining a sick body. But the *eidos* of the *Protagoras* cannot give language and speech the grounding it needs for our engagement in dialogues.

Alas, neither Socrates nor Diodotus are here to help us in the search for this inherently contradictory democratic *aidôs*. Thanks, however, to Thucydides and Plato, their words are, alerting us to the choices we make when we veer toward the shameless democracy with *parrhêsia* or toward an *aidôs* that restrains the uncovering equalizing potential of the ancient practices of free speech. As the trial of Socrates suggests, as the speeches of Diodotus and Hermocrates reveal, as the Socratic manipulation of Protagoras shows, the polity enamored of the practices of free speech cannot exist without a sense of awe or shame. And yet the democratic regime by its very nature must rebel against it.

References

Aeschines. 1919. *The Speeches of Aeschines*. With an English translation by Charles Darwin Adams. Loeb Classical Library. Cambridge, MA: Harvard University Press.

Aeschylus. 1972. *Septem quae Supersunt Tragoedias*. Edited by Denys Page. Oxford Classical Texts. Oxford: Clarendon.

Amar, Akhil Reed. 1998. *The Bill of Rights: Creation and Reconstruction*. New Haven, CT: Yale University Press.

Andrews, James A. 1994. "Cleon's Ethopoetics," *The Classical Quarterly* 44:26–39.

Annals of Congress: The Debates and Proceedings in the Congress of the United States. 1834–56. "A History of Congress." 42 vols. Washington, DC: Gales & Seaton.

Aristophanes. 1906. *Comoediae*. 2 vols. 2nd edition. Edited by F. W. Hall and W. M. Geldart. Oxford Classical Texts. Oxford: Clarendon.

Aristotle. 1935. *The Constitution of Athens*. With an English translation by H. Rackham. Loeb Classical Library. Cambridge, MA: Harvard University Press.

Aristotle. 1957. *Politica*. Edited by W. D. Ross. Oxford Classical Texts. Oxford: Oxford University Press.

Baker, C. Edwin. 1989. *Human Liberty and Freedom of Speech*. New York: Oxford University Press.

Barber, Benjamin R. 1984. *Strong Democracy: Participatory Politics for a New Age*. Berkeley: University of California Press.

Barber, Benjamin R. 1996. "Misreading Democracy: Peter Euben and the *Gorgias*," in *Dêmokratia: A Conversation on Democracies, Ancient and Modern*, edited by Josiah Ober and Charles Hedrick. Princeton, NJ: Princeton University Press. Pp. 361–75.

Bartlett, Robert C. 2004. *Plato, "Protagoras" and "Meno."* Ithaca, NY: Cornell University Press.

Benardete, Seth. 1969. *Herodotean Inquiries*. The Hague: Martinus Nijhoff.

Benedict, Ruth. 1946. *The Sword and the Chrysanthemum: Patterns of Japanese Culture*. Boston: Houghton Mifflin.

Benhabib, Seyla. 1996. "Toward a Deliberative Model of Democratic Legitimacy," in *Democracy and Difference: Contesting the Boundaries of the Political*, edited by Seyla Benhabib. Princeton, NJ: Princeton University Press. Pp. 67–94.

Berger, Harry, Jr. 1984. "Facing Sophists: Socrates' Charismatic Bondage in *Protagoras*," *Representations* 5:66–91.

Berns, Walter. 1976. *The First Amendment and the Future of American Democracy*. New York: Basic Books.

Berti, Enrico. 1978. "Ancient Greek Dialectic as Expression of Freedom of Thought and Speech," *Journal of the History of Ideas* 39:347–70.

Biagini, Eugenio F. 1996. "Liberalism and Direct Democracy: John Stuart Mill and the Model of Ancient Athens," in *Citizenship and Community: Liberals, Radicals, and Collective Identities in the British Isles, 1865–1931*, edited by Eugenio Biagini. Cambridge: Cambridge University Press. Pp. 21–44.

Blackstone, William. [1723–80] 2002. *Commentaries on the Laws of England*. 4 vols. Chicago: University of Chicago Press.

Blasi, Vincent. 1987. "The Teaching Function of the First Amendment," *Columbia Law Review* 87:387–417.

Blasi, Vincent. 2002. "Free Speech and Good Character: From Milton to Brandeis to the Present," in *Eternally Vigilant: Free Speech in the Modern Era*, edited by Lee C. Bollinger and Geoffrey R. Stone. Chicago: University of Chicago Press. Pp. 60–95.

Bollinger, Lee C. 1986. *The Tolerant Society*. New York: Oxford University Press.

Bollinger, Lee C. and Geoffrey R. Stone. 2002. *Eternally Vigilant: Free Speech in the Modern Era*. Chicago: University of Chicago Press.

Braithwaite, John. 1989. *Crime, Shame, and Reintegration*. Cambridge: Cambridge University Press.

Brann, Eva. 1978. "The Offense of Socrates: A Re-reading of Plato's *Apology*," *Interpretation* 7:1–21.

Brickhouse, Thomas C. and Nicholas D. Smith. 2002. *The Trial and Execution of Socrates: Sources and Controversies*. New York: Oxford University Press.

Brown, Wendy. 1998. "Freedom's Silences," in *Censorship and Silencing: Practices of Cultural Regulation*, edited by Robert C. Post. Los Angeles, CA: Getty Research Institute Publications and Exhibitions Program. Pp. 313–27.

Burke, Edmund. [1790] 1987. *Reflections on the Revolution in France*, edited by J. G. A. Pocock. Indianapolis, IN: Hackett.

Burnyeat, Michael. 1980. "Aristotle on Learning to Be Good," in *Essays on Aristotle's Ethics*, edited by Amelie Oksenberg. Berkeley: University of California Press. Pp. 69–92.

Butler, Judith. 1997. *Excitable Speech: The Politics of the Performative*. New York: Routledge.

Cairns, Douglas L. 1993. *Aidôs: The Psychology and Ethics of Honor and Shame in Ancient Greek Literature*. Oxford: Clarendon Press.

Canavan, Francis. 1978. "John Milton and Freedom of Expression," *Interpretation: A Journal of Political Philosophy* 7:50–65.

Cartwright, David. 1997. *A Historical Commentary on Thucydides: A Companion to Rex Warner's Penguin Translation*. Ann Arbor: University of Michigan Press.

Castoriadis, Cornelius. 1991. *Philosophy, Politics, Autonomy: Essays in Political Philosophy*. Edited by David Ames Curtis. New York: Oxford University Press.

Chafee, Zechariah, Jr. 1920. *Freedom of Speech*. New York: Harcourt, Brace and Howe.

Chafee, Zechariah, Jr. 1941. *Free Speech in the United States*. Cambridge, MA: Harvard University Press.

Coby, Patrick. 1987. *Socrates and the Sophistic Enlightenment: A Commentary on Plato's* Protagoras. Lewisburg, PA: Bucknell University Press.

Coby, Patrick. 1991. "Enlightened Self-Interest in the Peloponnesian War: Thucydidean Speakers on the Right of the Stronger and Inter–State Peace," *Canadian Journal of Political Science* 24:67–90.

Cogan, Neil H. 1997. *The Complete Bill of Rights: The Drafts, Debates, Sources, and Origins.* New York: Oxford University Press.

Cohen, Joshua. 1997. "Deliberation and Democratic Legitimacy," in *Deliberative Democracy: Essays on Reason and Politics,* edited by James Bohman and William Rehg. Cambridge: MIT Press. Pp. 67–91.

Conacher, D. J. 1967. *Euripidean Drama: Myth, Theme and Structure.* Toronto: University of Toronto Press.

Congleton, Ann. 1974. "Two Kinds of Lawlessness: Plato's *Crito,*" *Political Theory* 2:432–46.

Connor, W. R. 1971. *The New Politicians of Fifth-Century Athens.* Princeton, NJ: Princeton University Press.

Connor, W. Robert. 1984. *Thucydides.* Princeton, NJ: Princeton University Press.

Connor, W. R. 1991. "The Other 399: Religion and the Trial of Socrates," in *Georgica: Greek Studies in Honor of George Cawkwell,* edited by Michael A. Flower and Mark Toher. London: University of London, Institute of Classical Studies. Pp. 49–56.

Constant, Benjamin. [1819] 1988. "The Liberty of the Ancients Compared with that of the Moderns," in *Political Writings,* edited by Biancamaria Fontana. Cambridge: Cambridge University Press. Pp. 307–28.

Cover, Robert. 1993. "Nomos and Narrative," in *Narrative, Violence, and the Law: The Essays of Robert Cover,* edited by Martha Minow, Michael Ryan, and Austin Sarat. Ann Arbor: University of Michigan Press. Pp. 95–172.

Craik, Elizabeth. 1988. *Euripides: Phoenician Women.* Edited with translation and commentary by Elizabeth Craik. Wiltshire, England: Aris and Philips.

Cropsey, Joseph. 1995. *Plato's World: Man's Place in the Cosmos.* Chicago: University of Chicago Press.

Curtis, David. 1996. "Translator's Foreword," in Pierre Lévêque and Pierre Vidal-Naquet, *Cleisthenes The Athenian: An Essay on the Representation of Space and Time in Greek Political Thought from the End of the Sixth Century to the Death of Plato,* with a new discussion of the invention of democracy by Pierre Vidal-Naquet, Cornelius Castoriadis, and Pierre Lévêque; translated from the French and edited by David Ames Curtis. Highlands, NJ: Humanities Press. Pp. ix–xxvii.

Curtis, Michael Kent. 2000. *Free Speech, "The People's Darling Privilege": Struggles for Freedom of Expression in American History.* Durham, NC: Duke University Press.

Darwin, Charles. [1872] 1955. *The Expression of the Emotion in Man and Animals.* With a preface by Margaret Mead. New York: Philosophical Library.

Demetriou, Kyriacos. 1996. "In Defence of the British Constitution: Theoretical Implications of the Debate over Athenian Democracy in Britain, 1770–1850," *History of Political Thought* 17:280–97.

Demetriou, Kyriacos N. 1999. *George Grote on Plato and Athenian Democracy: A Study in Classical Reception.* Frankfurt am Main: Peter Lang.

Demosthenes. 1926. *Speeches*. 7 vols. Loeb Classical Library. Cambridge, MA: Harvard University Press.

Diels, Hermann and Walther Kranz. 1961. *Die Fragmente der Vorsokratiker*. 3 vols. 6th edition. Berlin: Weidmann.

Diogenes Laertius. 1931. *Lives of Eminent Philosophers*. 2 vols. With an English translation by R. D. Hicks. Loeb Classical Library. Cambridge, MA: Cambridge University Press.

Dodds, E. R. 1951. *The Greeks and the Irrational*. Berkeley: University of California Press.

Dodds, E. R. 1977. *Missing Persons: An Autobiography*. Oxford: Clarendon Press.

Dover, Kenneth. 1974. *Greek Popular Morality in the Time of Plato and Aristotle*. Berkeley: University of California Press.

Dover, Kenneth. 1987. *The Greeks and Their Legacy: Collected Papers*. Vol. 2 of *Greek and the Greeks*. Oxford: B. Blackwell.

Dover, Kenneth. 1989. *Greek Homosexuality*. Cambridge, MA: Harvard University Press.

Dunn, Francis M. 1996. *Tragedy's End: Closure and Innovation in Euripidean Drama*. New York: Oxford University Press.

Eisenstadt, Oona. 2001. "Shame in the *Apology*," in *Politics, Philosophy, Writing: Plato's Art of Caring for Souls*, edited by Zdravko Planinc. Columbia: University of Missouri Press. Pp. 42–59.

Elshtain, Jean Bethke. 1995. *Democracy on Trial*. New York: Basic Books.

Elster, Jon. 1979. *Ulysses and the Sirens: Studies in Rationality and Irrationality*. Cambridge: Cambridge University Press.

Elster, Jon, ed. 1998. *Deliberative Democracy*. Cambridge: Cambridge University Press.

Elster, Jon. 2000. *Ulysses Unbound: Studies in Rationality, Precommitment, and Constraints*. Cambridge: Cambridge University Press.

Euben, J. Peter. 1990. *The Tragedy of Political Theory: The Road Not Taken*. Princeton, NJ: Princeton University Press.

Euben, J. Peter. 1997. *Corrupting Youth: Political Education, Democratic Culture, and Political Theory*. Princeton, NJ: Princeton University Press.

Euripides. 1913. *Fabulae*. 4 vols. 3rd edition. Oxford Classical Texts. Oxford: Oxford University Press.

Farrar, Cynthia. 1988. *The Origins of Democratic Thinking: The Invention of Politics in Classical Athens*. Cambridge: Cambridge University Press.

Fernie, Ewan. 2002. *Shame in Shakespeare*. London: Routledge.

Ferrara, Alessandro. 2001. "Of Boats and Principles: Reflections on Habermas's 'Constitutional Democracy,'" *Political Theory* 29:782–91.

Finley, M. I. 1971. *The Ancestral Constitution: An Inaugural Lecture*. Cambridge: Cambridge University Press.

Finley, M. I. 1988. *Democracy: Ancient and Modern*. 2nd revised edition. New Brunswick, NJ: Rutgers University Press.

Fisher, N. R. E. 1992. *Hybris: A Study in the Values of Honour and Shame in Ancient Greece*. Warminster, England: Aris & Phillips.

Fiss, Owen M. 1996a. *The Irony of Free Speech*. Cambridge, MA: Harvard University Press.

Fiss, Owen M. 1996b. *Liberalism Divided: Freedom of Speech and the Many Uses of State Power*. Boulder, CO: Westview Press.

Forde, Steven. 1989. *The Ambition to Rule: Alcibiades and the Politics of Imperialism in Thucydides*. Ithaca, NY: Cornell University Press.

Foucault, Michel. 1983. *Discourse on Truth: A Study of Parrhesia*. Transcript of lectures given in English at the University of California at Berkeley.

Foucault, Michel. 2001. *Fearless Speech*. Los Angeles, CA: Semiotext(e).

Frede, Dorothea. 1986. "The Impossibility of Perfection: Socrates' Criticism of Simonides' Poem in the *Protagoras*," *Review of Metaphysics* 39:729–53.

Fustel de Coulanges, Numa Denis. [1870] 1956. *The Ancient City: A Study on the Religion, Laws and Institutions of Greece and Rome*. Garden City, NY: Doubleday.

Garvey, Stephen P. 1998. "Can Shaming Punishments Educate," *University of Chicago Law Review* 65:733–94.

Gill, Christopher. 1996. *Personality in Greek Epic, Tragedy, and Philosophy: The Self in Dialogue*. Oxford: Clarendon Press.

Gomme, A. W., A. Andrewes, and K. J. Dover. 1945–81. *A Historical Commentary on Thucydides*. 5 vols. Oxford: Clarendon Press.

Goodhill, Simon. 1998. "The Seductions of the Gaze: Socrates and His Girlfriends," in *Kosmos: Essays in Order, Conflict, and Community in Classical Athens*, edited by Paul Cartledge, Paul Millet, and Sitta von Reden. Cambridge: Cambridge University Press. Pp. 105–24.

Graber, Mark A. 1991. *Transforming Free Speech: The Ambiguous Legacy of Civil Libertarianism*. Berkeley: University of California Press.

Grant, Ruth. 1997. *Hypocrisy and Integrity: Machiavelli, Rousseau and the Ethics of Politics*. Chicago: University of Chicago Press.

Grote, George. [1851–6] 1900. *Greece*. Vols. 4–8. Reprinted from the second London edition. New York: Peter Fenelon Collier.

Gurstein, Rochelle. 1996. *The Repeal of Reticence: A History of America's Cultural and Legal Struggles over Free Speech, Obscenity, Sexual Liberation, and Modern Art*. New York: Hill and Wang.

Guthrie, W. K. C. 1956. *Plato: Protagoras and Meno*. Harmondsworth: Penguin Books.

Habermas, Jürgen. 1996. *Between Facts and Norms: Contributions to a Discourse Theory of Law and Democracy*. Translated by William Rehg. Cambridge: MIT Press.

Habermas, Jürgen. 2001 "Constitutional Democracy: A Paradoxical Union of Contradictory Principles?," *Political Theory* 29:766–81.

Halliwell, Stephen. 1991. "Comic Satire and Freedom of Speech in Classical Athens," *Journal of Hellenic Studies* 111:48–70.

Halliwell, Stephen. 2002. "Aristophanic Sex: The Erotics of Shamelessness," in *The Sleep of Reason: Erotic Experience and Sexual Ethics in Ancient Greece and Rome*, edited by Martha C. Nussbaum and Juha Sihvola. Chicago: University of Chicago Press. Pp. 120–42.

Halperin, David M. 1990. *One Hundred Years of Homosexuality and Other Essays on Greek Love*. New York: Routledge.

Hamilton, Alexander, John Jay, and James Madison. 2001. *Federalist Papers*. Edited by George W. Carey and James McClellan. Indianapolis, IN: Liberty Fund Press.

Hammer, Dean. 2002. *The "Iliad" as Politics: The Performance of Political Thought.* Norman: University of Oklahoma Press.

Hansen, Mogens Herman. 1974. *The Sovereignty of the People's Court in Athens in the Fourth Century B.C. and the Public Action against Unconstitutional Proposals.* Odense University Classical Studies, Vol. 4. Odense, Denmark: Odense University Press.

Hansen, Mogens Herman. 1991. *The Athenian Democracy in the Age of Demosthenes: Structure, Principles and Ideology.* Oxford: Basil Blackwell Ltd.

Hansen, Mogens Herman. 1995. *The Trial of Sokrates – from the Athenian Point of View.* Copenhagen: Royal Danish Academy of Sciences and Letters.

Hansen, Mogens Herman. 1996. "The Ancient Athenian and the Modern Liberal View of Liberty as a Democratic Ideal," in *Dêmokratia: A Conversation on Democracies, Ancient and Modern,* edited by Josiah Ober and Charles Hedrick. Princeton, NJ: Princeton University Press. Pp. 91–104.

Havelock, Eric A. 1957. *The Liberal Temper in Greek Politics.* New Haven, CT: Yale University Press.

Hegel, G. W. F. [1807] 1967. *The Phenomenology of the Mind.* Translated by J. B. Baillie. New York: Harper and Row.

Heidegger, Martin. 1997. *Plato's Sophist.* Translated by Richard Rojcewicz and André Schuwer. Bloomington: Indiana University Press.

Heller, Agnes. 1985. *The Power of Shame: A Rational Perspective.* London: Routledge & K. Paul.

Henderson, Jeffrey. 1998. "Attic Old Comedy, Frank Speech, and Democracy," in *Democracy, Empire, and the Arts in Fifth-Century Athens,* edited by Deborah Boedeker and Kurt A. Raaflaub. Cambridge, MA: Harvard University Press. Pp. 255–73.

Herodotus. 1927. *Historiae.* 2 vols. 3rd edition. Edited by Carolus Hude. Oxford Classical Texts. Oxford: Clarendon.

Hesk, Jon. 2000. *Deception and Democracy in Classical Athens.* Cambridge: Cambridge University Press.

Hobbes, Thomas. [1628] 1975. *Thucydides.* Edited by Richard Schlatter. New Brunswick, NJ: Rutgers University Press.

Hobbes, Thomas. [1651] 1994. *Leviathan.* Edited with Introduction and Notes by Edwin Curley. Indianapolis, IN: Hackett.

Honig, Bonnie. 2001. "Dead Rights, Live Futures: A Reply to Habermas's 'Constitutional Democracy,'" *Political Theory* 29:792–805.

Hunter, Virginia J. 1973. *Thucydides: The Artful Reporter.* Toronto: Hakkert.

Hunter, Virginia J. 1994. *Policing Athens: Social Control in the Attic Lawsuits, 420–320 B.C.* Princeton, NJ: Princeton University Press.

Isocrates. 1928. *Speeches.* 3 vols. With an English translation by George Norlin. Loeb Classical Library. Cambridge, MA: Harvard University Press.

Jacoby, F. 1944. "*Patrios Nomos*: State Burial in Athens and the Public Cemetery in the Karameikos," *Journal of Hellenic Studies* 64:37–66.

Jefferson, Thomas. 1984. *Writings.* New York: The Library of America.

Kagan, Donald. 1991. *Pericles of Athens and the Birth of Democracy.* New York: The Free Press.

Kahn, Charles H. 1996. *Plato and the Socratic Dialogue: The Philosophical Use of a Literary Form.* Cambridge: Cambridge University Press.

Karp, David R. 1998. "The Judicial and Judicious Use of Shame Penalties," *Crime and Delinquency* 44:277–94.

Kaster, Robert. 1997. "The Shame of the Romans," *Transactions of the American Philological Association* 127:1–19.

Kerferd, G. B. 1981. *The Sophistic Movement*. Cambridge: Cambridge University Press.

Kersch, Ken I. 2003. *Freedom of Speech: Rights and Liberties under the Law*. Santa Barbara, CA: ABC Clio.

Kilborne, Benjamin. 1995. "Trust That Cannot go Naked: Shame in Many Forms," *Psychiatry* 58:278–97.

King, Martin Luther, Jr., [1963] 1985. "Letter from the Birmingham Jail," in *A Testament of Hope: The Essential Writings and Speeches of Martin Luther King, Jr.*, edited by James Melvin Washington. New York: Harper Collins.

Kitto, H. D. F. 1950. *Greek Tragedy: A Literary Study*. Garden City, NY: Doubleday & Company.

Klein, Jacob. 1965. *A Commentary on Plato's* Meno. Chapel Hill: University of North Carolina Press.

Kofman, Sarah. 1988. "Baubô: Theological Perversion and Fetishism," in *Nietzsche's New Seas: Explorations in Philosophy, Aesthetics, and Politics*, edited by Michael Allen Gillespie and Tracy B. Strong. Chicago: University of Chicago Press. Pp. 175–202.

Konishi, Haruo. 1980. "The Composition of Thucydides' *History*," *American Journal of Philology* 101:29–41.

Konstan, David. 2003. "Shame in Ancient Greece," *Social Research* 70:1031–61.

Lane, Melissa. 2001. *Plato's Progeny: How Socrates and Plato Still Captivate the Modern Mind*. London: Duckworth.

Lansky, Melvin. 1995. "Shame and the Scope of Psychoanalytic Understanding," *The American Behavioral Scientist* 38:1076–90.

Lattimore, Richmond, trans. 1951. *Homer: The Iliad*. Chicago: University of Chicago Press.

Lattimore, Steven, trans. 1998. *Thucydides: The Peloponnesian War*. Indianapolis, IN: Hackett Publishing Company.

Lévêque, Pierre and Pierre Vidal-Naquet. 1996. *Cleisthenes the Athenian: An Essay on the Representation of Space and Time in Greek Political Thought from the End of the Sixth Century to the Death of Plato*. With a new discussion of the invention of democracy by Pierre Vidal-Naquet, Cornelius Castoriadis, and Pierre Lévêque; translated from the French and edited by David Ames Curtis. Highlands, NJ: Humanities Press.

Levy, Leonard W. 1960. *Legacy of Suppression: Freedom of Speech and Press in Early American History*. Cambridge, MA: Belknap Press of Harvard University Press.

Levy, Leonard W. 1999. *Origins of the Bill of Rights*. New Haven, CT: Yale University Press.

Lewis, Helen B. 1971. *Shame and Guilt in Neurosis*. New York: International Universities Press.

Lewis, J. D. 1971. "*Isegoria* at Athens: When Did It Begin?" *Historia* 20:129–40.

Locke, Jill. 1999. "Hiding for Whom? Obscurity, Dignity, and the Politics of Truth," *Theory and Event* 3:3. http://muse.jhu.edu.proxy.lib.umich.edu/journals/theory_and_event/v003/3.3locke.html

Locke, John. [1689] 2003. "A Letter Concerning Toleration" in *Two Treatises of Government and A Letter Concerning Toleration*, edited by Ian Shapiro. New Haven, CT: Yale University Press. Pp. 211–54.

Lombardo, Stanley, trans. 1997. *Homer: Iliad*. Indianapolis, IN: Hackett Publishing Company.

Long, Anthony A. 1996. "The Socratic Tradition: Diogenes, Crates, and Hellenistic Ethics," in *The Cynics: The Cynic Movement in Antiquity and Its Legacy*, edited by R. Bracht Branham and Marie-Odile Goulet-Cazé. Berkeley: University of California Press. Pp. 28–46.

Loraux, Nicole. 1986. *The Invention of Athens: The Funeral Oration in the Classical City*. Translated by Alan Sheridan. Cambridge, MA: Harvard University Press.

Loraux, Nicole. 1987. *Tragic Ways of Killing a Woman*. Cambridge, MA: Harvard University Press.

Lynd, Helen Merrell. 1958. *On Shame and the Search for Identity*. New York: Harcourt, Brace and Company.

Lysias. 1943. *Speeches*. Translated by W. R. M. Lamb. Loeb Classical Library. Cambridge, MA: Harvard University Press.

Machiavelli, Niccolo. 1996. *The Discourses on Livy*. Translated by Harvey Mansfield and Nathan Tarcov. Chicago: University of Chicago Press.

MacKinnon, Catharine A. 1993. *Only Words*. Cambridge, MA: Harvard University Press.

Manin, Bernard. 1997. *The Principles of Representative Government*. Cambridge: Cambridge University Press.

Manville, Philip. 1990. *The Origins of Citizenship in Ancient Athens*. Princeton, NJ: Princeton University Press.

Mara, Gerald M. 2001. "Thucydides and Plato on Democracy and Trust," *Journal of Politics* 63:820–45.

Martin, Thomas R. 1996. *Ancient Greece from Prehistoric to Hellenistic Times*. New Haven, CT: Yale University Press.

Mastronarde, Donald J. 1994. *Euripides: Phoenissae*. Cambridge: Cambridge University Press.

McGrath, Patrick. 2002. "God Bless the Republican Who Saved America," *Guardian Unlimited*. http://www.guardian.co.uk/Archive/Article/0,4273,4388118,00.html.

Meiklejohn, Alexander. 1948. *Free Speech and Its Relation to Self-Government*. New York: Harper and Brothers Publishers.

Mill, John Stuart. [1859] 1978. *On Liberty*. Edited by Elizabeth Rapaport. Indianapolis, IN: Hackett Publishing Co.

Mill, John Stuart. [1862] 1998. "Considerations on Representative Government," in *On Liberty and Other Essays*, edited by John Gray. Oxford World's Classics. Oxford: Oxford University Press. Pp. 203–467.

Miller, Fred D. 1995. *Nature, Justice, and Rights in Aristotle's* Politics. Oxford: Clarendon Press.

Miller, Steven G. 2000. "Naked Democracy," in *Polis and Politics: Studies in Ancient Greek History*, edited by Pernille Flensted-Jensen, Thomas Heine Nielsen, and Lene Rubinsteinet. Copenhagen: University of Copenhagen, Museum Tusculanum Press. Pp. 277–96.

Miller, Susan. 1985. *The Shame Experience*. Hillsdale, NJ: The Analytic Press (distributed by Lawrence Erlbaum Associates).

Milton, John. [1644] 1999. "Areopagitica," in *Areopagitica and Other Political Writings of John Milton*. Indianapolis, IN: Liberty Fund. Pp. 3–51.

Momigliano, Arnoldo. 1973–4. "Freedom of Speech in Antiquity," in *Dictionary of the History of Ideas: Studies of Selected Pivotal Ideas*, edited by Philip P. Wiener. 4 vols. New York: Scribner.

Monoson, S. Sara. 1994. "Frank Speech, Democracy, and Philosophy: Plato's Debt to a Democratic Strategy of Civic Discourse," in *Athenian Political Thought and the Reconstruction of American Democracy*, edited by J. Peter Euben, John R. Wallach and Josiah Ober. Ithaca, NY: Cornell University Press. Pp. 172–97.

Monoson, S. Sara. 2000. *Plato's Democratic Entanglements: Athenian Politics and the Practice of Philosophy*. Princeton, NJ: Princeton University Press.

Mulgan, Richard. 1984. "Liberty in Ancient Greece," in *Conceptions of Liberty in Political Philosophy*, edited by Zbigniew Pelczynski and John Gray. New York: St. Martin's Press. Pp. 7–26.

Munn, Mark. 2000. *The School of History: Athens in the Age of Socrates*. Berkeley: University of California Press.

Nathanson, Donald, ed. 1987. *The Many Faces of Shame*. New York: Guilford Press.

Nehamas, Alexander. 1998. *The Art of Living: Socratic Reflections from Plato to Foucault*. Berkeley: University of California Press.

Nichols, Mary P. 1987. *Socrates and the Political Community: An Ancient Debate*. Albany: State University of New York Press.

Niedenthal, Paula M., June Price Tangney, and Igor Gavanski. 1994. "'If Only I Weren't' Versus 'If Only I Hadn't': Distinguishing Shame and Guilt in Counterfactual Thinking," *Journal of Personality and Social Psychology* 67:585–95.

North, Helen. 1966. *Sophrosune: Self-Knowledge and Self-Restraint in Greek Literature*. Ithaca, NY: Cornell University Press.

Nussbaum, Martha C. 1986. *The Fragility of Goodness: Luck and Ethics in Greek Tragedy and Philosophy*. Cambridge: Cambridge University Press.

Nussbaum, Martha C. 2001. *Upheavals of Thought: The Intelligence of Emotions*. Cambridge: Cambridge University Press.

Nussbaum, Martha C. 2004. *Hiding from Humanity: Disgust, Shame, and the Law*. Princeton, NJ: Princeton University Press.

Ober, Josiah. 1994. "Civic Ideology and Counterhegemonic Discourse: Thucydides on the Sicilian Debate," in *Athenian Identity and Civic Ideology*, edited by Alan L. Boegehold and Adele C. Scafuro. Baltimore and London: Johns Hopkins University Press. Pp. 102–26.

Ober, Josiah. 1996. *The Athenian Revolution: Essays on Ancient Greek Democracy and Political Theory*. Princeton, NJ: Princeton University Press.

Ober, Josiah. 1998. *Political Dissent in Democratic Athens: Intellectual Critics of Popular Rule*. Princeton, NJ: Princeton University Press.

Ober, Josiah. 2000. "Quasi-Rights: Participatory Citizenship and Negative Liberties in Democratic Athens," *Social Philosophy and Policy* 17:27–61.

Ober, Josiah. 2001. "The Debate over Civic Education in Classical Athens," in *Education in Greek and Roman Antiquity*, edited by Yun Lee Too. Leiden: E. J. Brill. Pp. 175–207.

Ober, Josiah. 2003a. *Moral Authority and the Useable Past: Precedent, Legacy, Amnesty*. Princeton, NJ: Ms. University Center for Human Values.

Ober, Josiah. 2003b. "Conditions for Athenian Democracy," in *The Making and Unmaking of Democracy: Lessons from History and World Politics*, edited by Theodore K. Rabb and Ezra N. Suleman. London: Routledge. Pp. 2–22.

O'Rourke, K. C. 2001. *John Stuart Mill and Freedom of Expression: The Genesis of a Theory*. London: Routledge.

Orwin, Clifford. 1984a. "Democracy and Distrust," *The American Scholar* 53:313–25.

Orwin, Clifford. 1984b. "The Just and the Advantageous in Thucydides: The Case of the Mytilenian Debate," *American Political Science Review* 78:485–94.

Orwin, Clifford. 1994. *The Humanity of Thucydides*. Princeton, NJ: Princeton University Press.

Ostwald, Martin. 1979. "Diodotus, Son of Eucrates," *Greek Roman and Byzantine Studies* 20:5–13.

Ostwald, Martin. 1986. *From Popular Sovereignty to the Sovereignty of Law: Law, Society, and Politics in Fifth-Century Athens*. Berkeley: University of California Press.

Paine, Thomas. [1776] 1995. *Common Sense* in *Collected Writings*. Library of America. Pp. 5–59.

Paine, Thomas. [1791–2] 1995. *Rights of Man* in *Collected Writings*. Library of America. Pp. 433–661.

Pangle, Lorraine and Thomas L. Pangle. 1993. *The Learning of Liberty: The Educational Ideas of the American Founders*. Lawrence: University Press of Kansas.

Pangle, Thomas L. 1992. *The Ennobling of Democracy: The Challenge of the Postmodern Age*. Baltimore, MD: Johns Hopkins University Press.

Parker, Robert. 1996. *Athenian Religion: A History*. New York: Oxford University Press.

Parry, Adam. 1956. "The Language of Achilles," *Transactions of the American Philological Association* 87:1–7.

Parry, Adam. 1972. "Thucydides' Historical Perspective," *Yale Classical Studies* 22:47–61.

Piers, Gerhart. 1953. "Shame and Guilt: A Psychoanalytic Study," in *Shame and Guilt: A Psychoanalytic and a Cultural Study*, edited by Gerhart Piers and Milton Singer. Springfield, IL: Charles C. Thomas Publishers. Pp. 3–41.

Plato. 1900. *Opera*. 5 vols. Edited by John Burnet. Oxford Classical Texts. Oxford: Clarendon.

Post, Robert C. 1990. "The Constitutional Concept of Public Discourse: Outrageous Opinion, Democratic Deliberation, and *Hustler Magazine v. Falwell*," *Harvard Law Review* 103:601–86.

Post, Robert C. 1991. "Free Speech, and Religious, Racial and Sexual Harassment: Racist Speech, Democracy, and the First Amendment," *William and Mary Law Review* 32:267–327.

Post, Robert C. 1993. "Meiklejohn's Mistake: On Individual Autonomy and the Reform of Public Discourse," *University of Colorado Law Review* 64:1109–37.

Post, Robert C. 1998. *Censorship and Silencing: Practices of Cultural Regulation*. Los Angeles, CA: Getty Research Institute for the History of Art and the Humanities.

Post, Robert C. 2000. "Symposium on Law in the Twentieth Century: Reconciling Theory and Doctrine in First Amendment Jurisprudence," *California Law Review* 88:2353–74.

Raaflaub, Kurt A. 1983. "Democracy, Oligarchy, and the Concept of the 'Free Citizen' in Late Fifth-Century Athens," *Political Theory* 11:517–44.

Raaflaub, Kurt A. 1996. "Equalities and Inequalities in Athenian Democracy," in *Dêmokratia: A Conversation on Democracies Ancient and Modern*, edited by Josiah Ober and Charles Hedrick. Princeton, NJ: Princeton University Press. Pp. 139–74.

Raaflaub, Kurt. 2004. *The Discovery of Freedom in Ancient Greece*. Translated by Renate Franciscono; revised and updated from the German. Chicago: University of Chicago Press.

Rabban, David M. 1985. "Historical Perspectives on the Free Press: Review Essay: The Ahistorical Historian: Leonard Levy on Freedom of Expression in Early American History," *Stanford Law Review* 37:795–856.

Rabban, David M. 1997. *Free Speech in Its Forgotten Years*. Cambridge: Cambridge University Press.

Radin, Max. 1927. "Freedom of Speech in Ancient Athens," *American Journal of Philology* 48:215–30.

Redfield, James M. 1975. *Nature and Culture in the Iliad: The Tragedy of Hector*. Chicago: University of Chicago Press.

Reinhold, Meyer. 1984. *Classica Americana: The Greek and Roman Heritage in the United States*. Detroit, MI: Wayne State University Press.

Riezler, Kurt. 1943. "Comment on the Social Psychology of Shame," *American Journal of Sociology* 48:457–65.

Roberts, Jennifer Tolbert. 1994. *Athens on Trial: The Antidemocratic Tradition in Western Thought*. Princeton, NJ: Princeton University Press.

Roberts, Jennifer Tolbert. 1995. "Myths of Democracy and Gender in Plato's 'Republic': A Reply to Arlene Saxonhouse," *Thamyris* 2:259–72.

Roberts, Jennifer Tolbert. 1996. "Athenian Equality: A Constant Surrounded by Flux," in *Dêmokratia: A Conversation on Democracies Ancient and Modern*, edited by Josiah Ober and Charles Hedrick. Princeton, NJ: Princeton University Press. Pp. 187–202.

Roisman, Joseph. 2004. "Speaker Audience Interaction in Athens: A Power Struggle," in *Free Speech in Classical Antiquity*, edited by R. Rosen and I. Sluiter. Leiden: Brill. Pp. 261–76.

Rood, Tim. 1998. *Thucydides: Narrative and Explanation*. Oxford: Clarendon Press.

Rosen, Ralph M. and Ineke Sluiter, eds. 2004. *Free Speech in Classical Antiquity*. Leiden: Brill.

Sandel, Michael J. 1982. *Liberalism and the Limits of Justice*. Cambridge: Cambridge University Press.

Sartre, Jean-Paul. [1943] 1984. *Being and Nothingness: A Phenomenological Essay on Ontology*. Translated by Hazel E. Barnes. New York: Washington Square Press.

Saxonhouse, Arlene W. 1986a. "Myths and the Origins of Cities: Reflections on the Autochthony Theme in Euripides' *Ion*," in *Greek Tragedy and Political Theory*, edited by J. Peter Euben. Berkeley: University of California Press. Pp. 252–73.

Saxonhouse, Arlene W. 1986b. "From Hierarchy to Tragedy and Back Again: Women in Greek Political Thought," *American Political Science Review* 80:403–18.

Saxonhouse, Arlene W. 1992. *Fear of Diversity: The Birth of Political Science in Ancient Greek Thought*. Chicago: Chicago University Press.

Saxonhouse, Arlene W. 1994. "Athenian Democracy and Modern Mythmakers: A Lesson from Plato about Democracy, Equality, and Gender," *Thamyris* 1:105–22.

Saxonhouse, Arlene W. 1996. *Athenian Democracy: Modern Mythmakers and Ancient Theorists.* South Bend, IN: Notre Dame University Press.

Saxonhouse, Arlene W. 1998. "Democracy, Equality and *Eidê*: A Radical View from Book 8 of Plato's *Republic*," *American Political Science Review* 92:273–83.

Saxonhouse, Arlene W. 2004. "Democratic Deliberation and the Historian's Trade: The Case of Thucydides," in *Talking Democracy: Historical Perspectives on Rhetoric and Democracy*, edited by Benedetto Fontana, Cary Nederman, and Gary Remer. State College, PA: Penn State University Press. Pp. 57–85.

Schauer, Frederick. 1982. *Free Speech: A Philosophical Enquiry.* Cambridge: Cambridge University Press.

Scheff, Thomas. 1988. "Shame and Conformity: The Deference-Emotion System," *American Sociological Review* 53:395–406.

Scheff, Thomas. 2000. "Shame and the Social Bond," *Sociological Theory* 18:84–99.

Schneider, Carl D. 1977. *Shame, Exposure and Privacy.* Boston: Beacon Press.

Schwartz, Joel. 1986. "Freud and Freedom of Speech," *American Political Science Review* 80:1227–48.

Sealey, Raphael. 1990. *Women and Law in Classical Greece.* Chapel Hill: University of North Carolina Press.

Seidler, Gunter Harry. 2000. *In Others' Eyes: An Analysis of Shame.* Translated from the German by Andrew Jenkins. Madison, CT: International Universities Press, Inc.

Shapiro, H. A. 1991. "The Iconography of Mourning in Athenian Art," *American Journal of Archaeology* 95:629–56.

Shiffrin, Steven H. 1990. *The First Amendment, Democracy, and Romance.* Cambridge, MA: Harvard University Press.

Shklar, Judith. 1998. *Redeeming American Political Thought.* Edited by Stanley Hoffmann and Dennis F. Thompson. Chicago: University of Chicago Press.

Sinclair, R. K. 1988. *Democracy and Participation in Athens.* Cambridge: Cambridge University Press.

Sinclair, Thomas Alan. 1952. *A History of Greek Political Thought.* London: Routledge Paul.

Singer, Milton. 1953. "Shame Cultures and Guilt Cultures," in *Shame and Guilt: A Psychoanalytic and a Cultural Study*, edited by Gerhart Piers and Milton Singer. Springfield, IL: Charles C. Thomas Publishers. Pp. 43–78.

Solon. 1970. "Poems," in *Greek Elegy, Iambus and Anacreontea I.* Loeb Classical Library. Cambridge, MA: Harvard University Press.

Stockton, David. 1990. *The Classical Athenian Democracy.* Oxford: Oxford University Press.

Stone, I. F. 1988. *The Trial of Socrates.* Boston: Little, Brown.

Stoner, James. 2003. *Common Law Liberty: Rethinking American Constitutionalism.* Lawrence: University of Kansas Press.

Strauss, Barry. 1993. *Fathers and Sons in Athens: Ideology and Society in the Era of the Peloponnesian War.* Princeton, NJ: Princeton University Press.

Strauss, Leo. 1941. "Persecution and the Art of Writing," *Social Research* 8:488–504.

Strauss, Leo. 1952. *Persecution and the Art of Writing.* Glencoe, IL: The Free Press.

Strauss, Leo. 1964. *The City and Man.* Chicago: Rand McNally.

Strum, Philippa. 1984. *Louis D. Brandeis: Justice for the People.* Cambridge, MA: Harvard University Press.

Sunnstein, Cass. 1995. *Democracy and the Problem of Free Speech*. With a new afterword. New York: The Free Press.

Tajfel, Henri. 1981. *Human Groups and Social Categories: Studies in Social Psychology*. Cambridge: Cambridge University Press.

Tangney, June Price. 1991. "The Moral Affect: The Good, the Bad, and the Ugly," *Journal of Personality and Social Psychology* 61:598–607.

Tangney, June Price. 1995. "Recent Advances in the Empirical Study of Shame and Guilt," *The American Behavioral Scientist* 38:1132–45.

Tangney, June Price and Rhonda L. Dearing. 2002. *Shame and Guilt*. New York: Guilford Press.

Tangney, June Price, Rowland S. Miller, Laura Flicker, and Deborah Hill Barlow. 1996. "Are Shame, Guilt, and Embarrassment Distinct Emotions," *Journal of Personality and Social Psychology* 70:1256–69.

Taylor, C. C. W. 1976. *Plato Protagoras*. Oxford: Clarendon Press.

Taylor, Gabriele. 1985. *Pride, Shame, and Guilt: Emotions of Self-Assessment*. Oxford: Clarendon Press.

Thucydides. 1942. *Historiae*. 2 vols. Oxford Classical Texts. Oxford: Oxford University Press.

Tocqueville, Alexis de. [1835–40] 2000. *Democracy in America*. Translated and edited by Harvey C. Mansfield and Delba Winthrop. Chicago: University of Chicago Press.

Tomkins, Sylvan. 1995. *Shame and Its Sisters: A Sylvan Tompkins Reader*. Edited by Eve Kosofsky Sedgwick and Adam Frank. Durham, NC: Duke University Press.

Trenchard, John and Thomas Gordon. [1720–3] 1995. *Cato's Letters: Essays on Liberty, Civil and Religious, and Other Important Subjects*. Edited and annotated by Ronald Hamowy. Indianapolis, IN: Liberty Fund.

Turner, Frank. 1981. *The Greek Heritage in Victorian Britain*. New Haven, CT: Yale University Press.

Tutschka, Monicka and Arlene W. Saxonhouse. 2002. "The *Thesmophoriazusae*: Aristophanes' Challenge to Essentialism." Paper presented at the annual meetings of the Midwest Political Science Association. Chicago, IL.

Urbinati, Nadia. 2002. *Mill on Democracy: From the Athenian Polis to Representative Government*. Chicago: University of Chicago Press.

Vellacott, Philip. 1961. *Aeschylus: Prometheus Bound, The Suppliants, Seven Against Thebes, The Persians*. Translated with an introduction by Philip Vellacott. Harmondsworth, England: Penguin Books.

Villa, Dana. 2001. *Socratic Citizenship*. Princeton, NJ: Princeton University Press.

Vlastos, Gregory. 1991. *Socrates: Ironist and Moral Philosopher*. Ithaca, NY: Cornell University Press.

Waldron, Jeremy. 1995. "The Wisdom of the Majority: Some Reflections on Book III, Chapter 10 of the *Politics*," *Political Theory* 23:563–84.

Wallace, Robert W. 1994. "Private Lives and Public Enemies: Freedom of Thought in Classical Athens," in *Athenian Identity and Civic Ideology*, edited by Alan L. Boegehold and Adele C. Scafuro. Baltimore, MD: The Johns Hopkins University Press. Pp. 127–55.

Wallace, Robert W. 1996. "Law, Freedom, and the Concept of Citizens' Rights in Democratic Athens," in *Dêmokratia: A Conversation on Democracies, Ancient and Modern*, edited by Josiah Ober and Charles Hedrick. Princeton, NJ: Princeton University Press. Pp. 105–19.

Wasserman, Felix Martin. 1956. "Post–Periclean Democracy in Athens: The Mytile-
    nean Debate (Thuc. III.37–48)," *Transactions and Proceedings of the American
    Philological Association* 87:27–41.
Weiss, Roslyn. 1998. *Socrates Dissatisfied: An Analysis of Plato's Crito.* Oxford:
    Oxford University Press.
Weiss, Roslyn. 2001. *Virtue in the Cave: Moral Inquiry in Plato's Meno.* Oxford:
    Oxford University Press.
Weiss, Roslyn. 2006. *Socratic Paradoxes.* Chicago: University of Chicago Press.
West, Thomas G. 1979. *Plato's Apology of Socrates: An Interpretation.* With a new
    translation. Ithaca, NY: Cornell University Press.
West, William C. III. 1973. "The Speeches in Thucydides: A Description and Listing,"
    in *The Speeches in Thucydides: A Collection of Original Studies with a Bibliogra-
    phy,* edited by Philip A. Stadter. Chapel Hill: University of North Carolina Press.
    Pp. 3–15.
Williams, Bernard. 1993. *Shame and Necessity.* Berkeley: University of California
    Press.
Williams, Bernard. 2002. *Truth and Truthfulness: An Essay in Genealogy.* Princeton,
    NJ: Princeton University Press.
Winkler, John J. 1990. *The Constraints of Desire: The Anthropology of Sex and
    Gender in Ancient Greece.* New York: Routledge.
Winnington-Ingram, R. P. 1965. "*Deonta eipein*: Cleon and Diodotus," *Bulletin of
    the Institute of Classical Studies* 12:70–82.
Wolin, Sheldon. 1989. *The Presence of the Past: Essays on the State and the Consti-
    tution.* Baltimore, MD: Johns Hopkins University Press.
Wolin, Sheldon. 1994. "Norm and Form: The Constitutionalizing of Democracy,"
    in *Athenian Political Thought and the Reconstruction of American Democracy,*
    edited by J. Peter Euben, John R. Wallach, and Josiah Ober. Ithaca, NY: Cornell
    University Press. Pp. 29–58.
Wollheim, Richard. 1999. *On the Emotions.* New Haven, CT: Yale University Press.
Wurmser, Leon. 1981. *The Mask of Shame.* Baltimore, MD: Johns Hopkins Univer-
    sity Press.
Xenophon. 1985. *Opera Omnia.* 5 vols. Edited by E. C. Marchant. Oxford Classical
    Texts. Oxford: Oxford University Press.
Yunis, Harvey. 1996. *Taming Democracy: Models of Political Rhetoric in Classical
    Athens.* Ithaca, NY: Cornell University Press.
Zakaria, Fareed. 2003. *The Future of Freedom: Illiberal Democracy at Home and
    Abroad.* New York: W. W. Norton.
Zimmern, Alfred. [1911] 1924. *The Greek Commonwealth: Politics and Economics
    in Fifth-Century Athens.* 4th edition revised. Oxford: Clarendon Press.
Zuckert, Michael. 1994. *Natural Rights and the New Republicanism.* Princeton, NJ:
    Princeton University Press.

Court Cases Cited

Abrams v. United States 250 US 616 (1919)
Schenck v. United States 249 US 27 (1919)
Whitney v. California 274 US 357 (1927)

Index